The Age of Anxiety:
Conspiracy Theory and the Human Sciences

A selection of previous *Sociological Review* Monographs

Life and Work History Anaylses[†]
ed. Shirley Dex

The Sociology of Monsters[†]
ed. John Law

Sport, Leisure and Social Relations[†]
eds John Horne, David Jary and Alan Tomlinson

Gender and Bureaucracy[*]
eds Mike Savage and Anne Witz

The Sociology of Death: theory, culture, practice[*]
ed. David Clark

The Cultures of Computing[*]
ed. Susan Leigh Star

Theorizing Museums[*]
ed. Sharon Macdonald and Gordon Fyfe

Consumption Matters[*]
eds Stephen Edgell, Kevin Hetherington and Alan Warde

Ideas of Difference[*]
eds Kevin Hetherington and Rolland Munro

The Laws of the Markets[*]
ed. Michael Callon

Actor Network Theory and After[*]
eds John Law and John Hassard

Whose Europe? The Turn Towards Democracy[*]
eds Dennis Smith and Sue Wright

Renewing Class Analysis[*]
eds Rosemary Crompton, Fiona Devine, Mike Savage and John Scott

Reading Bourdieu on Society and Culture[*]
ed. Bridget Fowler

The Consumption of Mass[*]
eds Nick Lee and Rolland Munro

[†] Available from The Sociological Review Office, Keele University, Keele, Staffs ST5 5BG.
[*] Available from Blackwell Publishers Journals, PO Box 805, 108 Cowley Road, Oxford OX4 1FH.

The Sociological Review Monographs

Since 1958 *The Sociological Review* has established a tradition of publishing Monographs on issues of general sociological interest. The Monograph is an edited book length collection of research papers which is published and distributed in association with Blackwell Publishers. We are keen to receive innovative collections of work in sociology and related disciplines with a particular emphasis on exploring empirical materials and theoretical frameworks which are currently under-developed. If you wish to discuss ideas for a Monograph then please contact the Monographs Editor, Martin Parker, at *The Sociological Review*, Keele University, Newcastle-under-Lyme, North Staffordshire, ST5 5BG. Email m.parker@mngt.keele.ac.uk

The Age of Anxiety:
Conspiracy Theory and the Human Sciences

Edited by Jane Parish and Martin Parker

Blackwell Publishers/The Sociological Review

First published in 2001

Blackwell Publishers
108 Cowley Road, Oxford OX4 1JF, UK

and
350 Main Street
Malden, MA 02148, USA

British Library Cataloguing in Publication Data

A CIP catalogue record for this book is available from the British Library

Library of Congress Cataloging-in-Publication Data applied for

ISBN 0 631 23168 4

Printed and bound by Page Brothers, Norwich.

This book is printed on acid-free paper.

Contents

The age of anxiety

Jane Parish

Both professor and prophet depress,
For vision and longer view
Agree in predicting a day
Of convulsion and vast evil,
When the Cold Societies clash
Or the mosses are set in motion
To overrun the earth,
And the great brain which began
With lucid dialectics
Ends in a horrid madness.
(W.H. Auden, *The Age of Anxiety* 1948: 122)

From the assassination of JFK in November 1963, through Watergate and
Lockerbie, conspiracies beset popular culture. Television programmes about
mysteries and 'inexplicable' events command peak time viewing schedules,
reinterpreting 'old' conspiracy theories with new evidence. Sky television
devotes a single channel to programmes about mysterious happenings. In the
tabloid papers, conspiracies have caught the public imagination, and the
broadsheets debate possible explanations – the restructuring of the capitalist
totality, the questioning of 'expert 'knowledge, the postmodern collapse of
fixed meanings, and so on. Reflecting this trend, the best-selling books of the
90s reflect a widespread fascination with conspiracy, intrigue and secret
organizations: *The Holy Blood and the Holy Grail*, *Gods of the New Millennium*,
and the predictions of Nostradamus.

There have always been conspiracies. It now seems, however, that there are
more than ever. While the existence of conspiracies can be acknowledged, is it
the case that they mark a new type of theorizing? If, as Beck (2000) writes, we
cannot understand how frameworks of reference developed in the eighteenth
century can be of use in understanding the cosmopolitan world in which we live
today, do conspiracy theories represent a new categorizing of truth and
certainty where the construction of both expert authority and subversive
discourse is under the gaze of an increasingly sophisticated consumer who
questions everything? Or, is conspiracy theorizing today simply an age-old
solution to the present anxieties of an uncertain world?

Twentieth-century social theorists always recognized that the relation
between anxiety and certainty, far from being one of opposites is a complex

dialectic (Hacking, 1987). Rather than magic and a belief in the supernatural being cast as superstition and defeated by rationalization and technological development, it is the case that both are part of the same worldview, a feature of a specific, historical cosmological framework which reflects the cultural and historical conditions of the time. What Giddens calls the 'darker side of modernity' (1990: 7) has not been neglected by social commentators. Marx saw the capitalist order as marked by class conflict. Durkheim described the anomie of industrial society and Weber wrote about the increasing disenchantment with the world as bureaucracy crushed individual spirit. In this fashion writes Prior, Weber's concept of the iron cage in industrial society provides the backdrop for an understanding of both uncertainty and control as the growth of sophisticated bureaucracies (supposedly) removes anxiety from daily life and risk assessment and risk management become big business. Prior shows how even death has become a technically controlled event and that misfortune can be avoided by eating the right foods and exercising (1997: 189). Yet, although risk calculations are about making the 'incalculable calculable' (Beck, 1992: 100), at the same time, the inexplicable still looms in the world. Occult cosmologies are prevalent throughout the world, while in Euro-American cultures, supernatural beliefs appear to be held by ever greater numbers of people. Gallup polls conducted amongst the American public over the final three decades of the twentieth century show that over a thirty year period, an increasing number of Americans believe in angels, miracles, ghosts and the Devil (see Vyse, 1997, and Skinner, this volume).

May the contemporary popularization of beliefs about UFOs and ghosts be distinguished from previous dangers involving supernatural spirits? Giddens thinks so. He contrasts misfortune today with an earlier stage of modernity where the danger characteristic of these societies is, in his words, individual and observable (1990). Commonly, the cause of misfortune was believed by victims to be embodied in occult and black magic practices. In sixteenth century England, traditional medicines such as those used by female midwives to aid childbirth were condemned as demonic, reflecting increasing tension between a burgeoning male-dominated medical profession and female practioners in the countryside whom it sought to persecute (Larner, 1984). The diabolicalization of such beliefs by the church led directly to the great European witchhunts of the sixteenth and seventeenth centuries, culminating in the evil frenzy which was the witches' sabbat. The medieval Catholic church recorded the details of the sabbat with 'great meticulousness and experts, confessors, judges, clergy, feudal landowners and philosophers sought to understand demonology' (Trevor-Roper, 1969: 18). Their records describe how the suspected witch met with her fellow conspirators with whom she had formed a pact to celebrate their diabolical religion. Amid sexual orgies, drinking and eating, the devil himself would appear to participate in sexual reveries, often appearing as an evil smelling goat, a large toad or a tall black-bearded man (Trevor-Roper, 1969: 16–17). Priests noted that the devil's embrace was cold, that worm-like creatures resulted from the sexual union between Satan and, in line with church theology, that the devil, being neutered, took his sperm from the organs of the dead (Trevor Roper, 1969).

Significantly, as we shall see throughout this collection, the links between progressive rationalization and a decline in mystical or spiritual belief are never so straightforward. Trevor-Roper argues that scientific development in early modern Europe did not counter demonology and mysticism but appeared to encourage its growth (1969). The European witch craze sprang from secular roots, Trevor-Roper explains, itself an extension of a Aristotelian cosmology and social rationalization. It was only when a rival faith successfully challenged the conceptualization of the workings of nature between God and Devil, and 'replaced it with the universal mechanical laws of nature, that finally demons were made unnecessary' (Trevor-Roper, 1969: 110). Only now in this specific social and intellectual context were mysticism, superstitions, astrology and fortune-telling condemned as primitive beliefs and shifted to one side (1969).

Similarly, in the twentieth century, the globalization of scientific and technological development has its own covert edge epitomized by ideas of hidden and mysterious conspiracies between governments, secret agencies and multi-national companies who seek to conceal information about what is really happening in the world. Here, danger refers to risk – what Beck terms a 'peculiar synthesis of knowledge and unawareness' (2000: 216). This is a process whereby so-called expert knowledge is the source of greater risk as knowledge is associated with uncertainty, danger and the impossibility of predicting the consequences of its implementation. This paradox becomes evident when, for example, technology is capable of catastrophic potential which is impossible to calculate. For instance, advances in genetics have blurred the boundary between healthy people and ill people. Yet this knowledge is uncertain. We do not know the effects of genetic engineering (Faredi, 1997). The greater the gap between actions and their impacts, the more risks are produced. Hazards such as CJD and BSE are examples of such invisible affects of 'the unbridgeable spatio-temporal gap between actions and their impacts' (Beck, 2000: 220). Invisible victims appear everywhere. Hence the need for institutions to protect society from danger, since risk is no longer a private and individual matter:

> The tendency to dread hidden dangers invites speculation of science-fiction proportions ... The WorldWatch Institute's state of the World 1996 ... does not merely warn of the dangers of climatic change or the decline of the aquatic environment. A whole chapter is devoted to the threat of bioinvasions ... the most banal daily encounter becomes transformed into a potentially life-threatening danger (Furedi, 1997: 36).

Lack of official recognition for a problem merely heightens public anxiety and what is invisible becomes more relevant than so-called facts. Our trust in so-called experts is also gradually eroded (Giddens, 1991; Beck, 1992, 2000). From church ministers, politicians and the monarchy, to the decline in legitimacy of scientists and medical consultants, we now see a fragile public reliance on traditional types of expertise. For example, the idea that the sun is dangerous may have come as a shock to generations who were told that the sun was good for them, as the exact relationship between melanoma and sun exposure is brought into question (Furedi, 1997: 37). On the other hand, so-called experts are believed to conceal vital evidence and deliberately mislead the public. Many different cases could be used to illustrate this point. A recent headline in the British newspaper, *The Observer*, screamed 'Revealed: air deaths cover up'. The paper described how airline companies in Britain had ignored the potentially fatal effects of blood clots on passengers on long-haul flights, despite medical warnings nearly thirty years previously. Moreover, the paper accuses British Airways of downplaying these fears and of attempting to highlight misleading counter evidence. Despite knowing of the risks for years, passengers had not been alerted. Complacency or ineptitude? In the current climate in which we find ourselves this becomes another conspiracy where the pursuit of profit at all costs undermines public confidence.

The workings of the global economy

Mix the increased uncertainty found in everyday life with the insecurities of the global economy and nothing seems straightforward. The new world order incurring massive shifts of capital and technology has become opaque in a way that was not the case previously. The lack of control which many of us have over our everyday lives means that we must all learn to ride what Giddens calls the 'juggernaut of modernity', despite the risks involved in this (1990: 146). Taussig describes these complexities of the social-economic-political world as in a state of perpetual nervousness in which shock and normality are related, and rupture destructive of normality:

> I am referring to a state of doubleness of social being in which one moves in bursts between somehow accepting the situation as normal, only to be thrown into panic or shocked into disorientation by an event, a rumour, a sight, something said, or not said – something that even while it requires the normal in order to make its impact, destroys it (Taussig, 1992: 18).

People all over the world experience the affects of this. How do they theorize their fears? Anxieties focusing especially on the abuse of children's bodies appear to circulate in the global economy. 'From Nigeria to Brazil, South Africa to China and India, child abuse has become the quintessential crime ... it condenses a multitude of anxieties about risk' (Castaneda, 2000: 149). Scheper-Hughes analyses a rumour about child organ stealing which reverberates throughout Brazil (2000). It is a way, she argues, by which a dispossessed people at the edge of global capital are able to express their fears that their bodies may become parts for wealthy others in the western world.

The rumour allows an analogy to be drawn between commodities: 'the capitalist exploitation of rubber in the eighteenth century versus the twentieth century transplantation of bodily organs from the poor to produce, literally, a gourmet capitalism' (Scheper-Hughes, 2000: 211).

Comaroff and Comaroff coin the phase 'occult economy' to embody this preoccupation with the theft of children's organs as well as popular discourses about sexual slavery and the satanic abuse of children (1999). The occult economy symbolizes a malaise that has become endemic as 'the rich and powerful use monstrous means and freakish familiars to appropriate the life force of their lesser compatriots in order to strengthen themselves or to satisfy consuming passions' (1999: 282). Occult economies are also violent ones in many parts of the world. Kidnapping, torture, disappearances and abductions are the status quo in some South American countries and in South Africa, ritual murder, zombies and Satanism symbolise a dark violence:

... Islamic vigilantes, drug dealers, car jackers ... an economy, as much underground as above board, in which 'new' black bureaucrats and businessmen, politicians, celebrities and criminals, grow rich while the rest struggle to survive (Comaroff and Comaroff, 1999: 292).

It is precisely these fears about witchcraft and Satanism that come to symbolize what Comaroff and Comaroff (1993) call 'the malcontents of modernity', a fascination itself closely tied to the rhetoric and risks of the global market and large scale economic restructuring. Witchcraft accusations, rather than disappearing when faced with modern economic development and scientific progress, reappear through the back door and thrive as moral commentaries in a global economy. Of course it is tempting to dismiss such beliefs as too implausible for words and to try to discover a more down-to-earth explanation for their widespread existence. Therefore, whether in twentieth century Africa or sixteenth century Europe, witchcraft accusations are often explained away as the consequence of strains in the social structure, tension especially prevalent among social groups experiencing rapid economic and social change (Marwick, 1982). Taussig's fieldwork among Columbian mineworkers sees social tension as a consequence of the modernizing project in South America where evil is believed to be embodied in certain western commodities. La Fontaine, in trying to account for a sudden outbreak of accusations of Satanic abuse in Britain in the late 1980s among the marginal members of society living in 'sink' estates, identifies more mundane reasons for a sudden outbreak of supernatural danger. She points to the widespread malaise in Britain at this time: the widening of the gap between the rich and poor, an undermining of respect for those in authority, an increase in one-parent families and divorce and media hysteria about police corruption and government cover-ups (1997).

If in a disordered world witchcraft accusations represent the 'elusive effects of transnational forces' (Comaroff and Comaroff, 1993: xxv), in response to the social nervousness generated by the massive restructuring of late capitalism, conspiracies are often portrayed as 'the poor man's cognitive mapping' (Jameson, 1995). In all instances, a fear of the hidden, occult and mysterious becomes linked to the desire to find closure amidst the uncertainties of late capitalism. In other words, the popularity of the 'traditional' conspiracy lies in its function to provide neat explanations in an untidy and big world where there is no great centre anymore.

Doubtful conspiracies

Do the current explosion of conspiracies represent a novel and distinctive way of articulating anxiety and certainty? Commonly, as we have seen, conspiracy theorizing takes on what Englund and Leach call the meta-narrative of modernity (2000). This is the tendency to depict the economic and social transformations of late capitalism as illustrative of change, rupture and socio-economic breaks. Discontinuity and, by necessity, continuity revolve around a dialectic of emplacement/displacement, fact/fiction, and certainty/doubt (England and Leach, 2000: 237). The act of bringing together what was previously kept apart lies at the heart of the conspiracy, but it is this very movement of connecting and separation which is lost in looking at the sort of questions which conspiracies answer. Inevitably, the conspiracy becomes an event which stands out in an ordered world and which refers to the displacement of objects. The conspiracy comes to frame instability in a world where it is presumed that actors and objects are allocated specific places in what Deleuze calls 'striated space', a space that can be ordered and counted, and that models the chaotic into a common structure of cause and effect (1983, 1988). Along these surfaces, events are invariably constituted as breaks which tear into ordered connections. In this sense, the 'event' appears as a rupture against a plane of homogeneity (see Parker, this volume).

Deleuze and Guattari (1988) distinguish between different scales of discontinuity. First there are the segments that divide us up in everyday life: family/school, work/home. At the same time there are lines which are much more intimate or personal. They mark out feelings and attractions and do not have the same rhythms as our history. We can no longer put up with things in the way that we did yesterday. Things become imperceptibly different as we divide rich/poor, success/failure, love/indifference and so on. Then there are the great breaks that seem to come from 'outside' and consist of processes and movements between macro and micro structures which manifest themselves as sudden catastrophes. Sometimes, in answer to the question, 'what happened?', the inexplicable may also be given the ungraspable feeling of the sublime (Lyotard, 1991). This is the sudden instant when everything comes unexpectedly. Lyotard attributes to these events a feeling of fear and pleasure which he calls the sublime. On the one hand, certain objects carry a threat to our self preservation. They induce terror and silence. On the other hand, the threat to ourselves is always postponed (Lyotard, 1991: 82). So faith and uncertainty live side by side, constructed from a finite number of causal links which answers the questions, 'What?' 'Where?' and 'When?'

If conspiracies are constructed as answers to these specific questions, the search commonly becomes one for a lost truth, as when Merleau-Ponty is able to argue that speech 'tears out or tears apart meanings in the undivided whole of the nameable' (cited in Owens, 1992: 8). Lyotard terms this a force, the libidinal band:

> The whirling bar slows down, the mad aleatory movement which engenders the libidinal band brakes sufficiently for the this and the not-this (which its high speed had confused at every point in the field) now to be distinct, now the this, not the not-this, here it is, now it's gone (cited in Bennington, 1989: 22).

For Lyotard, to answer the question 'Why?' is a nostalgic search for the absent cause. It presumes a slowing down of the bar, the division, such that subjects and objects are emplaced. The question 'why?' ignores the idea that disjuncture not only separates, but brings together and mediates a process of betweeness that enables us to see the real, not as a final closure or the recovery of a lost totality as 'conventional' conspiracy theory would have us find, but as an open origin (see also Cooper, 1992). In this scenario, the lost whole can never be known for its very visibility is dependent on interpretation, a going-between, a backwards and forwards journey (Cooper, 1992). So there is no definite answer to a grand mystery, only a going-between. It is this in-between movement which, paradoxically, undermines the search for a final truth and which also provides us with a new and fascinating way of mapping disorder and order (Cooper, 1997).

A good example of the futile search for a hidden answer is brought to our attention by Beer in her account of the missing link (see also Cooper, 1997). She studies the Victorian idea of the missing link which caught the public's imagination at the same time as the detective novel became increasingly popular. However, while Sherlock Holmes in Conan Doyle's novel, *The Hound of the Baskervilles*, finds the tie between humans and primates, the missing link had no basis in nineteenth century science. Rather, it caught the popular imagination because it raised questions about 'questions of boundaries: what's in, what's out: the object and the abject' (Beer, 1992: 10). The missing link became an absence, a crossing over which was always asking questions rather than seeking final answers, 'a quest that finds that the link is not there' (1992: 13).

In an age of anxiety, perhaps we are always questioning and moving ideas on. Indeed, suggests Beer, 'overinterpretation is a familiar outcome of anxiety ... the itch to notice everything, to control by constant replaying' (Beer, 1992: 7). The tendency to overinterpret becomes common with the paradoxical acknowledgement that in revealing more and more, increasing diversity reveals less and less (Beer, 1992; Strathern, 1991). In an age of increasing risk, amid the questioning of expert knowledge, 'fraudulence and disconfirmation become pleasures' and more necessary than the need for discovery' (Beer, 1992: 13). Authenticity/inauthenticity become inseparable (see also Cooper, 1997). So might present conspiracy theorizing also become a way of assembling possibilities and information, rather than recovering a truth, in a culture obsessed with connections and interpretation?

Truth and a culture of possibility

How might then a new type of conspiracy thinking conceptualize people-objects relations in late capitalist society? Cooper refers to 'a hybridization of mass culture, science and technology' which intends to capture the contingent (1997: 690). Truth, he suggests, in this age refers to 'the emergence of reality out of possibilities' as opposed to a truth which relates to an external fact (691). To account for this, Cooper shows how Vattimo (1997) in *The Transparent Society* uses the analogy of the library to late twentieth-century living. The librarian knows where to look for books and how to look for them, but the library does not belong to the librarian. It cannot 'be grasped in a single look or unity, but requires innumerable perspectives and is constantly remade in an act that defies representation' (Cooper, 1997: 691). A feature of cultural production today is to celebrate this very space where dialogue and exchanges between readers take place (Owens, 1992). This, argues Owens, shifts attention from the work and the producer of this work and onto its frame, its context. Nowhere is this more apparent than in Adorno's analysis of mass culture which has shifted aside the autonomous author and subject:

> If mass culture has already become one big exhibition, then everyone who stumbles into it feels as lonely as a stranger on an exhibition site. This is where information leaps in. The endless exhibition is also the endless bureau of information, which forces itself on the hapless visitor and regales him with leaflets, guides and radio recommendations, sparing each individual from the disgrace of appearing as stupid as everyone else (Adorno, 1991: 71).

The endless stream of information is also best exemplified, argues Cooper (1997) by electronic media where information creates and dissolves fields which are both bounded and open, neither original or copy. Baudrillard distinguished four phases of the image: it is the reflection of basic reality; it marks and perverts a basic reality; it masks the absence of a basic reality; it bears no relation to any reality whatever and it is its own pure simulacrum (1981). Each image is a different way of seeing and of discerning, as in the case of the television advertisement.

> With great flexibility the ad constructs a mini-reality in which things are set in juxtapositions that violate the rules of the everyday. In particular, TV ads

associate meanings, connotations and moods that are inappropriate in reality subject to objections in dialogic communication ... (Poster, 1995: 612).

Simulation occurs through the mirror, not in the world. The medium of the message is somewhere between A and B. Reality in this sense may be understood as a surface where things scatter, a surface that has neither beginning and end but both beginning and end, here and there, and this and that (see Cooper, 1997: 699). Reality is weakened by the interference between what is and whatever might be. Location is both text and context, sign and signifier. More information means more improbability and less understanding as it becomes harder to construct stable canons when knowledge becomes fragmented (Mulgan, 1996: 11). In this unstable world, the conspiracy encompasses a particular style of dissemination, belonging to and cutting through a world of displacement.

The contradiction of cultural confinement characteristic of this type of conspiracy theorizing is made clearer by examining what Lyotard calls 'the set up', the way in which background and foreground interact. He analyses the processes involved in such a dialogue and distinguishes three limits or frames. The theatre walls correspond to the place of the painting, the art book, the place where what is inside is separate from the outside world. The second limit is the stage where the place of the observer is distinguished from the place observed. Finally, there is the frame from which depth is achieved, so that the surface recedes and becomes invisible, forgotten, but which, in a sense, must also be there in order for visibility to be achieved (Cooper, 1992: 297). Likewise, conspiracy theorizing is an attempt to move and fuse boundaries so that the spectator might frame the 'locating' apparatus itself. Owens records how Daniel Buren's art work entitled 'Within and Beyond the Frame', is actually a series of connected and interconnected parts which, to my mind, captures the contingent world of conspiracy theorizing:

> A series of striped banners strung down the middle of the gallery extended out the window and across West Broadway. Similarly, the 'missing parts' of a 1975 installation at the Museum of Modern Art in New York – the imaginary sections of Buren's work 'concealed' by a staircase – were posted on billboards in Soho, thereby reminding viewers that these two parts of the city were already connected by the art economy (Owens, 1992: 129).

Like the patterns created by a child's cats cradle, conspiratorial knowledge may also be woven by one person and then passed between different people, cut and joined together:

> Cat's cradle is about patterns and knots; the game takes great skill and can result in some serious surprises. One person can build up a repertoire of

string figures on a single pair of hands, but the cat's cradle figures can be passed back and forth on the hands of several players who add new moves in the building of complex patterns. Cat's cradle invites a sense of collective work of one person not being able to make all the patterns alone ... It is not always possible to repeat interesting patterns, and figuring out what happened to result in intriguing patterns is an embodied analytical skill (Haraway, 1997: 268).

This is also the success story of the modern conspiracy. If it was once an attempt at totalizing knowledge, spun by a select band of powerful people, today, by its very nature, it also proliferates because there appears to be no real explanation, only more interpretation which involves us all practising some type of conspiracy theorizing. It is perhaps these contingent conditions which account presently for the popularity of conspiracy theorizing where inter-pretation (and not just discovery) is the mark of our age.

Outline of the book

Conspiracy theorizing at the end of the twentieth century marks a new way of governing our relationship with others and our involvement with key social and economic institutions. As Alisdair Spark (this volume) illustrates, if 'old' conspiracy *theories* were about, in Jameson's words, a poor person's mapping of the world, conspiracy *practices* are popular today because there are no overarching cosmologies to explain the world to ourselves. Information is in overload with nothing to tie it together and conspiracy practices are a way of imaginatively moving doubt and suspicion around in a world of conjecture. Peter Knight and Warren Smith, in this volume, also make a distinction between 'old' and 'new' forms of conspiracy culture. Smith characterizes a movement away from what he calls 'traditional' conspiracy paranoia towards the state of antagonistic, jaded playfulness seen in the film *Fight Club* and the television 'detective' work of Chris Morris and Michael Moore. Knight, in turn, identifies an 'insecure' paranoia as characterizing a recent form of 'conspiracy culture' itself generated by the increasing awareness of risk to the self. No longer, Knight argues, are we able to make a distinction between us and them, friend and foe. The older scapegoats of paranoia such as the red under the bed have been replaced by the invasive enemy of the lone hacker and the computer virus. The invisibility of risk, the hidden threat which lurks around every corner, the secret workings of the global economy, mean that there is no safe place to hide.

Knight reasons that since we find ourselves living in a time where there are no satisfactory causal explanations, conspiracy theories provide a sense of agency when faced by the inexplicable. Talk of clusters and syndromes creates more uncertainty and agency panic. If contemporary conspiracy culture is distinguished by the absence of a determined enemy, the highly charged language of paranoia leads to a new conceptualization of identity, of otherness, as the old relationship between victim and conspirator breaks down. The idea of the self-contained, autonomous individual is deeply engrained in social theory and self and society are invariably seen as two distinct entities. Yet Knight illustrates how, quite literally, one's own body can turn against itself in the case of autoimmune diseases. Or, in the case of computer viruses such as the LOVEBUG, the virus infiltrates our home and our PC becomes an agent for the enemy.

In Mark Featherstone's chapter, the paranoia felt when everybody becomes a nobody translates into something quite different, the idea that the self will be anniliated. Featherstone considers how social inclusion is managed at an ideological level, given that the paranoid condition causes a misrecognition of the communicative relationship between self and other. Featherstone pictures a scenario where the self and other become so close, as which happens in the claustrophobic non-distance of paranoia, that the distance which allows the two parties to exchange knowledge breaks down. He highlights the consequence of this politics of absolute difference for social collectivity and justice. The truth is no longer 'out there', but an ideological bias that the post-modern state makes for itself. This disguises the other as inclusion-exclusion behind an imaginary notion of transcendental truth and conceals the violence endemic in the communicative relation in the self/other. Citing Žižek, Featherstone shows how 'traditional' conspiratorial thinking is unable to step outside the capitalist ideology of nomadic independence and understand the value of communicative recognition. Instead, conspiracy ideology perpetuates the paranoic frame of a hell which is other people through the image of the monstrous puppet maker who is blamed for the terrible workings of the world.

The Machiavellian world of the arch manipulator described in Feather-stone's paper is of course most readily apparent in the work of the spin-doctor, a pivotal figure in the contemporary democratic political arena where conspiracy lies at the heart of the political process. Spark in his chapter shows how conspiracy theories about a New World Order are shared by the Left wing and the far Right. He argues that their prevalence cannot be explained by a psychologistic diagnosis of paranoia alone, since conspiracy theory is ever present in contemporary America. So rather than proposing that a paranoia is currently sweeping the United States, Spark maintains that conspiracy theories about a New World Order enact a sort of playfulness. They allow for identities to be fought out, disseminated and exchanged in a contemporary *glocalization*, to use Bauman's phrase, of networks and connections.

Often, however, it suits politicians to downplay the widespread popularity of conspiracies in order to portray conspiracy theorizing as the demonic rantings of a lunatic fringe. Nigel James illustrates this in his analysis of the American far-right which, he contends, is demonized by the middle-ground in order to justify the exclusion of fringe groups from the central political process. According to 'centrists' it is only those individuals at the extreme edge of politics who are suffering from alienation or status anxiety and who hence indulge in conspiracy theorizing around central political figures. This of course, remarks James, diverts attention from the covert activities of key central political figures such as Hoover, Nixon and Clinton. James highlights how conspiracy theorizing is endemic in popular eschatology which is brought to the mass market via the preaching of TV evangelists such as Pat Robertson. He shows how the language of conspiracy and the Christian right has many strands, among them tax protests, anti-governmentalism, socialism and multiculturalism. American is seen to be a Christian nation and Americans are encouraged to defend their nation against global forces of immorality and the New World Order. Moreover, Christian Patriots are to be vigilant against enemies within the United States, namely their own government and federal state representatives. Outrages perpetuated at Waco, Texas become resources that can be deployed to demonstrate the truth of the 'patriot' world view.

In case we should believe that conspiracies are the preserve of the far right, Jonathan Skinner's fieldwork on Montserrat looks at how one man's anti-colonial conspiracies are integral to his belief systems. 'Mr Grey' holds a conspiratorial set of beliefs that allow him easily to accommodate and throw away information, linking minor narratives together to create a wider fantastic narrative. As Gluckman and Evans-Pritchard record, witchcraft beliefs in Africa are not 'closed' systems of thought, but actually absorb 'rational' attacks from colonialist discourses. Likewise, 'secondary elaboration' is also present in conspiracy theory belief systems. Thus, suggests Skinner, like Gluckman *et al.*, perhaps it is possible to look at the processes which are used to substantiate beliefs and conspiracies rather than dismissing them (as perhaps we tend to do in the social sciences) as illogical or based on inadequate evidence. Further, Skinner's chapter illustrates nicely that (as Lilley and Parker argue later in the volume) the process of linking together 'causes' and 'effects' is part of the very construction of narrative itself. In telling stories of, in this case, oppression and injustice, we construct conspiracy.

Often however, the media plays a key role in the spinning of these political conspiracies, whether in Montana or Monserrat, and these are conspiracy models which Adrian Quinn suggests cannot be dismissed as simplistic and naive in their view of power. Quinn analyses the complex dialectics of conspiracy between the media and the National Front in his account of far-right politics in France. The idea that everything is connected, *tout est lié*, is used by the Front to make sense of French society and to enable it to perpetuate a myth of French decadence. It is not necessarily a myth either, suggests Quinn, that the French media takes its lead from the political elite and is controlled by 'outside' forces. This message is used both by Le Pen's National Front both to advance its politics and to portray itself as a victim of a media conspiracy. The media thus plays a paradoxical role in this process. It has a key role in the Front's political thinking – in both assisting it in this role as conspiratorial victim, and also bringing it down through encouraging internal division.

Both James and Quinn make the important point that fringe beliefs are no longer as stigmatized as they once were. They have moved to the centre. This is also the theme tackled by David Bell and Lee-Jane Bennion-Nixon when they query whether the cult has been commoditized. Bell and Bennion-Nixon trace the movement in American television from Fordism to post-Fordism. This was a move away from 'lowest denomination' and 'consensus television' as television companies developed the concept of segmented audiences and 'knowing' viewers. Their analysis focuses on one of the most popular specialized TV shows, *The X-Files*, hailed by them as both the epitome of postmodernism and a modernist adventure, and certainly the by-word for niche TV marketing. Like conspiracy culture itself, Bell and Bennion-Nixon ask whether *The X-Files* is simply an ironic gesture or a sign of more critical intelligence? Their answer is to place Mulder and Scully firmly in the 'excluded middle' as both purveyors of a fake truth and renunciators of all things postmodern. Could the X-Files be a dangerous thing if, as Featherstone forcefully asks, identity politics distract us from what is really going on? As the title of their chapter suggests, 'The Popular Culture of Conspiracy/The Conspiracy of Popular Culture', Bell and Bennion-Nixon take to task those intellectuals who readily consign conspiracy theory to what is derided as the uncredible and incredible realm of popular culture. It is very easy, they argue, to dismiss popular culture as illusional, paranoid and intellectually impoverished and followed by an audience drawn into a state of passivity and dependence. Of course, as they identify in their chapter, this is the view of mass culturalists such as Adorno who makes links between the ideology of the prevailing cultural industry and what he terms the irrationalism of astrology and occultism. Nevertheless, Bell and Bennion-Nixon doubt whether populist pleasure really does indeed distract us from what is really going on. That would be to claim rather too much for one TV show.

If paranoia has perhaps become an essential feature of successful commoditization, returning again to Featherstone, has the preoccupation with identity politics been at the expense of losing authenticity? Is 'real' culture more authentic than popular culture in providing profound insights into the workings of government and society. Or might 'real' culture and 'popular' culture be inextricably intertwined? At the end of the twentieth century, conspiracy theories about alien abductions enjoy a circulation among global audiences and Bell and Beenion-Nixon consider that 'cult' TV is nothing of the sort anymore. Television programmes such as *Star Trek*, *Buffy the Vampire Slayer*, *Angel* and *Charmed* are marketed, so to speak, at the fringe. In this sense, major corporations create cult fashions and trends – Area 51 trading cards, SF comics, *X Files* figures, and toy alien eggs are 'cult' collectors items designed to be cultish.

Warren Smith, in a chapter on corporatism and conspiracy, points out that it is precisely this desire to be first and most fashionable which actually sustains the multinational companies who are behind the global cultural industry. Smith examines how cultural corporatism creates, following Naomi Klein's *No*

Logo (2000), a third culture entirely made up of corporate involvement, brand names, brand people and brand made media. He looks at the ability of consumers to play subtly with this practice of conspiracism, often adding an ironic twist so that they partake in an semi-independent consumption of mass produced objects. In the same way global corporate culture constantly looks to the cultural industry for marketing opportunities to the extent where marketing is even able to subsume subvertising which seeks to undermine the corporate message. Cultural jammers who seek to twist and subvert the media message increasingly see their efforts incorporated into market campaigns such as Nike's slogan 'I am not/A target market/I am an athlete'. Smith asks if there a way of making an identity which is not also a target market? Is it a case of ridding ourselves of our disenchantment with global corporatism through anti-consumerism? Or do we just have to grow up and learn to live with our angst?

Crucial questions posed by contributors about shifting ownership, organization and control are relevant not only in the wider cultural realm, but also within the academy itself. This is not necessarily to accuse social scientists of marketing their own conspiracies, although the authors and contributors in this volume might well have been, but to also recognize, as do both Parker and Lilley, that the human sciences, like conspiracies, share a narrative structure which seeks to order and explain the workings of mass society. Perhaps the ultimate horror lies, as Simon Lilley discovers, not in finding a hidden conspiracy, but realizing that there is no grand plot, only different organizations which (through their own momentum) follow a blind path? Within an 'antagonistic stream of interpretations', Lilley's desire to be identified as an 'able' researcher may, he rues, run contrary to what others believe is 'good' research. This chapter is particularly apt since the author believes himself to be the victim of such a mindless cycle of antagonisms, antagonisms also uncovered in his own research. Having successfully gained state funding to look at the issue of ownership and control in a large paper manufacturer, Lilley finds that within the company, shifting ownership does not necessary equate to shifting control. Yet on presenting these findings, Lilley finds himself at odds with the management ethos of the state funder which responds that the final report is at odds with the original objectives and grades (and hence defines) his research as 'problematic'. So heroic researcher or waster of public money? Or are we merely fooled into thinking that we can be either of these? That depends on how we understand the culture of audit and accountability that brings such managerial conspiracies into being. Since both Lilley and the funders and assessors of his research are brought together through myths of utility and transparency, the blind consequences of their mutual misunderstandings may be tragic, but perhaps not reflect a hidden mechanism.

Martin Parker, in the final chapter, returns to the question of whether there are simply more conspiracies today or, alternatively, are there conditions which encourage conspiracies in the absence of other forms of cognitive mapping? He proposes that both the 'will to connect' and the defining of an event as 'inexplicable' are both part of the same logic of the desire to find order behind the mystery of the surface. In an oddly conspiratorial mapping, conspiracy theorizing and theories about conspiracy perpertuated by academics both share a quest to discover the truth against all odds. Parker's dilemma is that whether it is Jameson or Chomsky, when theorists argue that conspiracies today are the results of changes in global capitalism or a result of the postmodern collapse between fact/fiction, are we not elevating ourselves to that high place occupied by the human sciences to draw on a further explanation? Is it not the case, asks Parker, that we are simply left with a wider conspiracy, but now that now occupies a putatively 'higher' or 'deeper' perspective than the one occupied by the masses? And so he concludes with the suggestion that, while resisting the logic of the question mark is not really possible, it is possible to celebrate and multiply conspiracies rather than condemning them. In this way, truth might also become multiple, and an universalized scepticism become a force which assists resistance to blindness to the 'real' conspiracies that shape the world behind our backs.

In summary then, this is a collection of essays which might entice the reader into seeing conspiracies everywhere. Or it might even encourage the reader to decide which is the most convincing conspiracy out of all the dizzying variety deployed within these pages. Or, have we concealed from the reader our own agenda cleverly hidden amongst the clues and secrets you might find here? I will leave you to decide what it all means, and whether there is something else going on behind this text.

Bibliography

Adorno, T.W., (1991), *The Culture Industry:Selected Readings on Mass Culture*, Bernstein, J. (ed.), London: Routledge.

Auden, W.H., (1948), *The Age of Anxiety*. London: Faber & Faber.

Baudrillard, J., (1981), 'Simulacra and simulations' reprinted and translated in Poster, M. (ed.) (1988), *Jean Baudrillard. Selected Writings*, Cambridge: Cambridge University.

Beck, U., (1992), *Risk Society. Towards a New Modernity*, London: Sage.

Beck, U., (2000), 'Risk Society Revisited:Theory, Politics and Research Programmes', in Barbara Adam, Ulrich Beck and Joost Van Loon (eds), *The Risk Society and Beyond. Critical Issues for Social Theory*, London: Sage.

Bennington, J., (1989), *The Lyotard Reader*, Oxford: Blackwell.

Beer, G., (1992), *Forging the Missing Link: Interdisciplinary Stories*. Cambridge: Cambridge University Press.

Castaneda, C., (2000), 'Child Organ Stealing Stories: Risk, Rumour and Reproductive Technologies', in Barbara Adam, Ulrich Beck and Joost Van Loon, (eds), *The Risk Society and Beyond. Critical Issues for Social Theory*. London: Sage.

Comaroff, J and Comaroff, J. (eds) (1993), *Modernity and Its Malcontents. Ritual and Power in Postcolonial Africa*. Chicago: University of Chicago Press.

Comaroff, J. and Comaroff, J., (1999), Occult Economies and the Violence of Abstraction: Notes From the South African Postcolony, *American Ethnologist*: 279–303.

Cooper, R., (1992), 'Technologies of Representation', in Ahonen, P. (ed.), *Tracing the Semiotic Boundaries of Politics*. Mouton de Gruyter: New York.

Cooper, R., (1997), Millennium notes for social theory, *The Sociological Review*, 45 (4): 690–703.

Deleuze, G., (1983), *On The Line*. New York: Semiotext.

Deleuze, G. and Guattari, F., (1988), *A Thousand Plateaus: Capitalism and Schizophrenia*. London: Athlone.

Englund, H. and Leach, J., (2000), Ethnography and the Meta-Narrative of Modernity, *Current Anthropology*, 41 (2): 225–248.

Furdei, F., (1997), *Culture of Fear. Risk-Taking and the Morality of Low Expectation*, London: Cassell.

Giddens, A., (1990), *The Consequences of Modernity*, Oxford: Polity.

Hacking, I., (1987), *The Emergence of Probability*, Cambridge: Cambridge University.

Haraway, D., (1997), *Modest_Witness@Second_Millennium_FemaleMan_Meets_OncoMouse*. London: Routledge.

Jameson, F., (1995), *The Geopolitical Aesthetic: Cinema and Space in the World System*, London: British Film Institute.

Klein, N., (2000), *No Logo*, London, Flamingo.

La Fontaine, J.S., (1998), *Speak of the Devil. Tales of Satanic Abuse in Contemporary England*, Cambridge: University of Cambridge.

Larner, C., (1984), *Witchcraft and Religion: the Politics of Popular Belief*, Oxford: Blackwell.

Lyotard, J.F., (1991), *The Inhuman*. Cambridge: Polity Press.

Marwick, M., (1982), *Witchcraft and Sorcery*, London: Penguin.

Mulgan, J., (1996), High Tech and High Angst in Sarah Dunant and Roy Porter (eds), *The Age of Anxiety*, London: Virago Press.

Owens, C., (1992), *Beyond Recognition. Representation, Power and Culture*, Berkeley: University of California Press.

Poster, M., (1995), *The Second Media Age*, Oxford: Polity Press.

Prior, L., (1997), 'Actuarial Visions of Death: Life, Death and Chance in the Modern World', in Peter Jupp and Glennys Howarth (eds), *The Changing Face of Death. Historical Accounts of Death and Disposal*, London: MacMillian Press.

Scheper-Hughes, N., (2000), The Global Traffic in Human Organs, *Current Anthropology*, Vol 41 (2): 191–224.

Strathern, M., (1991), *Partial Connections*. Savage, Maryland: Rowman and Littlefield.

Taussig, M., (1992), *The Nervous System*. London: Routledge.

Taylor, M., (1995), Rhizomic Fields of Interstanding, *Tekhnema*, 2: 24–36.

Trevor-Roper, H.R., (1969), *The European Witch-Craze of the 16th and 17th Centuries*, London: Pelican Books.

Vyse, S.A., (1997), *Believing in Magic. The Psychology of Superstition*, Oxford: Oxford University Press.

ILOVEYOU: Viruses, paranoia, and the environment of risk

Peter Knight

Early in the morning of 4th May 2000, an electronic virus began to sweep across computer systems at an astonishing rate. The outbreak started in Asia before spreading to Europe, then hitting computer systems in the USA, as users logged online and checked their email as their first task of the day. Within a few hours 100,000 systems had been infected; by the end of the week when the epidemic had begun to subside, the virus had struck 45 million computers in 20 countries, causing an estimated \$8 billion in damage (Suplee, 2000). Individual users and major organizations alike were crippled by the virus. From the Pentagon to Parliament, and from Microsoft to the BBC, it seemed that no one was immune. The virus (or, more technically, a worm) came in an email headed 'ILOVEYOU', and the text of the message read, 'Kindly check the attached love letter from me!' Once opened, the viral programme embedded in the attachment began to rename and relocate image and music files on the user's computer. Then it redirected the user's web browser to a site which downloaded an additional viral component, allowing all the passwords stored on the computer to be redirected to an anonymous site. Finally the 'Love Bug' (as it quickly became known) sent copies of the original email to everyone in the user's address books – and so on it spread, in a rapid proliferation across the globe.

Given the extent of the damage, it was little surprise that across the world's networks and airwaves the ILOVEYOU virus generated much alarm, a fair amount of which was framed in the rhetoric of paranoia and conspiracy. The Love Bug was not in itself an altogether new phenomenon. Its digital architecture and tactics resembled the Melissa virus of the previous year, which had likewise spread rapidly by sending copies of itself to names in a user's email address book – although, in that case, the rate of infection was fifteen times less because the virus only used the first fifty names in the address book (Rae-Dupree, 2000).

Indeed, conspiracy-minded anxieties about viral infiltration are not especially new occurrences. Since the middle of the nineteenth century, and especially in America, fears about invasive enemies – both real and imagined, both internal and external – have been framed in a conspiracy-infused language drawn from immunology and epidemiology (see Tomes, 1998). The idea of the national and the individual immune system under threat from alien invaders, be they from microbes, Mars, or Moscow, has repeatedly captured the public imagination. Most prominently, the popular and political culture of the 1950s in America teemed with images of germophobic invasion, mind control and bodysnatching, from anti-Communist propaganda to Hollywood films. These demonological attacks typically conjured up the spectre of an undesirable enemy suddenly infiltrating and corrupting the vulnerable body politic of WASPish America.[1] By imagining a temporary and eradicable threat from a distinctive enemy, these fears of invasion paradoxically served to bolster a sense – albeit a very restrictive one – of national or communal identity.

In the last two decades the paranoid rhetoric of quarantine and infiltration has returned with a vengeance, first during the AIDS epidemic, and now with the threat of computer viruses. Some commentators framed these episodes in the familiar rhetoric of an isolated invasion from undesirable influences (once again the usual suspects included, in the former case, blacks and gays, and, in the latter, disaffected youth). The real lesson, however, was that the safe distinction between imperilled self and undesirable other had begun to collapse. Unlike the sudden invasion by demonized monsters (whether from outer space or from the id or from society's unconscious) in the horror films of the 1950s, the nightmares of turn-of-the-millennium America – urban crime, random violence, economic insecurity, drugs, pollution and viral contamination – create an omnipresent and quite visible environment of risk which is centred less on the nation than on the vulnerable individual body (or its neural extension in electronic circuitry). In his introduction to *The Politics of Everyday Fear*, Brian Massumi offers an astute and acerbic commentary on this situation (which in his view is as cynically exploited as the former Cold War terror):

> The cold war in foreign policy has mutated into a state of generalized deterrence against an enemy without qualities. An unspecified enemy threatens to rise up at any time at any point in social or geographical space. From the welfare state to the warfare state: a permanent state of emergency against a multifarious threat as much in us as outside (Massumi, 1993: 10–11).

The superpower face-off has given way to a policy of 'low intensity conflict', producing a continuous but often unspecific sense of threat that is now located everywhere but nowhere in particular, just the kind of diffused, decentred notion of power for which the Internet (and its viral plagues) provide the perfect example and model.

The secure paranoia of the tense yet clear geopolitical division between self and other has given way to the troubling confusions that have emerged since the late 1960s, with uncertainty about the distinction between friend and foe, from American military intervention in Vietnam to peace-keeping missions in Africa. After the revival of Cold War demonology during the Reagan years, the 'New World Order' of the 1990s has introduced an insecure paranoia in which there is no longer a single recognizable enemy or indeed a clear sense of national identity. We have met the enemy, the logic goes, and it is us.

Given the close link between the rhetoric of germophobia and national politics, it comes as no surprise that there has been a corresponding shift in the vocabulary of immunology (and hence digital immunology) during this period. Since its emergence as a discipline towards the end of the last century, immunology has primarily been concerned with identifying the mechanisms by which bodies defend themselves from attack by foreign antigens. Its fundamental principle has been the distinction between self and non-self. In immunological discourse in the last three decades, the frontline of the battle against disease has shifted from the surfaces of the body (the skin as a protective barrier and personal hygiene as one's best defence) to the complex mechanisms of the immune system as a regulatory process at work within the body in the blood and lymph systems. More recently immunologists have been concerned with the complicated and troubling erosion of the supposedly bedrock distinction between self and other, provoked by an interest in autoimmune diseases in general and HIV/AIDS in particular. There has also been a corresponding slow erosion of the distinction between the material and the immaterial, as biological viruses have come to be seen as packages of code, and computer viruses have come to be described in the language of biology.

In immunology, the focus of attention is now 'The Wars Within', in the words of the subtitle of a famous article by Peter Jaret (with photographs by Lennart Nilsson) in *National Geographic*. The article offers dramatic pictures and accounts of the struggles waged in 'inner space', with, for example, macrophagocytes enveloping a bacterium in a scene that looks like nothing so much as an episode from *Star Wars*. The text uses a militarized language of enemies and invasion, but, when it comes to discussing HIV, the body-as-battlefield becomes fused with elements from an espionage tale:

> Many of these enemies have evolved devious methods to escape detection. The viruses that cause influenza and the common cold, for example, constantly mutate, changing their fingerprints. The AIDS virus, most insidious of all, employs a range of strategies, including hiding out in healthy cells. What makes it fatal is its ability to invade and kill helper T cells, thereby short-circuiting the entire immune response (Jaret, 1986: 709).

The inert virus is imbued with malicious agency, while the self is repeatedly metonymized into ever more microscopic particles of defence, forming immunological homunculi which are figured as miniaturized special agents. Though its metaphors are still mainly militaristic, immunology now draws on images of messy wars, civil unrest, domestic terrorism, and so on, precisely the kind of troubled, low-intensity conflict that has come to dominate the post-Cold War world. Furthermore, I want to suggest, events like the ILOVEYOU outbreak represent a significant mutation in the evolving history of conspiracy culture because they are not isolated irruptions into the stable status quo but

19

an inevitable consequence of the normal order of things in the wired world. Conspiracy-minded fears about viruses, whether digital or biological, therefore need to be understood in the context of a new and pervasive environment of risk.

Risky business

Anthony Giddens, Ulrich Beck and others have argued that in recent decades society has become dominated by risk (see Giddens, 1990, 1999; Beck, 1992; Franklin, 1998). The idea is not that life is any more dangerous than in the past, but that people (primarily in the First World) are being forced to rethink their attitude to the hazards of life. Since the Enlightenment most people have come to believe that natural disasters are not blind acts of God but are part of a predictable universe. Until recently, science has held out the promise of predicting and therefore controlling risks. For the events that can't be controlled technologically, there is the safety net of insurance, which is based on a statistical projection of the patterns of hazard. This safety net extends from commercial insurance to the welfare state, and is part of a larger social framework based on stability and tradition as coping structures. In recent decades, however, it has become clear that the kinds of technological intervention designed to gain mastery over the forces of nature and to reduce risk have in fact only served to increase risk. As Beck and Giddens have pointed out, we now worry less about what nature can do to us than about what we have done to nature. Risks are no longer necessarily external interruptions of everyday modern social and economic activity but are an inevitable (albeit unintended) consequence of technological progress. Who knows what the long-term effects of industrial production on the global climate will be, or whether the BSE outbreak (so-called mad cow disease) will produce a huge health problem at some point further down the line? The unparalleled global concatenation of trade and industry now means that risks are not only unpredictable but also uncontrollable. If life-threatening world-wide phenomena such as global warming or the AIDS epidemic can be neither traced back to a single cause nor confined to a single location, then individual national governments are unlikely to be able to bring them under control. Such events are the seemingly inescapable but unforeseeable by-products of modernization, with its global movement of people and manufacture of goods. Risks in the age of globalization are therefore not isolated interruptions of normal service but are part of business as usual.

Man-made 'natural' disasters are a part of the process of postmodernity, whose interwoven global complexities mean that cause and effect can never be mapped with certainty or simplicity. We now need to think in terms of clusters of causes, convoluted feedback mechanisms, syndromes, and decentred agency. If this is the case, the argument goes, then it would be a mistake always to try and blame misfortunes on a single, simple scapegoat – as conspiracy theories traditionally do. As Beck contends, 'risks are no longer attributable to external agency' (1998: 15). On the street and on the Web, however, Beck's pronouncement has not been heeded. Since we find ourselves living in times for which there are as yet no satisfactory 'cognitive maps' (Jameson, 1988) and no adequate popular forms of causal explanation to replace the older varieties of naming and blaming, it comes as no surprise that there has been a dramatic rise in recent decades in the popularity of conspiracy thinking.[2] Conspiracy theorists have traditionally sought to blame current misfortunes on a shadowy cabal of secret plotters. A conspiracy theory typically claims that there is a hidden agenda and a hidden hand behind current events. In effect conspiracy theories have tended to restore a sense of agency, causality and responsibility to what would otherwise seem the inexplicable play of forces over which we have no control. Even as they draw attention to the people's lack of power (since the conspiracy controls everything), they offer a compensatory fantasy that at least things are still controllable by an all-powerful individual or group. As with the current popularity of astrology and other new age forms of belief, in some cases talk of conspiracy returns to an older and hence more comforting belief system, even as it gives narrative expression to a sense of victimhood and widespread distrust of authorities. In effect it attempts to make the convoluted, decentred processes of contemporary global capitalism more rational and more dramatic – in short, to put a name and a face to otherwise unrepresentable and impenetrable systems.

In the case of the Love Bug, conspiracy-minded blame for the chaos hitting the world's computer networks was pinned not old demonological favourites like the Masons, the Bilderbergers or even the CIA, but on those corporate groups most likely to benefit from the disruption. Almost as fast as the virus itself spread its way across the globe, rumours about the origin of the e-plague ricocheted around the Net. The online version of *Wired* magazine, for example, quickly received emails about the event which identified three different culprits (King, 2000). Since the ILOVEYOU worm seemed to corrupt MP3 music files (in fact it merely renamed and relocated them), some correspondents argued that the music industry in general – and the Recording Industry Association of America (RIAA) in particular – must be behind it all. The RIAA, conspiracy theorists were quick to point out, is currently trying to get the courts to outlaw Napster, a software programme which allows people to trade and distribute music files easily and freely over the Internet – and which, it claims, will destroy the whole music industry. What better way to bring the free downloading of MP3 files to a halt than the release of virus which would make any user think twice about accepting files from strangers? And just so that no one would cast suspicion on the industry, the reasoning proceeds, the worm was given several destructive features so as to hide the true one. In a similar vein, other armchair detectives noted that the bug also appeared to destroy JPEG image files. Since most people who download porn would be unlikely to take back-ups of their digital pictures, the argument continued, the online porn industry would benefit enormously if all those consumers were forced to download everything again. Finally, some commentators speculated that the one organization with access to the source code of the email programme which the virus used to propagate itself was none other Microsoft, whose plans for global domination (the correspondents pointed out) have recently been thwarted by legal attempts to curb their monopoly position.

Although this conspiracy-minded hearsay follows a well-trodden line of blaming calamities on shadowy cabals, it is also in the spirit of a newer form of conspiracy culture. They are a long way from traditional right-wing conspiracy theories with their rigid and hate-filled doctrines of faith which blame current woes on an often blameless scapegoat. They are also far from the earnest, countercultural allegations about the secret activities of the so-called military-industrial complex that have become increasingly familiar since the 1960s. In contrast, these conspiratorial rumours were on-the-fly speculations that seemed to be mooted with a degree of irony and uncertainty. If their proponents didn't totally believe in the theories, neither did they fully disbelieve them either. Even if factually inaccurate, to many minds these conspiracies theories *might as well* be true. They functioned not so much as full-blown conspiracy theories as an opportunistic commentary on some of the key issues facing the Internet today. Just how much should be free and who should control it? What is the future of the Web if the only business regularly to make a profit is pornography? And has the success of Microsoft enabled near universal compatibility of file formats, or has its monopoly position left the digital world as vulnerable to catastrophic viruses as the mono-cultured potato which led to Ireland's famine in the nineteenth century?

Although these conspiracy-minded rumours offered a popular rationalization of the seemingly irrational chaos of the connected world, they were not the most significant feature of the Love Bug episode. For one thing, this and other similar virus scares vividly brought home the astonishing connectedness of the wired world. Unlike previous generations of computer virus which were spread one-by-one through corrupted floppy disks, the Melissa and ILOVEYOU worms spread like a nuclear chain reaction out of control, exponentially infecting whole networks with amazing speed. They not only caused damage for each recipient, but the sheer volume of email traffic they caused as they propagated caused network servers to crash, if system administrators had not already shut them down for fear of that happening. Like the unprecedented expansion in the electronic flow of currency and information (a trillion dollars are exchanged *each day* on the international finance markets [Giddens, 2000: 10]), the increasing ubiquity of the Internet in personal and professional lives in the First World is rapidly changing the way we do business with one another. More than any government report or television advert hyping up the infinite connectedness of the planet, the Love Bug offered a compelling demonstration of the power – and the danger – of everything and everyone on the Net being connected.

It also seemed a textbook example of the unpredictable and uncontrollable 'manufactured risks' produced by the march of progress (think of the IBM ads which offer not products but 'solutions'). As many commentators ruefully pointed out, the price to be paid for the fast and free exchange of information over the Internet is vulnerability to malicious invasion. Whatever its origin, this digital fireball quickly escaped the ability of any one agency or company or government to control it. If the strength and innovation of the Internet is its distributed and decentred architecture (designed originally by the American military to allow communication to continue in the event of a nuclear strike), then it is also its Achilles heel.

But the Love Bug was also quite *literally* a manufactured risk. The FBI, working with the National Infrastructure Protection Center, soon announced that they had traced the origin of the virus to an email address in the Philippines.[3] Onel de Guzman, a 23-year-old computer student from Manila, was arrested by the Filipino authorities, and accused of releasing the malicious software. Since the Philippines did not have laws about computer hacking and vandalism, he was charged with credit card fraud, as the Love Bug acted in part to search and deliver users' passwords, including credit card details; but the case against him under the existing laws was deemed insufficient, and he was later released. Given that de Guzman had been cautioned at a local computer college for trying to present a thesis which detailed how to engineer an illegal password-sniffing programme, and given that various hidden clues buried deep in the virus code seemed to point to him and his friends, de Guzman's digital fingerprints were all over the crime. Yet in his defence de Guzman claimed that he hadn't intended to cause global computer destruction, but merely to steal some passwords. (It was also perhaps to take revenge on his college for rejecting the thesis proposal: one line of the bug's code read, 'I hate go to school'). De Guzman's assertion that it was an accident is perhaps somewhat ingenuous, but looked at another way his claim of innocence makes some sense. 'Spyder' (the signature name embedded in the bug's code) may have deliberately plotted to create a deadly virus, but he had no way of knowing how it would react in the messy complexity of the digital environment. David Smith, the convicted creator of the Melissa virus, likewise insisted in his defence that 'I did not expect or anticipate the amount of damage that took place ... I had no idea there would be such profound consequences to others' (Martinson, 1999: 28). Leaving aside the twenty-nine deliberately engineered copycat variations on the original ILO-VEYOU worm, computer viruses are susceptible, like actual biological viruses, to mutation and hence unpredictable futures. (Significantly, a forerunner to Melissa and ILOVEYOU was called Chernobyl, that most dramatic symbol of a risky world). More likely than a carefully plotted act of global terrorism, it began to seem that the Love Bug was just an ill-thought-out prank that got out of hand. What once might have been an act of disgruntled arson that ended up flaming out of control until the school burnt down became in the age of globalization a worldwide (if temporary) computer meltdown. The Internet in particular and the global trade of goods and information in general simply cannot be controlled or interfered with in any reliable and predictable way, for good or ill, by lone hackers or corporate conspiracies.

The worldwide web of connections ensures that there is no guarantee that intended actions will produce the anticipated results. What looks like the product of a deliberate conspiracy for global domination might in fact be no more than the unplanned collusion of vested interests or a lone hacker's experiment that gets out of control. In the decentred ecosystem of the global economy, what we can only describe as conspiracies seem to emerge without there being any particular act of intended conspiring. In this climate, both 'lone gunman' theories and conspiracy theories – traditionally the only two options – rely on outmoded notions of effective causality and agency, in their bid to offer perceptual and moral purchase on current events. Where conspiracy theories might once have nostalgically tried to name and blame a single cause and a single cabal, in their proliferating complexity and uncertainty they now paradoxically end up gesturing towards the conceptions of decentred and endlessly displaced power that have become in vogue in the social sciences inspired by chaos and complexity theory – the very opposite, in fact, of traditional conspiracy theories.[4]

No word for rational fear

In common with other manufactured risks, it is never easy to decide whether apocalyptic fears about computer viruses and hackers are justified or exaggerated, or, to put it another way, whether scare stories are paranoid or prescient. With the Love Bug and other computer virus outbreaks, it is hard to know where the dividing line between a justified suspiciousness and a scaremongering paranoia lies. And in many ways that is precisely the point about contemporary conspiracy culture: no longer can the pathologizing accusation of paranoia be made with any certainty, because in many cases it is far from clear what the rational position should be. With so much conflicting scientific expertise, how do you choose which expert to believe? Indeed, a permanent, low-level and sceptical form of everyday paranoia now seems to be a necessary and understandable default approach to life in risk society. As risk society theorists have noted, authorities are often caught in a double bind when it comes to giving warnings in conditions of uncertain knowledge about episodes like BSE, global warming and the AIDS epidemic (eg, Giddens, 1999: 29–32). If they issue dire warnings that do not come to pass, they are accused of scaremongering and lose credibility even if the worst case scenarios do not pan out *precisely because* people heeded the advice and changed their behaviour accordingly, as happened to some degree in the case of AIDS (though HIV infection levels are once again rising in the UK). Conversely, if the authorities fail to take potential dangers seriously, then they are accused, in an increasingly common conspiratorial expression of distrust of experts and officials, of a cover-up (the BSE crisis is the obvious example here).

In the case of the ILOVEYOU outbreak, as much as network servers were clogged up with email traffic generated by the worm itself, they were also inundated by people sending warnings about the virus and desperately trying to download anti-virus software.[5] According to various virus-watching websites (eg, Vmyths.com), most virus warnings are hoaxes which are then passed on unwittingly: most of us never know which warning we should take seriously. Sceptics warn that passing them on to everyone in your address book (as several of my colleagues have earnestly done) only serves to take up bandwidth. The inevitable effect is a follow-up round of multi-forwarded emails which warn in equally authoritative terms that the original warning should be ignored and not circulated, and so on, potentially forever. Given the choice between two equally plausible warnings, both of which arrive in your inbox through entangled chains of forwarding, most people find it impossible to know what is the sensible course of action. What makes the situation worse is that online perils no longer necessarily come from strangers. You only received Melissa and the Love Bug from people you knew. In this heady climate of ignorance, gullibility and justified paranoia, conspiratorial rumours often circulate on the Net that panic about hackers and viruses – and perhaps even the viruses themselves – are spread by the burgeoning computer protection industry (the 'viral-industrial defence complex' was worth $1 billion in 1999–2000 [Suplee, 2000; on similar rumours from the early 1990s, see Ross, 1991]). One astute but vicious variant of the Love Bug posed itself as an anti-virus fix for the original worm from one of the major virus protection companies, instructing recipients to click on the attachment to obtain protection. The result was near total destruction of all the files and the operating system on the unlucky user's PC. With no obvious or watertight way to tell the difference between irrational fears and warranted suspicions, rumours, theories and counter-claims circulate around the Net in an ever-quickening spiral.

Total immunity

In the face of such threats, many people have begun to wonder whether total immunity from online hazards is possible. At a hearing of the US House Science Committee's Technology Subcommittee in the aftermath of the Love Bug outbreak, Representative Anthony David Weiner (D, NY) gave vent to popular anger that that there had been an 'utter, abject failure' of the anti-virus industry's promise of protection (Clausing, 2000). 'I don't understand why it is', Weiner continued, 'that with all this technology we have, this couldn't have been predicted'. After all, he argued, the Love Bug had been assembled out of bits of code already widely known, not least from the previous year's Melissa virus. But in response the computer security experts called to give witness on Capitol Hill insisted that a guarantee of total protection was impossible, since no programme could ever anticipate all possible developments in malicious software creation. Even if such a programme were logically or technically possible, in the unregulated global realm of the Internet there is no consensus on whose responsibility it is to provide protection from invasion: the anti-virus industry, the skeleton non-government agencies nominally in control of the Internet, government intelligence agencies, Internet service providers, company system administrators, or individual users?

Leaving aside suspicions that the industry was trying to cover up its vested interest in the never-ending arms race of destruction and protection, its warning is in tune with the arguments of risk society theorists. In an age of unforeseeable risks, Giddens warns, it is pointless (although understandable) to seek the guarantees of security and immunity from harm that we have been used to in the past (1989). Peter Tippett, an epidemiologist-turned-computer security expert at ICSA.net, warned the congressional committee that 'you can't generically stop viruses unless you stop your computer from running programs' (Clausing, 2000). On this line of thinking, viruses are an unpredictable (but also fairly inevitable) by-product of having highly connected computer networks that allow fast and unregulated exchange of data. 'If you want a closed Internet', observed Harris Miller, president of the Information Technology Association of America, 'you can have that, but you'll have to pay the price'. Unfortunately, he continued, 'the openness of it is its vulnerability' (Clausing, 2000). It seems that the possibility of infection is the price of instant intimacy, both digital and emotional (after all, the Love Bug email promised a love letter from an unacknowledged admirer, a poignant ruse which disabled the defences of many otherwise savvy Net users).

The sense of unease at the impossibility of complete immunity from digital infection has become a familiar feature of our current environment of risk. The AIDS epidemic most notably reintroduced the 1950s germophobic (and often homophobic) rhetoric of contamination and quarantine into the social arena. In the 1980s, amid fears that a disease which infected 'them' (read: deviant) might begin to infect 'us' (read: the virtuous mainstream), there emerged a moralizing 'body McCarthyism' (Kroker and Kroker, 1987) which sought to reinforce traditional social and sexual divisions through the scaremongering rhetoric of a *cordon sanitaire*. Not only did the containment strategy of dividing society into the 'general populations' and 'at risk' identities collapse under its own incoherence, but a host of other seemingly watertight distinctions began to blur: gay and straight; official knowledge and pseudo-science; the material and the informational; the human and the viral; host and parasite; the self and the non-self, and so on (see Treichler, 1988). In the last few years, for example, even the 'safe sex' promise of a fully quarantined self has begun to give way to more realistic advice on strategies for 'safer sex'.

Fears about potential environmental hazards, from acid rain to GM (genetically modified) food likewise speak to a realization that there is nowhere completely safe to hide – not even in the home or in one's own body. In contrast to the rhetoric of body panic in the 1950s whose ultimate point of reference was the body politic, current fears of infiltration from alien forces have become quite literal, for all the ideological baggage they still carry with them. Food safety scares, the prominence in the popular imagination of newly emerging diseases, and an increase in allergies all contribute to an age of anxiety in which the self and the body are under attack not just from without but also from within. We find ourselves immersed in an environment of risk, with no way of escape or safe place to hide, and no certain knowledge about how our daily environment affects us. Is asthma caused by the increase in pollution, or is it due to our immune system's intolerance to household dust which in turn is a result of our *lack* of exposure to dirt in modern, hyper-hygienic homes? The scientific jury is still out, but the need to protect ourselves is pressing.

From secure to insecure paranoia

It was, however, not just the threat of corrupted files and email traffic jams that made people so aptly paranoid about the ILOVEYOU worm. I would argue that it was also the Love Bug's nature as a form of *virus* that made it and its mutations such potent symbols of the current age of anxiety. Fears about microbial invasion, both literal and metaphorical, have long been part of the cultural landscape, from nineteenth-century scaremongering concerns about disease, dirt and immigration (see Kraut, 1994) to the anti-Communist and anti-deviance germophobia of the 1950s in America: 'Is your washroom breeding Bolsheviks?', a contemporary paper tissue poster asked (Ross, 1989: 150). By dramatizing the self or race or nation under threat from an external enemy, however tiny, these immunological scare stories have traditionally served to bolster the sense of identity of the imperilled individual and national body. Only by imagining a coherent and determined enemy, the logic goes, can one conceive of the self or nation as a coherent entity that can survive the threat. From its outset the science of immunology has taken the division between self and non-self as its basic premise, and this bedrock distinction has made its language available for recycling in the wider cultural arena (see Featherstone, this volume).

In recent years, as I have suggested, that hard-and-fast division between self and other has begun to be questioned both within immunology and within the culture at large (see Martin, 1994; Haraway, 1991). Prompted by an interest in newly emerging autoimmune diseases such as ME, multiple chemical sensitivity and of course HIV/AIDS, some revisionist immunologists have begun to speculate that the relationship between self and non-self is much more fluid than previously thought. In the case of autoimmune diseases, the body appears to attack itself, as the division between invader and resister – conspirator and victim – breaks down. Indeed, the nature of viruses in general erodes the conceptual clarity of the unshakeable difference between self and other. Unlike bacteria, which are more easily thought of as alien invaders, viruses are inactivate strings of code covered in protein, which require a suitable host to spring into action. The protein coatings allow the virus to penetrate a host cell by mimicking a non-threatening organism. Once inside, the virus's genetic code fuses with the host cell's RNA or DNA, that most intimate, but also most inhuman, location of unique identity. It rewrites the cell's biological instruction book, telling it to produce further copies of the virus, which then go on to infect other cells in their search for a host. At this most fundamental level, then, there is a blurring between self and other, as the body's defences are turned into agents for the enemy. In the case of the Love Bug, computer users found to their horror that their PC, that increasingly indispensable extension of our own neural circuits (in Marshall McLuhan's terms), had seemingly taken on a life and a mind of its own.

As the literary critic Timothy Melley has argued, however, the highly-charged metaphorical language of infiltration in which immunological dramas are cast (as my own account above demonstrates) can in fact serve once again to bolster a sense of a unique and self-contained self under threat (Melley, 1999: 173–78). Fears about addiction, mind control or viral take-overs of the body's will, Melley suggests, end up restaging the distinction between an autonomous besieged self and unauthorized infiltration at one remove. The romantic rhetoric of *agency panic* (in Melley's phrase) returns with a vengeance, as the humanist conception of a struggle between an independent self and external influences is dramatized in minuscule.

The host cell becomes a homunculus, a displaced but miniature version of the larger self, preserving the fantasy of freedom of will and immunity from alien control, if only by attributing those qualities of agency to the blind interactions of cells.[6] Melley's account of this rhetorical manoeuvre in popular and literary discourses of corporeal invasion is often persuasive. But at a certain stage increasingly desperate attempts to maintain a conceptual distinction between self and other, inside and outside, autonomous agency and 'deterritorialized' desire, begin to buckle under the pressure of fact. As much as viral invasion, whether biological or digital, is couched in the traditional, conspiracy-minded lingua franca of agency panic, it can delay but not deny the ultimate conclusion that at a fundamental level the carefully policed border of identity is forever compromised.

It is in this situation that the traditional function of corporeal paranoia enters a distinctive new phase. Whereas everyday paranoia about enemy invasion has in the past functioned paradoxically to conserve a secure sense of Them and Us, now the increasing awareness of being immersed in a permeable environment of risk produces what might be termed *insecure paranoia*. If people used to voice fears that the individual or national body was under threat from conspiring enemies from within, then more recently the truly scary proposition is that there is no longer any sure-fire way of telling the difference between self and threatening other, between friend and foe. One extremely destructive variant on the ILOVEYOU worm, for example, continually mutated itself by changing the subject line of the email it sent out to propagate itself. It cunningly used the name of a randomly snatched file recently opened by the computer's user. Not only did this mean that it was very difficult to devise anti-virus programs that could capture this 'NewLove' variant (since

28   © The Editorial Board of The Sociological Review 2001

such programmes tend to scan for known danger words), but that the recipient would far more easily be gulled into believing that the virus-laden file was quite legitimate – not only would it come from someone familiar, but its title referred to something recognizable (Schwartz, 2000). The significance of paranoia-inducing events such as the Love Bug outbreak, then, is not so much that older scapegoated enemies (Russia, deviant 'enemies within', or even one's own government) have been replaced by a new source of fears (a solo disgruntled hacker from the Far East). It is, rather, that the safe distinction between enemy and ally has come unstuck. In the environment of risk, a love letter might well turn out to be hate mail.

Notes

1 According to recent interpretations of the sci-fi/horror genre of the 1950s, candidates for the role of un-American included not just Communists but also blacks, gays and women, all of whom were seen to constitute a threat to the status quo (see Knee, 1997; Benshoff, 1997; Rogin, 1984).
2 The emergence of risk society is, however, not the only explanation for the current prevalence of conspiracy theories and popular paranoia. There are more particular stories to be told about the local functions and contours of conspiracy thinking in various countries and communities. For an outline of the different roles that talk of conspiracy plays in the United States, see Knight (2000).
3 Despite the heavy-handed way in which the US authorities attempted to intervene in the Philippines' jurisdiction, the case outlined how impotent any single national agency is to deal with crime which is located everywhere but nowhere in particular. The irony is also that, just over a century after the United States' arrogant imperial invasion of the Philippines in 1898, a single disaffected Filipino hacker managed to invade vital security and business interests in the USA without leaving his living room (or, more accurately, the living room of his hapless sister, who was initially arrested in place of her brother by the Philippines Bureau of Investigation).
4 For an extended discussion of the convergence of conspiracy theory and other ideas of interconnectedness, see Knight, 2000, chapter 6.
5 There were many conflicting claims about the estimated total cost of the Love Bug outbreak, and how much damage it caused. One report reckoned that 98% of US business received the virus, and 65% were infected (Clausing, 2000); in the UK it was estimated that between 10 and 30% of businesses were hit (Meek, 2000). Another preliminary survey, however, suggested that only 15% of all adult emailers in the US received the virus, but only a quarter of them opened the attachment (Schwartz, 2000).
6 Although there are many comparisons between computer viruses and their biological forerunners, the former have agency programmed into them in quite literal ways which the latter do not. But even the most carefully contrived software agents can accidentally turn coat, either through mutation in the wild, or because they themselves contain accidental coding 'bugs'.

References

Beck, U., (1992), *Risk Society: Towards a New Modernity*. London: Sage.
Beck, U., (1998), 'Politics of Risk Society', in Franklin (1998).
Benshoff, H.M., (1997), *Monsters in the Closet: Homosexuality and the Horror Film*. Manchester: Manchester University Press.

Clausing, J., (2000), 'In Hearing on "Love Bug", Lawmakers Go After Software Industry'. *New York Times* (*Cybertimes*), 11 May. < http://www.nytimes.com > .

Franklin, J. (ed.) (1998), *The Politics of Risk Society*. Cambridge: Polity Press.

Giddens, A., (1990), *Consequences of Modernity*. Cambridge: Polity Press.

Giddens, A., (1999), *Runaway World: How Globalisation is Reshaping Our Lives*. London: Profile Books.

Haraway, D., (1991), 'The Biopolitics of Postmodern Bodies: Constitutions of Self in Immune Systems Discourse'. In *Simians, Cyborgs, and Women: The Reinvention of Nature*. London: Free Association Books.

Jameson, F., (1988), 'Cognitive Mapping', in Cary Nelson and Lawrence Grossberg (eds), *Marxism and the Interpretation of Culture*. Basingstoke: Macmillan, pp. 347–358.

Jaret, P., (1986), 'Our Immune System: The Wars Within'. *National Geographic*, June 1986, pp. 702–735.

King, B., (2000), 'Love Bug: The Conspiracy'. *Wired*, online version, 6 May 2000. < http://www.wired.com/news/print/0,1294,36166,00.html > .

Knee, A., (1997), 'The American Science Fiction Film and Fifties Culture', unpublished PhD diss., Cinema Studies, NYU.

Knight, P., (2000), *Conspiracy Culture: From the Kennedy Assassination to 'The X-Files'*. London: Routledge.

Kraut, A.M., (1994), *Silent Travelers: Germs, Genes, and the 'Immigrant Menace'*. Baltimore: Johns Hopkins University Press.

Kroker, A. and Kroker, M., (eds) (1987), *Body Invaders*. London: St. Martin's Press.

Martin, E., (1994), *Flexible Bodies: Tracking Immunology in American Culture – From the Days of Polio to the Age of AIDS*. Boston: Beacon Press.

Martinson, J., (1999), 'E-finance: Guilty Plea in the Melissa Case'. *Guardian*, 10 December, p. 28.

Massumi, B., (1993), 'Everywhere You Want to Be: Introduction to Fear'. In Massumi (ed.), *The Politics of Everyday Fear*. Minneapolis: University of Minnesota Press.

Meek, J., (2000), 'Love Bug Virus Wreaks Chaos'. *Guardian*, 5 May, p. 1.

Melley, T., (1999), *Empire of Conspiracy: The Culture of Paranoia in Postwar America*. Ithaca, NY: Cornell University Press.

Rae-Dupree, J., (2000), 'A Twisted Kind of Love'. *U.S. News and World Report*, 24 May, p. 24.

Rogin, M., (1984), 'Kiss Me Deadly: Communism, Motherhood, and Cold War Movies'. *Representations*, Vol. 6: 1–36.

Ross, A., (1989), *No Respect: Intellectuals and Popular Culture*. London: Routledge.

Ross, A., (1991), 'Hacking Away at the Counterculture', *Strange Weather: Culture, Science, and Technology in the Age of Limits*. London: Verso, pp. 75–100.

Schwartz, J., (2000), 'New Virus Hits World Computer Networks'. *Washington Post*, 20 May, p. A1.

Suplee, C., (2000), 'Anatomy of a "Love Bug"'. *Washington Post*, 21 May 2000, p. A1.

Tomes, N., (1998), *The Gospel of Germs: Men, Women, and the Microbe in American Life*. Cambridge: Harvard University Press.

Treichler, P., (1988), 'AIDS, Homophobia, and Biomedical Discourse: An Epidemic of Signification'. In Douglas Crimp (ed.) (1988), *AIDS: Cultural Analysis, Cultural Activism*. Cambridge: MIT Press pp. 32–70.

The obscure politics of conspiracy theory

Mark Featherstone

1. Difference versus ideology

This chapter suggests that we may regard conspiratorial thinking as a pathological effect of the dissolution of social recognition, a paranoid form of non-knowledge caused by the rise of political ideologies which foreground the rights of the individual at the expense of those of all others. In the first section, the chapter looks at Minogue's book *Alien Powers* (1985) as an example of such a political argument. According to an analysis of this theory of difference, which attempts to see the ideological critique of social inequality as emblematic of a form of totalitarian paranoia, we can understand how conspiracy theory represents an attempt to compensate for the repression of sociability. The paradox of Minogue's exercise is clear: at the same time that he attempts to problematize the ideological critique of social inequality as a subjective stance which limits the unfolding of difference, he continues to advance his own manifesto of absolute difference/freedom behind the veil of undecidability/ objectivity. Reading this reversal, which sees the absolute openness of difference contract towards the inflexibility of total closure, through Žižek's dialectical view of the popular science fiction film *The Matrix*, the second part is concerned to show how theories of absolute difference may inadvertently create an atmosphere for conspiratorial thinking. Through their disavowal of the reality of sociability one can argue that authors like Minogue hide both the motivated reality of the law and the violence which necessarily under-writes the integrity of such symbolic rule. Caught inside this nonsensical machine, where absolute openness to others inverts towards the absolute closure of claustrophobic solipsism, the alien-ated individual attempts to create meaning through the degraded medium of conspiratorial thinking. As such, the chapter will show how in an age that sees everybody cast outside the bounds of sociability, the obscure politics of conspiracy theory de-scribe the dark-side of theories of difference and mark the vicious mechanics of the state of post-modern second nature/capital which such political ideologies appear to support.

Jodi Dean's book *Aliens in America* (1998) suggests that the post-modern ideas surrounding the collapse of the meta-narrative and the end of the modern truth claim can be associated with the increasing popularity of conspiracy theory. In my *Knowledge and the Production of Non-Knowledge* (2001), I refer to Dean's work in order to explore her argument that the invention of new communication technologies, such as the internet, and the advance of conspiratorial non-knowledge, which questions the legitimacy of all forms of thinking about the world, are inter-related developments which should be celebrated as emancipatory openings that may allow other voices to escape from the limiting nature of modern truth/knowledge. Recalling the work of Lyotard, and in particular his book *The Postmodern Condition* (1984), Dean's take on the Wittgensteinian concept of the 'language game' uses the idea of conspiracy theory to un-fold truth onto the undecidability of knowledge relativism. Although such a programme is aimed at increasing freedom by attacking elite forms of political articulation, the actual conclusion of Dean's argument is one that threatens to abandon all notions of social justice to the un-differentiation of a post-modern abyss. Like Lyotard's anti-utopian space, this undecidable state embraces radical difference at the expense of a recognition of structural power relations, such as those engendered by post-modern capital, and may actively contribute to an increase in conspiratorial violence by advocating the development of an economic state of nature.

John O'Neill's paper 'Oh My Other, There is No Others!' (2001) summarizes this idea by showing how the post-modern political economy stimulates a paranoid obsession with alien others. Against Dean, who views the proliferation of difference as a positive effect, O'Neill argues that the invention of absolute difference may result in a condition which provokes rivalrous violence by abolishing the communicative bind that allows for a recognition of human distinction. Regarding this form of un-differentiation, O'Neill refers to a state called 'alien-ation' whereby absolute individualism over-writes human sociability and erodes channels of self/other communication by advancing the claims of the self at the expense of those of all others. For O'Neill, the result of this process is a form of generalized solipsism which fails to acknowledge anything beyond the idea of the isolated individual. Moreover, apart from hardening the concept of the solitary monad, the inter-related effect of this movement away from Hegelian recognition is that everybody is threatened with anonymity. Here, a lack of social relationality illuminates the emergence of a paradoxical double bind, a circular effect which is constitutive of a pathological consequence of the ideology of monadism's augmentation of the concept of the individual. According to an examination of this machine we can see how the ideological reinforcements which bolster the concept of the self are opposed by the appearance of a proportionately powerful contrasting emotion that causes the solitary person to experience a heightened fear of their own dissolution. The presence of this Sartrean (1989) anxiety shows that while the idea of collective organization may wither at the level of ideological articulation, the actual company of other bodies leads the monad to associate its own fear of annihilation with a discovery of human collectivity. This psycho-pathology allows one to understand why the post-modern individual is plagued by a claustrophobic feeling that the world is saturated with otherness.

In textual terms this uneasiness, which revolves around a discovery that the world is inhabited by many alien bodies that the isolated self will invariably collide with from time to time, is comparable to the recognition of otherness that both Descartes and Freud attempted to avoid through their respective theories of egoistic independence (Oughourlian, 1991; O'Neill, 1992). Akin to both these thinkers' theoretical enterprises, it is clear that the work of the isolated self becomes one of continual evasion. This is because the politics of absolute difference view any collision with otherness as a strange and dangerous occurrence which may shake the confidence of the self by providing it with a recognition of its own sociability that contradicts the ideology of possessive individualism. During these chance meetings the other appears to threaten the independence of the monadic subject to such an extent that it starts to take on the form of an alien invader whose role is to corrupt the integrity of the self and exploit any weakness which the individual may inadvertently display.

O'Neill argues that this paranoid condition is caused by the erosion of a politics of Hegelian recognition (civic responsibility) and the advancement of the asocial ideologies of post-modern capitalism. Against this understanding, which claims that we should associate paranoia with social dislocation, authors such as Kenneth Minogue (1985) have argued that positions which attempt to stem the tide of difference by imposing a particular point of view as an universal truth claim are constitutive of a form of conspiratorial thinking that is responsible for framing other opinions in pathological terms. An example of a theoretical work which appears to advance this claim is Deleuze and Guattari's book *Anti-Oedipus* (1984). In this famous essay on capitalism and schizophrenia the authors show how Freudian psychoanalysis has re-written a particular point of view (Oedipal repression) as an universal claim about the reality of human existence (psycho-sexual trauma). Yet, despite the fact that *Anti-Oedipus* regards Freudian psychoanalysis as a conspiratorial structure which limits our understanding of other voices, Deleuze and Guattari's aim was never to un-fold truth onto the undecidability of post-modern knowledge relativism. Rather, their thesis attempts to show how the true source of psychic repression is the disciplinary social structure adopted by capital organization (Deleuze and Guattari, 1984; Massumi, 1992). With regard to this assertion Minogue may suggest that Deleuze and Guattari's theory seeks to replace one conspiratorial matrix with another equally limiting position. However, one could also use this understanding of Deleuze and Guattari's theory of capitalism and schizophrenia to illuminate the paradoxical logic at work in Minogue's own book. That is, Deleuze and Guattari's recognition of the necessity of advancing a position, whatever that may be, can allow one to see that Minogue's attempt to view the Hegelian politics of power as a conspiracy theory contradicts his own idea of difference by banning any position which disagrees with the thesis outlined by *Alien Powers*.

Therefore, it appears that the major fault with Minogue's attempt to un-cover the conspiratorial structures which under-write the politics of power is that his own strategy for advancing theories of difference is based on the exclusion of other voices. What separates this position from those of the capital theorists, such as Deleuze and Guattari, is that texts like *Anti-Oedipus* recognize the reality of a politics of exclusion and advance a thesis based on this understanding. In contrast authors like Minogue mis-recognize actual processes of social inequality even though they base their own work on a form of abandonment which mimes the inside/outside nature of social organization at the level of extensive textuality (Bandera, 1981). Indeed, one may suggest that it is precisely because of the existence of this form of textual abandonment that the mis-recognition of actual social injustice continues to problematize theories of power and oppression. In essence, then, it is this exclusionary feature which may consign Minogue's thesis to the category of ideological thinking he is so critical of throughout his own book.

Further evidence of this possibility is provided by *Alien Powers*' built-in defence mechanism. This textual system, which is able to absorb the critique advanced by the politics of power by acknowledging that any argument which disputes the validity of ideology, or sees it as a psycho-pathological theory, will be viewed as ideological by conflict theorists, only strengthens the position which suggests that Minogue performs the very activity he is so keen to dismiss as conspiratorial thinking. In other words, the ability of Minogue's thesis to assimilate any oppositional argument, and dismiss theories which critique his own position as fantastic, mirrors the form of Marxist ideology which *Alien Powers* condemns as a despotic attempt to impose a particular conspiratorial world-view as a universal truth claim. Again the key difference between the conflict theorists critique of capital ideology and Minogue's position is that the politics of oppression/repression attempt to respond to the conditions of social injustice while the advocates of radical difference escape a recognition of actual structural inequality by performing exclusionary violence at the level of text/discourse.

Related to this recognition, an understanding of Minogue's ability to incorporate critiques, yet escape the conspiratorial slur by advertising his own technique for damning opponents as ideologists, shows how *Alien Powers* attempts to hide its own exclusionary practices behind a strategy which aims to throw doubt upon our central assumptions about conspiracy theories. Against one of the key motifs of conspiracy theory, which suggests that heinous plotting is always hidden, or obscured, by constructions such as technical language, Minogue visibilizes his exclusionary technique through the pre-emptive claim that any conflict theory which disagrees with his thesis must be characterized by conspiratorial thinking. Here, the visibility of Minogue's strategy represents an attempt to naturalize his own position against the technical argumentation of conflict theorists. Such reasoning suggests that because *Alien Powers*' attempt to exclude dissenting voices is couched in the immediately perceptible terms of a 'fundamental language' it cannot represent political abandonment. By contrast, the same logic then focuses on the philosophical terminology of Marxism in order to imply that the technicality of conflict theory appears to refer to the constitutional form of a monolithic ideology which is designed to mask some heinous conspiratorial matrix. According to a consideration of this technique, which tries to advance the validity of a natural order of reality and problematize any oppositional stance by arguing that critical thinking is constitutive of an 'un-natural' construction, one is led to question *Alien Powers* equation of Marxism and conspiracy theory. Indeed, we may be left in doubt as to who represents conspiratorial thinking, the Marxist theorists or the advocates of difference like Minogue.

Recent critiques of theories of radical difference (Goux, 1998) suggest that we can reach a similar conclusion through an examination of other texts which attempt to advance notions of openness and difference at the expense of a politics of power. Work by Abercrombie, Hill, and Turner, whose books *The Dominant Ideology Thesis* (1980) and *Sovereign Individuals of Capitalism* (1986) criticise the Marxist notion of ideology as out-dated, can be seen to represent such an example. Throughout their books Abercrombie, Hill, and Turner suggest a project aimed at over-writing the politics of power with an (a)social form that recognizes the sovereign position of monadic subjectivity. Akin to Dean, they imply that if we can begin to see totalizing forms of knowledge, such as Marxism, in terms of an attempt to seize the moral high-ground or advance a particular point of view as a universal truth claim then we can start to understand the undecidable reality of politics. Two critics who feed into this thesis and appear to confirm the conspiratorial nature of conflict theory by attempting to advance a particular point of view as a universal truth claim are Therborn (1994) and Žižek (1994). Both these thinkers repeat our critique of Minogue by arguing that recent attacks on the theory of ideology are themselves grounded in an ideological position. In the first instance, Therborn maintains that Abercrombie, Hill, and Turner's thesis can be viewed as an ideological attempt to silence theories of peripheral domination by claiming that Marxist notions such as 'interpellation' and 'hegemony' over-state the extent to which the subject class is incorporated into the dominant ideological position.

Similarly, Žižek's thesis suggests that Abercrombie, Hill, and Turner's assertion that there is no dominant ideology is questionable because of their limited definition of the concept of ideology. In his essay 'The Spectre of Ideology' (1994) Žižek argues that the notion of ideology as a belief-system is one that relies on a mis-recognition of ideology in the instances where it is most effective. From this perspective, Abercrombie, Hill, and Turner's understanding of ideology neglects the most powerful forms of political bias. That is to say, those ideas which have moved beyond the sphere of internal belief and become part of the external social, political, and cultural fabric. Here, Žižek repeats our analysis of Minogue by arguing that ideology resides in apparently neutral forms of communication. His suggestion is that it is precisely because Abercrombie, Hill, and Turner miss this dimension of ideological bias, a level of particularity that is illustrated by Minogue's attempt to ban conflict theories by visibilizing, and thus attempting to naturalize, his assault on Marxism, that their thesis should be seen as a tautology which views ideology as indeterminate strictly because it accepts the most pervasive forms of political dominance as objective fact. In contrast to this level of external bias, Abercrombie, Hill, and Turner's definition of ideology includes only the weaker form of political leaning as internal belief. This is why they see ideology as indeterminate and find fault with strong versions of the dominant ideology thesis.

Of course, from Minogue's point of view this idea, which relies on an acceptance of the existence of invisible bias, supports the position which argues that conflict theorists see evidence of conspiracies everywhere they look. Indeed, he may argue that Žižek's essay allows one to see how, for conspiracy theorists, an absence of hard evidence only confirms the existence of ever more cunningly disguised plotting (Fenster, 1999). Initially Minogue's argument is persuasive. However upon further inspection an important flaw begins to emerge which re-states the value of Žižek's critique. Once again, we can see that the problem with Minogue's attempt to consign conflictual arguments to the realm of conspiracy theory revolves around his idea which suggests that if political bias is not immediately apparent then it does not actually exist. Against this stance, that upholds the equation between visibility and a natural order of reality, a consideration of Giorgio Agamben's book *Homo Sacer* (1998) allows one to regard a form of political abandonment which shows how the sphere of legal visibility may be based on a system of exclusion which renders alien bodies invisible. According to Agamben's study of the Roman figure, Homo Sacer, who could be killed but not sacrificed to the divine/judicial law (1998: 8), one can understand how the expulsion of other voices founds the sphere of modern politics. Related to this understanding, we can now see how Žižek's critique of Abercrombie, Hill, and Turner's thesis aims to illuminate the condition of those who are banned from the sphere of political/legal visibility. Here, the figure of Homo Sacer, who was cast out into the pre-human state of nature, works against Minogue's *Alien Powers* by suggesting that just because political bias is not visible, or obviously apparent, does not mean that it is a fantastic product of conspiratorial thinking.

On the contrary, Agamben's thesis allows one to understand that Homo Sacer's abandonment is discernable precisely because of his invisibility to the sphere of political/legal discourse. Thus the reason Minogue is unable to detect forms of structural oppression or social injustice is that his frame of reference is a politics of difference which regards inequality from the primacy of political/legal visibility. Furthermore, this point, which shows how the visible space of difference may be based on the invisibility of exclusionary practices, permits an understanding of how Minogue's critique of Marxist communism, as an attempt to flatten all difference onto a utopic state of non-difference, is one which his own thesis performs by banning the politics of power according to a rule which suggests that conflict theory imposes universal truth claims at the cost of a recognition of individual particularities. In the case of *Alien Powers* these two inter-connecting points (the exclusionary base of a politics of difference leading to the invention of a state of un-differentiation/sameness) coincide at the site of the post-modern political economy. Here, the politics of radical difference collapse onto un-differentiation because of the abolition of a communicative relationship with otherness/opposition/critique. Therefore, we may argue that radical difference is based on a re-discovery of an atmosphere of absolute individualism/sameness which approximates that of a Hobbesian state of nature. Again Minogue is unable to see this process as an actual occurrence because the endless struggle for survival – the war of all against all – takes place within the confines of an ideological system which visibilizes a form of debased communism that views equality as the generalization of expendability. Considering this idea Minogue is able to view the politics of difference as free of structural inequality precisely because he associates his theory with the visibility of the notion of equality contained within the condition of the generalization of expendability. In contrast, he regards the politics of power as conspiratorial because they critique the violence of the exclusionary sub-text which underwrites the debased communism of the economic state of nature. Put another way, this chaotic under-current remains invisible to *Alien Powers* because of Minogue's exclusive frame of reference.

Other recent attempts to create a politics of inclusive difference have faltered at a similar impasse. For instance Derrida's recent book *Politics of Friendship* (1997) is a notable example which allows one to see how the visible space of absolute hospitality is necessarily under-written by a systematic process of exclusionary violence. As Richard Kearney explains in his essay 'Aliens and Others' (1999), the major problem with Derrida's attempt to invent a space of absolute difference is that he mis-recognizes the violence which accompanies the implementation of such an amoral stance. In contrast to deconstructive theories, Kearney refers to a dialectic of aliens and others in order to show how the sphere of openness and freedom is always shadowed by a state of closure and bondage:

> If there is a difference between Jesus and Jim Jones, between Saint Francis and Stalin, between Melena and Mengele, between Siddartha and the Marquis de Sade – and I think most of us would want to say there is – then some further moral decisions are needed to supplement the deconstructive gesture of hospitality (1999: 261).

Without the imposition of a degree of moral judgmentalism Kearney argues that the Derridean sphere of visible difference/un-differentiation will remain blind to the noisy chaos of the pre-human under-belly. As such, we can see why the novel form of radical difference, advocated by post-modern capital, makes the need for the re-discovery of a moral code a pressing matter. Like Derrida's theory, the doctrine of non-human hospitality advanced by this order of capital is absolutely against moral judgmentalism. Indeed, because the equation of equality with the generalization of expendability invents an atmosphere whereby 'everybody is a nobody' (O'Neill, 2001: 21) theorists of difference, like Derrida, have a tendency to justify the work of post-modern capital by celebrating the possible freedoms contained by such debased communism at the expense of a recognition of the fearful paranoia which increasingly plagues the fractured mass that lives within the world system. In this state, where each person has become acutely aware of their own vulnerability, we may, as Jameson (1993, 1995, 2000) argues in many of his books, perceive the detrimental effects which shadow the ideologies of difference through an excavation of a political unconscious that under-writes the increasing popularity of conspiratorial thinking. According to an exploration of this category of writing one can begin to understand how conspiracy theory appears to de-scribe the violence of the economic state of nature at the obscure level of a paranoid mythology (Featherstone, 2001).

2. Uncovering the master of puppets

Against the Derridean notion of friendship as absolute openness, Žižek suggests that the un-restricted passage of information between the self and its other may lead to the collapse of sociability and the violence of doubling. Opposing the deconstructive form of radical difference, he advises a more cautious mode of friendship which maintains a stable distance between the communicative partners:

> Most of us know from personal experience how unpleasant it is when a person in authority whom we deeply admire, and even want to know more about, grants our wish and takes us into his confidence, sharing with us his deepest personal trauma – the charisma evaporates all of a sudden, and we feel the impulse just to run away. Perhaps the feature which characterizes true friendship is precisely a tactful knowledge of when to stop, not going beyond a certain threshold and 'telling everything' to a friend (1997: 69).

In this passage Žižek illuminates a process whereby absolute openness leads to a crisis of individual identity and the end of difference. When the self and its other become so close that the distance which allows the two parties to exchange information begins to fail, the communicative bind which previously held the couple together, through a process of inter-subjective recognition, also starts to vanish into the claustrophobic non-distance of paranoia. Here, the phenomenological distance that should separate the self from its other begins to collapse onto the plane of non-distance/un-differentiation. This violent crash, which is simultaneously representative of the invention of absolute distance, may be seen as the profound failure of inter-subjective communication that is celebrated by theories of post-modern identity. Through reference to the *X-Files* motto, 'the truth is out there', Žižek excavates the category of intra-subjective writing Jameson calls the political unconscious in order to explain how this process relates to psycho-pathology. In the first instance, he repeats his position which suggests a critique of Abercrombie, Hill, and Turner by arguing that the idea which states that 'the truth is out there' shows how a trace ideological bias is implicitly encoded in the external world that we make for ourselves. However, at a deeper level his equation of popular science fiction and ideology also allows one to understand how conspiratorial thought is related to the politics of possessive individualism and its fatal discovery of the impossibility of an absolute denial of otherness. With regard to this comparison, the notion that 'the truth is out there' concerns conspiracy theory's mis-recognition of human sociability and its consequent search for knowledge through the endless deferral of alienated meaning/non-knowledge. Such a process is constitutive of the ideological form which expands according to a logic of extensive verticality, the eternal repetition that works to sustain the veil of invisibility, hide the reality of communicative recognition, and defend the privileged place of monadic identity in western social organization.

Moreover, the example of the *X-Files* also recalls our examination of Agamben's *Homo Sacer* (1998). By returning to this study we can begin to see that otherness is not only hidden at the base of the communicative relationship. That is, because we can now recognize the idea of a natural order of reality as the imposition of a law, which renders those who fail to conform to the system of difference invisible to the political sphere, we can also discern the presence of a legislator who also occupies a place of sovereign invisibility. In terms of the *X-Files*, this recognition allows one to see why theories of alien invaders and government plots de-scribe the presence of a transcendental principle, or master signifier, through the eyes of an author whose understanding of structural power relations has been severely de-limited by the post-modern politics of difference (Jameson, 1995). Any exploration of the heinous powers which plague the heroes of the *X-Files* would surely show that this prohibition causes one to view top-down oppression from an irrational perspective that projects 'alien-ation' beyond the nauseating dislocation of post-modern (a)sociability. Thus, it is precisely because the authors of radical difference exclude any perspective which may lead one to see social injustice in terms of communicative relations that conspiracy theorists tend towards a form of thinking which equates social problems with the evil tendencies of non-human forms of administrative dominance and the techno-myths of extra-terrestrial super-nature (Featherstone, 2001).

In terms of writing, the obscure sovereign position, which completes the communicative bind with those rendered invisible by textual abandonment, is occupied by the figure of the author as legislator. It is clear that Minogue recognizes this situation in his *Alien Powers* when he criticises the work of the Marxist ideologist as a mechanism for the transformation of a particular world-view into an universal claim about the reality of the world. However, as we have already seen, Minogue's thesis is paradoxical. On the one hand he critiques the politics of power for trying to define reality, while on the other hand he attempts to conceal his own role as sovereign writer by advancing a position, disguised as a non-position, which is more concerned with creating spaces for contestation than contributing any positive commentary. The effect of this strategy is two-fold. In the first instance, the attempt to conceal a position behind a non-position shows how Minogue wants to maintain his sovereign state of exclusive-inclusion. According to this stance he is able create laws and advance a position, by virtue of being included in the socio-political system, without appearing to advance any particular view, due to his exclusive/outside non-position. The second, inter-related, effect of this strategy of invisible intervention is that those, such as Homo Sacer, who are banned from the sphere of politics are also rendered invisible because their exclusion appears to be based on the dictates of a law/position which is actually a natural principle/divine non-position. This division between the author of difference, as exclusive-inclusion, and those who are excluded from the sphere of political law, as inclusive-exclusion, at once upholds the primacy of visibility over invisibility, structures the relations of social inequality, and maintains the integrity of the boundaries which order the violence of the theories of radical openness.

However, theorists of difference, like Minogue, who try to look at the openness of the space that sits between the twin boundaries of the exclusive-inclusion and the inclusive-exclusion, are condemned to be understood as invisible, spectral figures who assert their influence at a distance by those conspiratorial thinkers that mis-recognize the attempt to exercise a political strategy as the appearance, and intervention, of a super-natural evil genius. In the case of *Alien Powers*, Minogue's attempt to exert a position (inclusion) by virtue of the maintenance of his neutral non-position (exclusive) makes him appear like Faust's master of puppets, the devil Mephistopheles, to those caught in the paranoiac frame of non-distance/absolute distance that is constitutive of post-modern capital's generalized state of asocial expendability. Thus we can understand what happens when the equation which summarizes this system, equality as the generalization of expendability, is separated by theorists of difference. As we have already discovered, Minogue extracts the debased communism advanced by post-modern capital and makes this point his visible (exclusive-inclusion) naturalized law. By contrast, the notion of generalized expendability is rendered invisible (inclusive-exclusion) even though it serves as the base for the (a)social order.

Now because this equation of post-modern capital (equality as the generalization of expendability) refers to everybody as they live through time, so that, like Girard's scapegoat (1986), we may be a villain one day and a hero the next, it is clear that the narrative form of conspiratorial thought should be understood as an obscure attempt to comprehend the Faustian pact that binds the solitary monad to the spectral ideologies of post-modern capital. In response to the dictates of this particular big Other, those notions which seem like super-natural laws due to the spectral nature of the technologies of exclusive-inclusion, conspiratorial thought may be viewed as a quasi-religious strategy for opposing the possibility of future exclusion. In other words, the increasing popularity of conspiracy theory represents a paranoid attempt to under-write the vulnerability that is written into the laws of the post-modern big Other by attempting to gain knowledge of the rules which govern its pact with the self and thus master the capital decision making process. Akin to Weber's (1992) Calvinists, who sought to secure entry into Heaven through worldly achievement, contemporary conspiracy theorists are obsessed with un-covering the hidden truth of a master of puppets. An evil genius who is in actual fact nothing more than a political theorist, with a clever strategy for naturalizing his positions, understood through a paranoid reading lens.

Žižek's essay on recent science fiction cinema, 'The Matrix, or, The Two Sides of Perversion' (1999), provides another nice example of this conspir-atorial effect at work. In this paper he allows one to see how a mis-recognition of structural power relations at the level of politics encourages the paranoid imagination to create mythical stories about hostile super-nature. In the case of the film *The Matrix*, this position suggests that a failure to perceive the actual presence of the legislator (exclusive-inclusion) leads to the conspiratorial vision of an evil super-computer. Moreover, according to Žižek's Lacanian theory, the film's description of the heinous machine conforms to the psychoanalytic theory of psychosis and, in particular, the paranoid idea of the other of the other. In this instance, the notion of the other of the other refers to the invisible conspirator who manipulates the collective big Other and makes the monad's life a living Hell. Like the Sartrean idea which suggests that 'Hell is – other people!' (1989: 45), for the conspiratorial mind-set which is banned from thinking along social lines, torment is the monstrous other who hides in the shadows and acts as the Satanic obstacle/stumbling block. As Žižek explains, this psychotic mind-set reflects the theory expressed by Morpheus, the leader of the rebels in *The Matrix*:

It's that feeling you have had all your life. That feeling that something was wrong with the world. You don't know what it is but its there, like a splinter in your mind, driving you mad. The Matrix is everywhere, it's all around us, here even in this room. It is the world that has been pulled over your eyes to blind you from the truth (*The Matrix* quoted in Žižek, 1999: 13).

This idea, which suggests that the hostile world is caused by the schemes of an evil master of puppets, rather than the violence which is constitutive of the relationship between the self and its other, resides in the mis-recognition of the Lacanian imaginary (Borch-Jacobsen, 1991). Following Lacan, Žižek shows how this state occupies the gap between the conspiracy theorist's pathological perception of the relationship between the real (invisible other) and the symbolic (visible political domain) and the actual inter-relation between these two psychic categories. According to this thesis he explains how, for the paranoid individual who is caught in the unifying arena of the textual symbolic/monadic mirror stage, the real as alienated sphere (invisible other) appears to represent the utopic truth that occupies an external place far away in time/space. As such, Lacanian theory suggests that the monad mis-recognizes the violence which banishes the other to the state of nature, where she is invisible to the sphere of political articulation, as the search for an alien landscape that contains the truth of the world.

In *The Matrix* this confusion leads to the transformation of the state of nature into 'the desert of the real', the Zionist paradise that stands for the birth place of humanity. Furthermore, at the same time that the Lacanian real as inclusive-exclusion is re-written as an Edenic landscape, the problems which illuminate the vulnerability of the psychotic self are also understood in terms of alien mythology. Here, the dictates of the political economy, the symbolic legislation as exclusive-inclusion, are seen as evidence of alien intrusion. Re-staged by conspiratorial thinking, the threats of capital expulsion represent the shadowy presence of the Satanic master of puppets, the figure that *The Matrix* de-scribes through the post-modern techno-myth of the evil super-computer.

Therefore, one can see how the conspiracy theorist's vision of the world recognizes a binary structure which, on the one hand, hides the other as inclusive-exclusion behind an imaginary notion of transcendental truth. *The Matrix* describes this place through the theological notion of Zion, the kingdom of God in Heaven. For those occupants of the Matrix who are able to crack machine code, and thus expose the conspiracy which is hidden behind the technical ideology, 'Zion' is the last human city, a sanctuary that sits at the heart of 'the desert of the real'. By contrast, the conspiracy theorist imagines the shadowy figure of the legislator as the heinous master of puppets. The evil other of the other who constructs the ideological veil which hides the utopic reality of the world from those who are concerned to discover the truth out there. In *The Matrix* the monstrous super-computer is the transcendental judge that occupies the sovereign position of the exclusive-inclusion. As the film shows, this invisible law-maker is only discernable through the bugs that cause things to go wrong. Thus, one can understand how conspiracy theory constructs a paranoiac model of the two poles of the social order. Essentially, it is a recognition of this relationship, the bind that ties the inclusive-exclusion (invisible other) to the exclusive-inclusion (invisible legislator), that leads Žižek to conclude that:

> Therein resides the correct insight of *The Matrix*: in its juxtaposition of the two aspects of perversion – on the one hand, reduction of reality to a virtual domain regulated by arbitrary rules that can be suspended; on the other hand, the concealed truth of this freedom, the reduction of the subject to an utter instrumentalized passivity (1999: 18).

According to this passage we can see how Žižek reads the film's notion of a separation between mind and body as a metaphor for the sado-masochistic brutality of post-modern social organization. In *The Matrix* this discovery is represented by the idea that for the computer simulation to remain vital at the level of symbolic cognition, the body must be butchered in the huge processing plants of 'the desert of the real'. Here, one of the film's central scenes, which shows how human bodies are used as batteries, may be compared to Deleuze and Guattari's Marxist theory of the vampyric nature of capital (1984: 228). Re-staged at the obscure level of conspiratorial thinking, the blood-sucking super-computer from *The Matrix* mimes Deleuze and Guattari's idea by showing how capital lives by killing the body while keeping the mind narcotized with a mythology of individual agency (Featherstone, 2000). However, what separates Deleuze and Guattari's Marxist argument from the story of *The Matrix* is that both *Capital* (1990) and *Anti-Oedipus* (1984) suggest that what drains people is a particular form of social relationship, rather than the schemes of an evil genius.

We can see that while the authors of the politics of power, like Marx and Deleuze and Guattari, argue for a re-discovery of communicative association and civic responsibility, the critique of post-modern discipline advanced by *The Matrix* remains trapped within the ideology of monadic isolation. Due to this situation the film's conspiratorial commentary is destined to reproduce the logic of alien-ation, whereby the self continues to see its other as nemesis, according to the feed-back effect of a paranoiac spiral. Within this system, which we may describe as the conspiratorial narrative, the roles may reverse, so that the content of the utopian image may change and the figure of the alien can alter, but the antagonistic relationship remains constant. This structural feature is discernable through the film's techno-mythology which, rather like the Cathar theories of super-nature that saw the material world as the creation of an evil devil and the spiritual domain as the arena of a loving God, pits the monstrous super-computer (which conjures the visible world) against the messianic saviour figure, as represented by Keanu Reeves' character Neo (the One who is able to out-pace the calculations of the machine and thus de-realize the heinous simulation).

Here, the narrative which sees the film exchange the One for the evil super-computer and 'the desert of the real' for the Matrix illuminates the conspiratorial/monadic thinking which is unable to understand the value of communicative recognition/human sociability. Instead, its strategy advocates an endless search for the One who can negotiate the other, that appears as a perennial obstacle/stumbling block to the explosion of the heinous conspiracy, and supply the true knowledge of the master of puppets, the monstrous creator of the hostile world. Centrally, this mythology of the One, the super-human, who is invulnerable to the vicissitudes of the furious capital machine, remains the utopic truth of a conspiratorial thinking that is unable to step outside the ideologies of possessive individualism. Thus, what Žižek's study excavates is the sociological meaning of the paranoiac text. He allows one to understand how the obscure politics of conspiracy theory re-stage the ideologies of monadic independence and their fatal attempt to deny the phenomenological reality of human sociability through a psychoanalytic critique which treats conspiracy theory like ideology.

Put another way, Žižek allows one to see conspiracy theory as an obscure attempt to understand the reality of sociability from the myopic perspective of a non-social political ideology. As such, his essay on *The Matrix* explains how the politics of difference dissolve the social bond and create a conspiratorial mind-set, a world-view that is forever agitated by the progress of a vicious 'everybody for themselves' socio-political system. Against this machine, Žižek's attempt to un-cover the fictive-truth of the conspiratorial text advances the politics of Hegelian recognition. Like the Lacanian notion of truth-as-communication, this *form* of zero-degree speech has the ability to institute the re-organization of a social pact. The emergence of such a communicative order, which Lacan might have called the analytic society, represents a vision of the social unconscious, a hard kernel of critical resistance which can oppose the imperialism of the ideology of monadic individualism.

Acknowledgments

I would like to thank Siobhan Holohan for her thoughts on *The Matrix* and John O'Neill for his invaluable advice and continued direction. His supervision continues to inspire my work.

Filmography

Matrix, The. The Wachnowski Brothers, 1999.

Bibliography

Abercrombie, N., Hill, S. and Turner, B., (1980), *The Dominant Ideology Thesis*, London: Allen and Unwin.

Abercrombie, N., Hill, S. and Turner, B., (1986), *Sovereign Individuals of Capitalism*, London: Allen and Unwin.

Abercrombie, N., Hill, S. and Turner, B., 'Determinacy and Indeterminacy in the Theory of Ideology', in Žižek, S. (ed.) (1994), *Mapping Ideology*, London: Verso.

Agamben, G., (1998), *Homo Sacer: Sovereign Power and Bare Life*, Stanford: Stanford University Press.

Bandera, C., (1982), 'Notes on Derrida, Tombstones, and the Representational Game' *Stanford French Review*, Volume 6: Number 213.

Borch-Jacobsen, M., (1991), *Lacan: The Absolute Master*, Stanford: Stanford University Press.

Dean, J., (1998), *Aliens in America: Conspiracy Cultures from Outerspace to Cyberspace*, Ithaca: Cornell University Press.

Deleuze, G. and Guattari, F., (1984), *Anti-Oedipus: Capitalism and Schizophrenia: Volume I*, London: Athlone Press.

Derrida, J., (1997), *Politics of Friendship*, London: Verso.

Featherstone, M., (2000), 'Cracking Cube: Cryptology and Ichnography' *Ctheory* online at http://www.Ctheory.com/.

Featherstone, M., (2001), *Knowledge and the Production of Non-Knowledge*, New Jersey: Hampton.

Fenster, M., (1999), *Conspiracy Theories: Secrecy and Power in American Culture*, Minneapolis: University of Minnesota Press.

Girard, R., (1986), *The Scapegoat*, Baltimore: Johns Hopkins University Press.

Goux, J-J., 'General Economics and Postmodern Capitalism', in Botting, F. and Wilson, S. (eds) (1998), *Bataille: A Critical Reader*, Oxford: Blackwell.

Jameson, F., (1993), *The Political Unconscious: Narrative as a Socially Symbolic Act*, Ithaca: Cornell University Press.

Jameson, F., (1995), *The Geopolitical Aesthetic: Cinema and Space in the World System*, Bloomington: Indiana University Press.

Jameson, F., 'Cognitive Mapping', in Hardt, M. and Weeks, K. (eds) (2000), *The Jameson Reader*, Oxford: Blackwell.

Kearney, R., (1999), 'Aliens and Others: Between Girard and Derrida' *Cultural Values*, Volume 3: Number 3.

Lacan, J., (1993), *The Psychoses: The Seminar of Jacques Lacan: Book III 1955–1956*, London: Routledge.

Lyotard, J-F., (1984), *The Postmodern Condition: A Report on Knowledge*, Manchester: University of Manchester Press.

Marx, K., (1990), *Capital: Volume I*, London: Penguin.

Massumi, B., (1992), *A User's Guide to Capitalism and Schizophrenia: Deviations from Deleuze and Guattari*, Massachusetts: MIT Press.

Minogue, K., (1985), *Alien Powers: The Pure Theory of Ideology*, Weidenfeld and Nicolson: London.

O'Neill, J., (1992), *Critical Conventions: Interpretation in the Literary Arts and Sciences*, Oklahoma: University of Oklahoma Press.

O'Neill, J., (2001), 'Oh My Others, There is No Other!' *Theory, Culture and Society*, Volume 18: Number 2–3.

Oughourlian, J-M., (1991), *The Puppet of Desire: The Psychology of Hysteria, Possession, and Hypnosis*, Stanford: Stanford University Press.

Sartre, J-P., (1989), *No Exit and Three Other Plays*. New York: Vintage Books.

Therborn, G., 'The New Questions of Subjectivity', in Žižek, S. (ed.) (1994), *Mapping Ideology*, London: Verso.

Weber, M., (1992), *The Protestant Ethic and the Spirit of Capitalism*, London: Penguin.

Žižek, S., (1989), *The Sublime Object of Ideology*, London: Verso.

Žižek, S., 'The Spectre of Ideology', in Žižek, S. (ed.) (1994), *Mapping Ideology*, London: Verso.

Žižek, S., (ed.) (1994), *Mapping Ideology*, London: Verso.

Žižek, S., (1997), *The Plague of Fantasies*, London: Verso.

Žižek, S., (1999), 'The Matrix, or, The Two Sides of Perversion' online at http://www.anticopyright@britannica.co.

Conjuring order: the new world order and conspiracy theories of globalization

Alasdair Spark

On January 29th 1991, President Bush gave his second State of the Union address. He spoke as the Gulf War was well underway, and he was keen to promote the new era he claimed the conflict represented. To do so, Bush repeated a term he had already used in several speeches, claiming that abroad in the world was:

> a big idea, a new world order, where diverse nations are drawn together in common cause to achieve the universal aspirations of mankind – peace and security, freedom, and the rule of law. Such is a world worthy of our struggle and worthy of our children's future.
>
> (http://thisnation.com/library/sotu/1991gb.html)

Bush was not the first to speak of a 'New World Order', but like the others, his words rested on a generally held perception that with the ending of the Cold War something transformational had begun, and that the world (which is to say, the future) would inevitably be different. Other visions which saw sunlit uplands as lying just ahead had already been offered, most obviously two years earlier when Francis Fukuyama had proclaimed that the 'the End of History' had arrived. While this 'endist' concept of a universal order was aptly summed up as 'liberal democracy ... combined with easy access to VCRs and stereos', such talk of the end of History and a differently ordered world did seem to capture for many people a desirable potential for change (Horsman and Marshall, 1994: 70). This was not least because the future now imagined was both opposite to and better than that previously available, in which History endlessly stayed the same, frozen in the Cold War.

Ten years later, after the conflicts in Bosnia and Kosovo and with Saddam surviving in power long enough to see Bush's son (just about) elected President, the world no longer seems quite so novel or so ordered. Instead, the favoured descriptor for what has happened/is happening/might happen is 'globalization' and, as Anthony Giddens, one of its foremost theorists, argues, it most of all lacks a discernible order:

> We are the first generation to live in this society, whose contours we can as yet only dimly see. It is shaking our existing ways of life, no matter where we

happen to be. This is not – at least at the moment – a global order driven by collective human will. Instead it is emerging in an anarchic, haphazard fashion, carried along by a mixture of economic, technological and cultural imperatives.

(http://www.lse.ac.uk/index/Giddens/rcith_99/week1/week1.htm)

Zygmunt Bauman likewise writes of history's advance into 'the foggy and slushy "no man's land" stretching out beyond the reach of the design and action capacity of anybody in particular' (Bauman, 1998: 39). This shift, from the presumption that a desirable and manageable new order would inevitably emerge in the post-Cold War world, to a present conviction that any such order – not least as it affects the individual – now rests on contingency is striking. If so, is it merely a coincidence, simply a contingency, or just an irony that this past decade has also been marked by the profusion and heightened popularity of conspiracy theories, not least those dominated by perceptions of a threatening New World Order? Since conspiracy theories seek totality and impose order, it might even seem that they are purpose built for the contemporary world which Giddens and Bauman describe. It is striking then that use of the term in a conspiratorial sense has *not* been limited to the radical Right's visions of total global control; the New World Order has been an equal opportunity conspiracy theory. Left wing and progressive arguments about the post Cold War world and most recently the rhetoric behind the mass protests against globalization, have also constructed the world conspiratorially. By examining both these versions of the New World Order and how they converge and conflict, interesting insights into how contemporary conspiracy theories operate and thrive can be learnt.

While talk of the New World Order was heard frequently in the United States in the 1990s, it was rarely in the affirmative sense Bush had intended. Instead, it quickly gained mass market notoriety as a code-phrase for the conspiracy theories of global control which were being disseminated in print, over short-wave radio, and most of all, over the world-wide web (so much so that the term very soon dropped out of use by American policymakers). For the radical Right, Bush's mere use of the phrase had been enough, since these three words were already very familiar to groups such as the John Birch Society. The pre-eminent Right wing conspiracy-mongers of the 1950s and 1960s (and the focus of Richard Hofstadter's analysis of the paranoid style in 1964), the Birchers had for a long time popularized its use in their literature to describe the socialistic 'one worldism' they were convinced was being promoted by the United Nations. Needless to say, they greeted Bush's employment of it with the happy fear so typical of vindicated conspiracy theorists. In the 1990s however, the term would become synonymous not with traditional radical Right organizations such as the Birchers (though religious Right figures such as Pat Robertson did dabble a little), but with the new grassroots militias and other self-styled 'patriot' groups that sprang up so rapidly in the United States during the decade (see James, this volume). Often now written up as the acronym NWO, it became emblematic of a set of Right wing conspiracy theories about America's subversive slide towards global domination that made the claims of the Birchers look modest in comparison.

The vision put forward – for instance, in the views of the Michigan Militia or the Militia of Montana – was (and still is) of a dedicated 'globalist' conspiracy which works ceaselessly to overthrow American liberties and incorporate America into a World state and World government. Genuine organizations such as the Council for Foreign Relations, the Trilateral Commission, the World Trade Organization and the Bilderberger group are said to conspire together to advance this goal. Treaties such as the North Americans Free Trade Agreement (NAFTA), the General Agreement on Trade and Tariffs (GATT), and various United Nations environmental agreements are all claimed to be part of a super-plot. Texts detailing this are legion and little is left out; the following is from 'Operation Vampire Killer' by the 'Police Against the New World Order':

> Behind the scenes is a plan for an oligarchy of the world's richest families to place 1/2 the masses of the earth in servitude under their complete control, administered from behind the false front of the United Nations. To facilitate management capabilities, the plan calls for the elimination of the other 2.5 billion people through war, disease, abortion and famine by the year 2000. As we can plainly see, their plan for population control (reduction) is well under way. (Mulloy, 1999: 426–7).

Some advocates see the global take-over as only potential, while for others it is near complete, following centuries of dedicated plotting. As a phrase, NWO conspiracy advocates have charted New World Order backwards through Henry Kissinger, Henry Wallace, the Versailles Peace Conference, Cecil Rhodes and British imperialism, to traditional bogeymen of many American conspiracy theories, the Freemasons and the Bavarian Illuminati. Wherever the river has its source, in all the patriot/militia NWO scenarios one thing is made clear: this time the globalist forces are here already and are being actively assisted in their schemes to deprive of Americans of their collective and individual sovereignty by a traitorous Federal government and its many agencies. As a militia text asked in 1994: 'Do you know there are more than a million among us who are trained as traitors to the American constitutional way of life [and] are slated to be our slavemasters under the New World Order?' (Mulloy, 1999: 437). In support of all this, a profligate mish-mash of detail has been put forward as 'evidence'. This ranges from the very specific – that Highway Department notations on the back of road-signs are in fact secret codes to enable foreign troops to find their way (with the typical excess logic of conspiracy theories, they are written on the back because foreign troops will prefer to drive on the wrong side of the road) – to the sweeping, such as the claim that a government agency such as FEMA (the Federal Emergency Management Agency, responsible for floods, hurricanes and the like) is a cover story for the preparation of concentration camps for dissident American patriots. Among other claims made are that electronic implants can control individuals, the military can control the weather, and (as I have written elsewhere, (Spark, 1998)) that hovering above America is the all-seeing, all-knowing black helicopter, the 'Strikeforce for the New World Order' as Jim Keith called it.

Such a deeply convoluted and paranoid discourse invites ridicule, and often gets it. Here for instance, is Linda Thompson, an Indiana attorney but also in 1994, the self-styled 'Adjutant General of the Unorganized Militias of America' (this is part of the preamble to her proposed 'Re-Declaration of Independence'):

> The Federal Government, at this time, is transporting large Armies of foreign mercenaries to complete the works of Death, Desolation and Tyranny, already begun, often under the color of the law of the United Nations, and with circumstances of Cruelty and Perfidy, scarcely paralleled in the most barbarous Ages, and totally unworthy of a civilized Nation.
> (http://10hpt.com/pub/blackcrwl/patriot/linda-thompson-dec.txt)

While such views seem absurdly inconceivable (particularly for Europeans and others who have learnt to have little faith in the abilities of the United Nations), such rhetoric does, of course, sometimes connect to action. Militia opinion often invokes anti-semitism or racism, and militia activities can easily be read as inevitably leading to the terrible events of April 19th 1995, and the bombing of the Alfred P. Murrah Building in Oklahoma City. However, despite this atrocity, to consider Right wing authored conspiracy theories about a New World Order as latently terrorist, or held solely by a Right wing fringe would be a mistake. Thus, while militia membership has been estimated at only about 100,000, the dissemination, casual use and appeal of these ideas among people has clearly gone much wider (leaving aside for the moment the Left wing). It is not the just the atrocious acts of the very few, or the gun-toting antics of the membership that requires an enquiry – the wider effects of the sheer promiscuity of the New World Order conspiracy's imagination are also important. Take for instance this comment by Phyllis Schafly – no liberal she, but equally not a militia militant. Schafly wrote in 1996, a year after the Oklahoma bombing, and she phrased her views interestingly:

> It's becoming clear that the 'New World Order' is not just a fantasy of conspiracy-minded right-wingers. President George Bush popularized its use in 1990 in order to legitimize the Gulf War by resuscitating the then dormant United Nations. Like Saddam Hussein, the New World Order concept survived the Gulf War and now we're seeing the unintended consequences. The New World Order is a handy label to describe the various politics that are challenging our sovereignty, trying to bore into our bank account, and turning over US service personnel to the UN. The World

Trade Organization (WTO) which the United States officially joined when Congress ratified the GATT treaty in its lame duck session in December 1994, recently ruled against the United States in its first case. Why is anybody surprised!

(http://www.eagleforum.org/column/feb96/2–22.96.hmtl)

How broadly does this suspicion that there might be something in it, that the vocabulary of the paranoid might have some 'handy' application, extend? Clearly, in regard to NAFTA, GATT and the WTO, more broadly indeed and I will examine this issue at length later in a discussion of the rhetoric and practice of anti-globalization. It is worth noting here that Mark Fenster and Peter Knight have both convincingly argued that Hofstadter's concept of the 'paranoid style' no longer works in an America in which conspiracy theories have become generally far more prevalent, popular and powerful – personal paranoia simply isn't a sufficient explanation (Fenster, 1999: 61; Knight, 2000: 36). Kathleen Stewart expressively sums up this approach, claiming that we now all live in a world which 'has made conspiracy theory not only possible and popular, but ever present, unavoidable, pervasive, compulsive, fun, frightening, and fascinating often to the point of a paranoid-mystical urgency' (Marcus, 1999: 13).

If so, any analysis of conspiracy theories and the New World Order has to recognize that these three words have had as much employment on the Left as on the Right, and question whether they have been conspiratorially aligned. Both Left and Right used the term as a convenient and apt descriptor for their views about the nature of the post War order, and the question of whether the Left's views are not also conspiratorially aligned demands attention, not least because some on the Left see the congruence of terms and subject matter as offering an easy route for contamination by promiscuous Right wing conspiracy theories. For the Left, use of the term seems to come about as part of a process of counter definition. For instance, political scientist John Agnew described the New World Order as follows in 1994:

the New World Order being made under American auspices is a 'transnational liberal economic order' that now detracts from rather than augments the material conditions of life both for the average and for the poorest people ... in the United States (Demko and Wood, 1994: 70).

Like much of the Left, Agnew's focus lay with NAFTA, jobs, and the economic exploitation made possible by a newly unfettered corporate capitalism. The process of criticising by counter definition (sometimes by using the modifier 'New World Disorder') inevitably led to results such as the fact that any internet search offers as many Left wing as Right wing usages.

The name on the Left one comes across most often is Noam Chomsky – no other author is so associated with a coherent viewpoint on the post Cold War order of the world and the place of the United States within it. Chomsky offered a succinct definition in *Deterring Democracy* in 1992:

> The Gulf War has torn aside the veil covering the post-Cold War era. It has revealed a world in which the United States enjoys unchallenged military supremacy and is prepared to exploit this advantage ruthlessly. The New World Order (in which the New World gives the orders) has arrived.
> (http://www.znetwork.org/chomsky/dd/dd.html)

Writing on this subject (with titles such as *World Orders, Old and New*) and developing these ideas has been Chomsky's work in the last ten years. By the end of the decade his meaning of the term was solidly fixed, as this announcement (from the World Socialist Website), on the occasion of another military intervention, reveals:

> **US-NATO bombs fall on Serbia: the 'New World Order' takes shape**
> The aim of these assaults is to establish the role of the major imperialist powers – above all the United States – as the unchallengeable arbiters of world affairs. The 'New World Order' is precisely this: an international regime of unrelenting pressure and intimidation by the most powerful capitalist regime against the weakest.
> (http://www.topix.com/~sean/yugo1.htm)

For all that, it is a little surprising that the Left's employment of the term was not blunted by the Right's. This may be because the Left view of the New World Order appeared so fundamentally different, speaking of an excess of US sovereignty (and its effects abroad), and not its subversion or demise. As such, the Left might seem safe and secure, immune from the conspiracy theories of the 'other' New World Order. However, Left commentators often warned of the risk. In *Z Magazine* Michael Albert warned of the voyeurism of conspiracy theories and Holly Sklar of the 'snake oil' of scape-goating, while Chip Berlet of Political Research Associates cautioned Leftists to beware being suckered by the conspiracy theories of the Right. Berlet cites among those seduced the West Coast progressive radio station Pacifica radio and the Christic Institute.

It is certainly true that an eclectic mixture of materials can be found as ingredients of most Right wing conspiracy theories, and perhaps the New World Order most of all – for instance, great chunks of Noam Chomsky can be found waiting patiently for readers on patriot and militia websites. Despite fears, the favour is much less often returned by the Left. The potentials of mixture were commented on by Michael Kelly in an article in the *New Yorker* in 1995. Kelly wrote of the 'fusion paranoia' to be found when studying the views of those who believed in the New World Order and other such conspiracies. He argued that since the close of the Cold War, distinctions between Left and Right in America had lost meaning, and the 'fusion' this provoked suggested that new groupings and new perspectives were merging and emerging onto the US political and cultural scene. As Mark Fenster argues, seeing mixture and an intermingling is one thing, but claiming a workable fusion of New World Order conspiracy theories is a greater leap. (Fenster, 1999: 267) Given that, as Francis Mason has commented, conspiracy theories supply 'a heterodoxy of orthodoxies', they don't mesh as easily as Kelly claims. (Mason; 2001 forthcoming) In any case, it would be a mistake to see conspiracy theories on the Left as only stemming from contamination, or seduction or admixture. It is not necessary. The events (proven and disputed) of the Kennedy and King assassinations, Vietnam, COINTELPRO, and Watergate, Iran Contra, the Tuskegee syphilis study, all have offered the Left historical confirmation for contemporary fears of overseas military adventurism, government surveillance, corporate conspiracies, clandestine intelligence agency dirty tricks, or even Hillary Clinton's 'vast Right Wing conspiracy' against her husband. In other words, the New World Order as the Left saw it could not help but rest on a foundation of prior suspicion. Does this make the Left's concept of the New World Order a conspiracy theory? No, not if it is taken as baldly as stated above, namely that there is only one superpower left in the world, and it uses its power to satisfy its own interests. However, the larger edifice constructed on the foundation of Left conspiracy theories goes further. Daniel Pipes, author of *Conspiracy: How the Paranoid Style Flourishes and Where It Comes From*, claims that Chomsky is the prime architect of a Left wing:

> conspiracy theory that blames the U.S. government for virtually every ill in the world, including environmental pollution, militarism, economic poverty, spiritual alienation, and the drug scourge. It manipulates the mainstream media (to divert the revolutionary potential of workers), sponsors academic postmodernism (to bewilder the uninitiated), and encourages professional sports (to distract attention from serious issues) (Pipes, 1997: 160).

While this a slightly bowdlerized description of Chomsky, it does capture the totalizing tendency and the 'can do no good' flavour of his writings. The perception that Chomsky might offer a conspiracy theory because he connects issues together into a grander, revealing narrative of contemporary affairs, is also hinted at by the method used, namely the exhaustive plotting of a mass of detail – a skill for which many on the Left have praised Chomsky a great deal. Alexander Cockburn recalls:

> The nights I've stayed at Noam and Carol Chomsky's house in Lexington and I've watched him at even-tide working his way through a capacious box of the day's intake of tripe – newspapers, weeklies, monthlies, learned journals, flimsy mimeo-ed mailers – while Carol Chomsky does the same thing on the other side of the room.
> (Chomsky, *Chronicles*, 1992: x)

This mode of enquiry does seem very reminiscent of that classically employed by conspiracy theorists on the Right – the deep mining of the world's detail for bits of evidence. Of course, Chomsky would claim that the difference is that he is correct, but even if he is, that only leads to a further element. In an interview in 1999 he described the nature of the mainstream media:

Q: *So would you say that the elite groups are not so much co-ordinated in producing the system as they are unanimous in protecting it?*

A: There are matters on which they tend to be in overwhelming agreement. There are other matters on which there are internal differences. And in fact, when you investigate the media product, what you typically find is that on topics on which there is very broad consensus, there's no discussion. On topics where there's debate, there is discussion. A dramatic recent case was the Multilateral Agreement on Investments. On that there was near-uniformity in the corporate sector, the government, the media component of the corporate sector, the international financial institutions. They were all in favor of this treaty, overwhelmingly. They all understood very well that the public is not going to like it, so for years they just kept it secret. On that issue, no discussion. The same happened on NAFTA. The same sectors were overwhelmingly in favor, but they knew the population wasn't going to like it – which in fact remained true right until the end. So they simply would never allow debate on it.

(http://www.bostonphoenix.com/archive/features/99/04/01/
NOAM_CHOMSKY.html)

In effect, Chomsky accuses the media of participating in a conspiracy of silence which also includes the government and business. Actions such as the Gulf War, or NAFTA might be impossible to hide, but motives and meaning are disguised, and (of course) consent is manufactured. Does this not make Chomsky (and like-minded others) into at least a quasi-conspiracy theorist, that is, someone who theorizes about the actions of others who he claims are conspiring – whether they know they are doing it or not? On this very point, Chomsky stated in a 1995 interview with Michael Albert in *Z Magazine* (a journal that carries a great deal of Chomsky's writings and speeches):

We want to find out the truth about the way things work. There are doubtless cases in which people get together, in fact, every example of planning decisions is a case where people got together and used their power, or the power that they could draw from to try to achieve a result. If you like, that's a conspiracy. So with that definition, everything that happens is a conspiracy. So if the board of General Motors gets together and decides what kind of Chrysler, Ford, something to produce next year, that's a conspiracy. Every business decision, every editorial decision ... But we're not learning much about how the world works, in fact, nothing that generalizes to the next case.

(http://zena.secureforum.com/Znet/zmag/zarticle.cfm? Url = articles/chomalb.htm)

For this same reason Albert has argued that (even if it looks like it) the Left doesn't indulge in conspiracy theory, since it assigns responsibility to processes and institutions ('institutional theory'), and not to malign rogue individuals.

There are problems here. First of all, this is a rather classical Hofstadter-like definition, and many conspiracy theories on the Right, and certainly the milder Right, could pass Albert's test. There is a focus on actors such as Janet Reno, but equally now a strong tendency to dwell on the role of institutions such as the WTO, the Trilateral Commission and others identified as part of the New World Order. Secondly, as Mark Fenster notes, it is also a very narrow and functionalist definition of ideology, leaving out all symbolic operations of ideas and values. (Fenster, 1999: 61) In effect, the construction Albert makes is a simple syllogism: if it offers an ideological critique, it can't be conspiracy theory, and if it is conspiracy theory, then it can't offer an ideological critique. Michael Parenti, a far more populist progressive, sets out a different position in his book *Against Empire*:

> To dismiss as conspiracy fantasy all assertions that elite power is consciously and intelligently exercised is to arrive at the implausible position that there is no self-interested planning, no secrecy, no attempt to deceive the public, no suppression of information, no deliberate victimization, no ruthless policy pursuits, no intentionally unjust or illegal gains ... The alternative is to have a coincidence theory or an innocence theory which says that things just happen because of unintended happenstance, or a muddling through, with a lack of awareness of what is at stake, of who gets what, when, and how. For some unexplained reason we are to assume that the rich and the powerful, so well schooled in business and politics, so at home in the circles of power, are unaware of where their interests lie, and they lift not a competent finger in support of them. Such an innocence theory appears vastly more far fetched than the idea that people with immense wealth and overweening power will resort to every conceivable means to pursue their interests. (Parenti, 1995: 156)

Parenti's distinction between coincidence and conspiracy – and so between 'innocence theory' and therefore guilt theory? – intriguingly again presents the vision of Left wing conspiracy theorizing working with its object of attention in plain sight, and actions and motives taken for granted – an open conspiracy. In effect, for Parenti, (unlike Albert) conspiracy and ideology are interchangeable, and there is nothing regressive about admitting it. Chomsky at times even seems to come to near agreement with this:

Q: *But I get the impression that a lot of people think that you're saying that it's a massive conspiracy?*

A: That's true maybe of people in the Harvard faculty, but that's because for them *conspiracy* is a curse word. If something comes along that you don't like, there are a few sort of four-letter words that you can use to push it out of the sphere of discussion. If you were in a bar downtown, they might have different words, but if you're an educated person what you use are complicated words like *conspiracy theory* or *Marxist*. It's a way of pushing unpleasant questions off the agenda so that we can continue in our own happy ideology.

(http://www.bostonphoenix.com/archive/features/99/04/01/
NOAM_CHOMSKY.html)

He also said in his 1995 interview with Albert:

If the word conspiracy is to have any sensible meaning, the question becomes whether there are groupings well outside the structure of the major institutions that go around them, that undermine them, pursue other courses without an institutional base, and so on.

(http://zena.secureforum.com/Znet/zmag/zarticle.cfm?Url = articles/
chomalb.htm)

Ironically however, by this very description Chomsky himself might be defined as exactly this sort of actor, a guerrilla academic from MIT who (under) mines the 'truth'. At least one of his readers seems to see it as so. The actor John Cusack recalls his first encounter with reading Chomsky as follows:

When I was seventeen', recalls Cusack, 'Joanie was going out with some anarchist from Madison, Wisconsin, who gave me *The Chomsky Reader*, this big fat thing – the most important thing I've ever read. I had my counterculture instincts, but this book validated them, gave them context, a genuinely radical way of looking at the world. I had always loved Orwell and had an interest in conspiracies, but I didn't want to be paranoid. Chomsky allowed me to understand the obfuscation of truth at the mass level and how to embrace the Big Conspiracy Theories without being too cynical'.

(http://premieremag.radicalmedia.com/archive/Mar_96/cusack/
cusack3.html)

For Daniel Pipes, the difference comes down to this alone; the skill and training of the conspiracy theorists:

In American life, the right tends to be crude and overt in its conspiracism. The left is elegant and sophisticated and subtle. And so take Noam Chomsky vs. Mark of Michigan. Mark of Michigan is a janitor by day and he has loudmouth ravings. Noam Chomsky is one of the brilliant intellectuals of this century, a man who changed our understanding of the human mind, a fluent polemicist who's written book after book on important subjects. Sophisticated is an understatement. And yet, his view of the United States government is as conspiracist as Mark of Michigan. So there is this mirror imaging on the two sides, and yet, the left gets away with a lot more, in large part because of the elegance with which it purveys its conspiracy theories.

(http://www.skeptictank.org/hs/conspir.htm)

In a curious way, Chomsky can even seem to be in partial agreement. He commented on the Oklahoma bombing:

People like Timothy McVeigh, the guy who is charged with putting the bomb ... they are exactly the kind of people who 60 years ago would have been building the CIO. They had something constructive to do then. Now they don't know what is going on. They don't know about the profits of the Fortune 500, but they do know about the bad government and the extra-terrestrials and Lucifer and the other really serious threats.

(http://www2.prestel.co.uk/littleton/nc95_nwo.htm)

However, Pipes, a skeptic about all conspiracies, leaves the most significant question hanging: if both sides do supply conspiracy theories or quasi-conspiracy theories to such an extent (and even if one does it more elegantly and with more validity than the other), then what general needs are being met by such, and how satisfactorily? Pipes' basic answer – none, because all conspiracy theories are mad, bad, and dangerous to know – offers little.

To answer this, it is helpful to return to Bush's 1991 speech. Zygmunt Bauman came back to it in 1998 and to the question of the New World Order. The idea of order, he wrote, relates:

not so much to things as they are as to the ways of managing them; to the capacity of *ordering*, rather than of any immanent quality of the things as they happened to be by themselves and at the moment. What George Bush must have meant was not so much the dissipation of the 'order of things' as the disappearance of the means and the know-how to *put things in order* and keep them there ... The present day 'New World Disorder' ... does not refer to the state of the world after the end of the Great Schism and the collapse of the power-block political routine. It reports, rather, our sudden awareness of the essentially elemental and contingent nature of things, which was before not so much non-existent as barred from sight by the all-energy consuming day-to-day reproduction of balance between the world powers. By dividing the world, power conjured up the image of totality ... - With the Great Schism out of the way, the world does not look a totality anymore, it looks rather as a field of scattered and disparate forces, sedimenting in places difficult to predict and gathering momentum impossible to arrest. (Bauman, 1998: 38)

The sudden visibility of the contingent therefore suggests a reason to account for the swift rise in popularity of conspiracy theories in the 1990s, namely as popular attempts to re-conjure a lost totality, and cope with the randomness which now seems to propel the world – and the one thing more frightening than thinking that all events are controlled, is thinking that none are (see Lilley, this volume).

Of great interest here is the apparent collapse of trust in government, and indeed in most forms of nation-state authority. Therefore, like many theorists of globalization, Bauman stresses the importance of global-local connections for re-asserting identity in a contingent world, a task which a 'local industry of self-differentiation [has turned] into a globally determined characteristic of the late 20th century'. (Bauman, 1998: 43) Therefore, conspiracy theories can be seen to supply another route for the essentially tribal process of 'glocalization'. Manuel Castells makes much this point in *The Power of Identity*, the second volume of his trilogy *The Information Age*, and draws not just on the militias, but other examples such as the Mexican Zapatistas and the Japanese Aum Shinrikyo sect as examples of 'refusals' to globalization (1997: 69–109). However, in considering such tribes, Frederic Jameson's comment from 1988 does inevitably come to mind – that conspiracy theories provide only a 'poor person's mapping of the post-modern world ... a degraded figure of the total logic of capital ... a desperate attempt to represent the latter's system, whose failure is marked by its slippage into sheer form and content' (Jameson, 1988: 356). Answering Jameson, Pat O'Donnell has argued that 'cultural paranoia' offers 'a way of seeing the multiple stratifications of reality, virtual and material, as interconnected or networked [in] an attempt to make order out of chaos' (Willman, 1998: 406). However, for all this affirmation, it is evidently true on reading an advocate like Thompson that such conspiracy theories evidently do supply a massively debased understanding. But, as Francis Mason has noted, Jameson's comment begs a question: just what would the 'rich person's mapping' be, not least in a contingent present such as Bauman and Giddens describe? (Mason, 2001 forthcoming) Thus a more significant response might be to ask if Jameson's point is even worth answering anymore, not least since it rests itself on the most lost totality of all, namely Marxism? Perhaps instead what we have to consider are not the views of the core tribes of conspiracy theory believers at all, but instead the dissemination and popular attractions of conspiracy theories and the uses to which they are put by individuals?

In fact, Bauman's argument on 'glocalization' does not speak to the tribal with any great fixity at all. Instead what he notes about the contemporary is the social, political, economic and informational mobility available, both voluntary and involuntary – his two models for glocalization are 'the Tourist' and 'the Vagabond' (Bauman, 1998: 47). The view that globalization is actually about connections and networks – economic, political, informational, military, governmental – has been given extensive voice by many, and it is now common to define globalization as the eradication of not just space but time. In regard to information, what is being created is an all but instantaneous and connected society, in which the Haves and the Have Nots are defined by their relative degree of access. Contemplating this, a curious link between conspiracy and contingency is again revealed by the internet, which has been the medium for the development and propagation of so much of contemporary conspiracy theory. The internet has allowed the potential connection of any item, any datum, to any other – producing latent connections which produce transitory, temporary, meanings out of the mass. As such, it models the contemporary use made of conspiracy theories by many. Elsewhere Bauman has written that today:

> the image more likely to grasp the nature of cultural identity is one of the eddy rather than the island. Identities retain their distinct shape only in as far as they go on ingesting and divesting cultural matter seldom of their own making. Identities do not rest on the uniqueness of their traits, but consist increasingly in distinct ways of selecting/recycling/re-arranging the cultural matter which is common to all, or at least potentially available to all.
>
> (Bauman, 1999: xlv)

Bauman's point about order is not that it is lost, but that it was never there in the first place, only its illusion, and only its illusion can be recaptured, and then only temporarily fixed. With this in mind, we must understand that the New World Order and other contemporary popular manifestations of conspiracy such as the so-called Roswell UFO incident, the crash of TWA flight 800, or government involvement in the drug trade, have gained both a broader, open, but just as importantly a more *casual* adherence in the contemporary world. As Mark Fenster puts it:

> [If] fear of the loss of employment, personal control, and identity in a continually transforming economy and shrinking civil society saturates the lives of a considerable portion of the public, then conspiracy theory constitutes a profoundly satisfying politics. It not only explains the victory of seemingly demonological forces and the emptiness and inaccessibility of politics, but it also establishes a particular logic based on the interpretation of phenomena within an explanatory narrative form that is profoundly skeptical of dominant discourse. Continuity and balance, increasingly unsustainable at the personal level, re-emerge in the theory and practice of following conspiracy.
>
> (Fenster, 1999: 72)

To understand such requires us not so much to think of conspiracy theories, but (following Fenster's clue) what we might better call conspiracy *practices*. By this, I do not mean participation in a conspiracy, but rather participation in *thinking* conspiratorially, in a conspiracy mind-set or a conspiracy expectation.

This allows extension beyond the literal question of, say, militia membership or progressive activism. A more relevant term than membership might be 'association' or perhaps even better 'suspicion'.

Thus, an awareness of conspiracy theories no longer signals being individually certain of a hidden plot or a secret order, but more of entertaining doubts, often about things which are quite openly visible, and the feeling that in a contingent world there is some truth, somehow, in certain elements of conspiracy's imaginations. This is something that most people will explore not in membership or intense devotion, but in visits to conspiracy webpages, the viewing of conspiracy-aligned movies and television series, or just – perhaps most – in situations such as water-cooler conversations about events in the news. They may take up an interest in elements of a specific conspiracy theory, and make contributions, but this would be better considered as a hobby than as an obsession. Some will find it guides their politics intensely, other will not. Contradictions will exist, and fusions will take place. Equally, the practice is transitory and passing, with elements being forgotten and remembered, sampled and retained. For most people therefore, what is on offer from the New World Order, particularly as the popularly fused together text of Left and Right, therefore is more frisson than faith. In effect then, conspiracy *practice* – the thrill of conjecture and the enlightening experience of apparently connecting things together – has become just as important as conspiracy *theory* – provision of the intense detail of the narratives as thought out and disseminated by a core, whether it be Noam Chomsky or Mark of Michigan.

All of this bears upon the most recent events to operate *within the text* of the New World Order conspiracy theories, the protests against the World Trade Organization and similar agencies. The protests drew to Seattle in late November-early December 1999 figures as different as Pat Buchanan (who a month before had quit the Republican party for the Reform party, and declared himself against the New World Order) and Situationist Anarchists intent on trashing the omnipresence of McDonalds and Starbucks. Organized via the Internet and co-ordinated 'live' via cellphones, this almost leaderless protest fused together for a few days a tribe of 50,000 protestors, and some of their encounters with the Police led to the so-called 'Battle of Seattle'. Follow-up protests have since taken place in Davos, Switzerland, Washington DC, London, and more are planned. Is it fair to say that these events were bred from a conspiratorial vision of the contemporary global order? I think so, which is not to diminish their importance or meaning, because thinking conspiratorially, or considering 'open conspiracies' as ideologically symbolic is not necessarily politically regressive. While the events in Seattle came as a surprise, this was not for want of economic globalization being an issue during the 1990s; indeed, a good part of the discourse about the New World Order, Left and Right, had to do with legislation for a global economy and fears that measures such as NAFTA would bring unemployment to Americans, as jobs were exported to Mexico. These sentiments were well expressed by journalist and film-maker Michael Moore, who made an explicit comparison to the Oklahoma bombing:

> Though most people are somehow able to keep their wits through these hard times, I believe thousands of Americans are only a few figurative steps away from getting into that Ryder truck. How terrifying that the vehicle chosen for terrorist acts [by Timothy McVeigh] should be the same one used by the vast diaspora of working class Americans who have spent the last decade moving from state to state in the hopes of survival.
>
> (Moore, 1997: 15)

It seems unlikely, however, that Seattle can be explained in these literal terms, not given that the American economy had undergone a decade of sustained growth, unemployment and inflation were at historic lows, and apocalyptic predictions of a meltdown provoked by NAFTA had not been realized. Why then did this hardly very secretive meeting of a rather dull and bureaucratic trade organization of 135 nations whose membership was publicly known, serve as a focus for such uproar? It seems more that the general sense of a lack of control and input into order noted by Bauman and Giddens were responsible. Parallel concerns (held rather more by the Left than the Right) that the economic management policies brokered by the WTO, GATT and the like, were giving large corporations release to ruthlessly exploit Third World peoples and ruin the global environment also appear to have provided significant motivation for many, especially young people. As an explicitly titled 'global' organization, the WTO did seem to symbolize a great deal to a great many people. Here is David Goldman, the Chairman of the Florida branch of the Reform party:

> The WTO represents the culmination of a trend in which the ability of ordinary Americans to have a say in how they are governed has reached a point of no return. The influence of large, predominantly corporate, special interest groups on our federal and state government has produced a crisis of confidence that has become so ingrained in our national consciousness that we now assume that our elected officials are all bought and paid for.
>
> (http://ronhoward.org/battle_in_seattle.htm)

This is a very strange thing to say about a meeting of a bureaucratic body that has only existed since 1995, but Tom Hayden made an even larger claim for the importance of the protests:

> For the first time in memory, the patriotism of the corporate globalizers is in question, not that of their opponents. Do the Clinton administration's investor-based trade priorities benefit America's interest in high-wage jobs, environmental protection and human rights? Are American democratic values and middle-class interests secondary to those of transnational

corporations? As a grass-roots movement seeking the overthrow of what it sees as an oppressive system, Seattle 99 was more like the Boston Tea Party than the days of rage we knew in the late 60s.

(http://www.portaec.net/library/mai_wto/tom_hayden_on_the_
battle_in html)

At the heart of the event therefore was a symbolic sense – not a perception, not a knowledge – that something was wrong, and that individuals felt disenfranchised and misrepresented. As Sarah Brown, a protestor interviewed on the street by CNN World News on 30 November, while standing amidst the tear gas, said:

> I think we've told the delegates that we're not just going to stand by and let them trade our sovereignty away, our ability to withstand, and our ability to stand up for ourselves, and our ability to get our points across. I think this is a really huge deal, and I think they got it.

One index of this (good and bad – it might never happen again) is simply the unexpected size of the demonstrations, a surprise for organizers and Police alike, neither of which had expected to experience the largest street disturbances in the United States since the 1992 Los Angeles Riots. Was this agglomeration merely a coincidence? It isn't a meaningful question. The fact is that large numbers of people for many different reasons that long weekend, took time to take part in something that somehow they had become aware of, which somehow motivated them, and somehow seemed to represent their sense of what we might call global 'mis-order'. In this regard, an observation *and* the conclusions drawn from it by one student protestor's recollections are revealing:

> 'I can't believe this is America', one woman said, her eyes red and her voice shaking.
>
> Those who had come for a march and a casual protest for human rights had left with much more. They had gotten a taste of just how much dominance the corporate world has in our government, and how far this country is willing to go to defend globalization.

(http//iahf.com/world/wto-eyewitness.html)

Bibliography

Agnew, J., (1994), 'Global Hegemony versus National Economy. The United States in the New World Order', in Demko, G. and Wood, W. (eds), *Re-Ordering the World*. Oxford: Westview Press, 269–279.

Albert, M., (1992), 'Conspiracy Theory', *Z Magazine*, May. (http://zena.secureforum.com/Znet/zmag/zarticle.cfm?Url = articles/oldalbert19.htm).

Bauman, Z., (1998), 'On Glocalization: Or Globalization for Some, Localization for Others', *Thesis Eleven*, 54: 36–49.

Bauman, Z., (1999), *Culture as Praxis*. London: Sage.

Berlet, Chip, 'Right Woos Left' (http://www.publiceye.org/rightwoo/Rwooz.htm).

Castells, M., (1997), *The Information Age*, Vol II: *The Power of Identity*. Oxford: Blackwell.

Chomsky, N., (1992), *Chronicles of Dissent: Interviews with David Barsamian*. Boston: Common Courage Press.

Fenster, M., (1999), *Conspiracy Theories. Secrecy and Power in American Culture*. Minneapolis: University of Minnesota Press.

Horsman & Marshall (1994), *After the Nation State: Citizens, Tribalism and the New World Disorder*. London: Harper Collins.

Jameson, F., (1988), 'Cognitive Mapping', in Nelson, C. and Grossberg, L. (eds), *Marxism and the Interpretation of Culture*. Urbana: University of Illinois Press, 347–360.

Keith, J., (1994), *Black Helicopters Over America: Strike Force for the New World Order*. Georgia: Illuminet Press.

Kelly, M., (1995), 'The Road to Paranoia', *New Yorker*, 19 June, 60–75.

Knight, P., (2000), *Conspiracy Culture. From Kennedy to the X Files*. London: Routledge.

Stewart, K., (1999), 'Conspiracy Theories' Worlds', in George, M. (ed.), *Paranoia within Reason. A Casebook on Conspiracy as Explanation*. Chicago: University of Chicago Press, 13–21.

Mason, F., (2001), 'A Poor Persons' Cognitive Mapping', in Knight, P. (ed.), *Trust No One*. New York: NYU Press.

Moore, M., (1997), *Down Size This!* London: Boxtree.

Mulloy, D., (ed.) (1999), *Homegrown Revolutionaries*. Norwich: UEA Press.

Parenti, M., (1995), *Against Empire*. San Francisco: City Lights Books.

Pipes, D., (1997), *Conspiracy: How the Paranoid Style Flourishes and Where It Comes From*. Boston: Free Press.

Sklar, H., (1995), 'The SnakeOil of Scapegoating', *Z Magazine*, May. (http://zena.secureforum.com/Znet/zmag/zarticle.cfm?Url = articles/may95sklar.htm)

Spark, A., (1998), 'Do Black Helicopters Hover over your House?' *Thresholds: Viewing Culture*, 11: 101–112.

Willman, S., (1998), 'Traversing the Fantasies of the JFK Assassination: Conspiracy and Contingency in Don DeLillo's, *Libra' Contemporary Literature*, 39/3: 405–433.

Militias, the Patriot movement, and the internet: the ideology of conspiracism

Nigel James

Representing the right: sociological debates

The literature on the Patriot movement explicitly links the newly emergent 'militia movement' with the well-established racist right in America. It is the employment of conspiracy theories by both new and old right wing groups that is regarded as the proof of this link, especially amongst 'watchdog' academics and activists. However, an understanding of popular eschatology points to the fact that a different type of conspiracism[1] is being employed here, not necessarily racist in origin but rooted in Christian Manichaeism,[2] fundamentalism and 'end times' Prophecy. This is not to suggest that Christian Patriot ideology is immune from racism, it is to acknowledge that race as a referent is obscured, contested, and sometimes genuinely opposed. As well as covering these themes, in this chapter I will explore how the internet emerges as a medium that is uniquely receptive to conspiracism, and put forward an argument that suggests that conspiracism should properly be seen as an ideological phenomenon.

The militias that have formed across the USA since the early 1990s have troubled academics and 'watchdogs' because of their success in reaching out to new segments of alienated middle class Americans (Hardisty, 1995; Sklar, 1995). Initially, they received little coverage apart from alarms raised by human rights groups and 'watchdog' organizations such as the Southern Poverty Law Center (SPLC) and the Anti-Defamation League of B'Nai B'rith (ADL). The SPLC wrote to Janet Reno in October, 1994, alerting her to the danger the militias represented (Berlet and Lyons, 1995). But it was not until the Oklahoma City federal building was blown up by a terrorist bomb on April 19th 1995 that there was widespread public interest in the militias and the wider Patriot movement, out of which the perpetrator of the bombing, Tim McVeigh, was said to have emerged. Since then there have been hundreds of articles and books on the subject, with a consensus gradually emerging which effectively demonizes 'Christian Patriotism' as a front for racists and anti-Semites (for example, Dees and Corcoran, 1997).

Mark Fenster argues that the demonization of the militias by both watchdogs and law enforcement agencies is based on flawed assumptions regarding the nature of conspiracism, and that the most likely result is 'the militarization of confrontation between a more empowered state disciplinary machinery and marginal, well-armed groups whose very fears would thereby be realized' (Fenster, 1999: 51). Other analysts have viewed with alarm 'delegitimization as a mutual and reciprocal process' as both the radical right and state authorities employ antipathetic dualism (Kaplan, 1995: 74). According to Fenster, watchdog activists and academics, such as Morris Dees and Ken Stern, effectively mirror the right-wing conspiracy theorists they are concerned with, in that both groups seek the exclusion of certain other groups from the marketplace of democratic political processes. This, he argues, is because of the simplistic approach regarding the concept of extremism, which has its origins in the work of Richard Hofstadter, Seymour Lipset and other 'pluralist' academics of the 1950s and 60s.

Hofstadter's work on the 'paranoid style' of radical rightists depicted a dividing line between rational (healthy) political views and irrational (pathological) ones. Fenster argues that what such analysts were doing, in Gramscian terms, was helping to build the 'historic bloc' of forces and culture which ensured the continued triumph of American capitalism during the post-World War Two era. These 'consensus' historians downplayed genuine conflicts in American society and, basing their ideas on the notion of 'American exceptionalism' (ie, the unique lack of a feudal past) they promoted a conception of 'Americanism' linked to shared liberal democratic values. The pluralist model, which has continued to hold sway within the academic mainstream, argued that it was only 'alienated' people who fell foul of a 'paranoid' fear of conspiracy. The conditions of American exceptionalism therefore dictated that the unique stability of the American system justified the exclusion of 'extremists' (of both the left and the right) for the greater good. This de-legitimization of radicalism, Fenster argues, originates with the fear of 'mass society', which is perceived as threatening to annihilate the consensus of 'normal' politics. Hofstadter and others employed dichotomies that constructed dominant society as 'normal' versus an 'Other' which comprised those who are marginalized, outside of the mainstream. For instance, he drew a distinction between 'interest politics' (revolving around economics and bargaining power) and 'status politics' (based on emotion and ideology). Movements based on the former were regarded as healthy, those based on the latter as unhealthy.

Fenster cites a critic of the consensus historians who in 1959 argued that they had 'substitute[d] a schism in the soul for a schism in society' and had thereby trivialized conflict as 'psychological adjustments to institutional change'. Ultimately, for Fenster, the application of 'a theory of individual pathology to a social phenomenon' should be rejected as anything other than an interesting analogy. The problem with the 'paranoid style' analysis is that it is 'limited in its ability to analyse, challenge, and redirect the populism of conspiracy theory' and becomes problematic when seeking to explain the populist political dissent of the 1990s. (Fenster, 1999: 21).

Fenster's critique of the pluralist standpoint is grounded in the work of Michael Rogin whose retrospective of American demonology (and countersubversion) focuses on central political figures, such as J. Edgar Hoover and Ronald Reagan. He argues that extremism and the 'paranoid style' are generated by forces at the heart of American capitalism, rather than emanating from the fringes of society: 'The important bearers of American political demonology have not been extremists or subversives, but their foes'. (Rogin, 1987: 274) Rogin is critical of the inferred pluralist tradition of hostility to 'masses', within which exclusion is justified for those who behave 'irrationally' and are motivated by 'status concerns' instead of more rational, class-based interests. (Rogin, 1967: 15) In seeking to understand the process of political demonology he also explicitly rejects the dichotomy between 'realist' and 'symbolist' explanations. A realist approach would regard countersubversion, instigated by elites, as ultimately serving capitalism and powerful interests. A symbolist approach would focus on a 'paranoid style', which mobilized outsiders or extremists, thus threatening the stability of the system. For Rogin, 'Realists saw political repression when they examined countersubversion; symbolists saw paranoia' (Rogin, 1987: 274). He wishes to bring these competing viewpoints together – they are not mutually exclusive.

The work of Lipset and Raab and other pluralists, in emphasizing 'symbolism', implicitly rejected Marxism and diverted attention away from class divisions and also away from racial oppression.

> But racial conflict placed the paranoid style at the centre and origin of American history, made it hard to argue for a happy, pluralist outcome, and broke down the easy distinction between interests and fantasies. The fantasies whites generated about peoples of colour exposed and intensified actual conflicts of interest; interests and fantasies could neither be reduced to nor separated from one another. (*op cit*: 277)

Rogin rejects 'class-status distinctions [which] diverted attention from deep cleavages and fundamental conflicts'. He calls for 'the problems of identity, anxiety, and mobility, the fears of identity loss and homogenization' to be examined in the context of 'class, race, gender and institutional stratification' rather than treated separately (279).

Rogin's perspective is being emphasized here because it points towards a more sophisticated understanding of demonology and conspiracism, in which the subconscious aspects of identity formulation are melded with interest-based politics focussing on power relations:

> The cultural power of mobility, far from undermining stratification, at once obscures social divisions and intensifies the need for them. To win, in the countersubversive tradition, is to be an English-speaking white man. To lose is to fall back among the undifferentiated mass of aliens, women and peoples of colour. Countersubversives desire the submergence of separate identities within an ideal America, but they also enforce divisions because they are threatened by boundary collapse. That oscillation between a fear of

the breakdown of all difference and a desire for merger lies at the core of American political demonology. (279–80)

Countersubversives need the myth of the American Dream – the belief that equality of opportunity exists for all and that there is an all-embracing 'Americanism' – but at the same time they need to be aware of what it means to be one of the chosen few, exercising God's will, morally and spiritually superior. Much of the discourse of the Patriot movement and the racist right is concerned with morality, arguing that the immorality exhibited by American society is part of a deliberate plan by anti-Christian élites. It is not surprising that the rhetoric of resistance employed by Christian Patriots frequently lapses into piety.

Ultimately, Rogin turns to the psychology of familial relations to lend greater depth to an understanding of demonology. In acknowledging that the psyche is socially constructed (287), he indicates that the search for pathology is misguided. Unconscious conflicts are not signs of pathology, they are part of the psychological makeup of normal people. For this reason countersubversion remains a powerful force in America, employed instrumentally by elites, but supported by non-elites as a means of shoring up their identity. 'Attending to the origins of individual identity', Rogin feels, 'helps explain the structure of the countersubversive imagination, its sources in sexual anxiety, and the connections in political demonology between political and sexual chaos' (290). He concludes by drawing attention to the nature of mass culture and the national-security state, with surveillance at its centre. These have become 'the distinctive and most important modern agents of social control within the borders of the nation-state. These twin developments ... place seeing and being seen at the centre of modern political integration' (296). The work of both Michel Foucault and Zygmunt Bauman is instructive in this respect. Both emphasize the role that the state has taken on in delivering 'security' to citizens, performing functions previously undertaken within communities but now imposed upon the remnants of communities. The anti-statism of the Patriot movement is part of the backlash from those who still harbour rose-tinted memories of a time when communities had enough salience to deliver security autonomously.

The massification of information technology has only served to dynamize these processes of countersubversion and identity construction. Extremism is rarely the product of pathology, but it is certainly generated by ideology. The following section deals with the ideology (and theology) of Christian Patriotism, and how it has been reflected in the literature on the radical right since the advent of the militia movement.

Christian Patriots, identity theology and conspiracism

There is widespread agreement that known racists and anti-Semites play a leading role within the Patriot movement. For instance, Ken Stern of the

American Jewish Committee quotes a human rights activist who states: 'The body work is painted with religion, patriotism, and the U.S. Constitution; but the motor is anti-Semitism and racism and the drivers are white supremacists'. (Stern, 1996: 245) What underpins this widely held assumption is the view that the common belief in conspiracy theories provides the glue between widely differing groups. This is overly simplistic, however. The Christian Patriot/ militia milieu is a complicated one, characterized by multiple allegiances to causes and groups. It is clear that not all Christian Patriot organizations are racist; what they do share is the employment of conspiracism as a means of cognitively mapping a complex world in which they feel politically powerless. Other analysts have argued that the movement employs 'fusion paranoia' which is neither left wing nor right wing. (Kelly, 1995) But watchdog academics such as Chip Berlet have warned against the dangers implicit in accepting right wing arguments based on the assumption of a 'common enemy'(1994). Daniel Pipes (1997) has argued that there are essentially just two types of 'global' conspiracism – the Jewish conspiracy and those of secret societies (eg, the Illuminati) – and that it is a mistake to see the latter, in which racism can be absent, as a coded version of the former, which is predicated upon racism. This chapter supports Pipes' contention, although I wish to emphasize the slippage that takes place between the two within the Patriot movement and the theocratic right.

Stern sees the militias and the Patriot movement operating as a 'funnel' which draws people in on issues such as gun control and taxes, then they get introduced to conspiracy theories about the federal government and secret societies, and then to anti-Semitic theories ... 'Finally, at the narrowest end of the funnel, you've drawn in the hard core, where you get someone like Tim McVeigh popping out ... [T]he bigger the front end of the funnel is, the bigger the number that get to the core'. (Stern, 1996: 107) Similarly, Michael Barkun sees the militias as 'bridges that take individuals from mainstream, albeit highly conservative, positions to activities and memberships that once lay beyond the pale'. (Barkun, 1996: 61) It is the language and style and assumptions behind conspiracism that appear to make this bridging function possible.

Predating the birth of the 'militia movement' in the early 1990s, James Aho was one of the first academics to focus on Christian Patriots from a sociological perspective, basing his research on right wing extremists in his home state of Idaho (Aho, 1990). Many analysts, it should be noted, use the term 'Patriot movement' when talking about the whole range of nationalist groups – from relatively moderate Second Amendment (pro-gun) activists to neo-Nazis and Christian Identity believers. This is useful as a much wider category, and it is also less offensive to other American Christians who consider themselves 'patriotic' whilst they would refute the beliefs espoused by those calling themselves 'Christian Patriots'. In this chapter I will use the term 'Christian Patriot' to denote the range of right wing activists who fulfil the following four criteria: support for the formation of armed militia; belief in conspiracies perpetrated by secret societies with internationalist agendas;

espousal of 'constitutionalist' arguments against federal government usurpation of power; and belief in the literal truth of 'End Times' prophecy as
contained in the Bible. Within certain groups, however, the disavowal of
racism may also be a factor. This may be genuine and sincere, or it may be
disingenuous or an act of self-deception. The point is that it is a variable within
Christian Patriot ideology and that racial inclusiveness is emphasized by
movement adherents and fervently believed by at least some of the Patriots I
have contacted. Both watchdog organizations and leading academics employ a
distinction between the racist right ('hate groups') and the Patriot/militia
milieu. But what is lacking is an overarching typology that can assist in
outlining the demarcations between the myriad political organizations of the
far right. The typology I am employing is based on the two key variables of
race and theocracy, considering how they are embedded in various modes of
conspiracism.

In his study focussing on the Pacific Northwest, David Neiwert asserts,
'there can be little mistaking the nature of the Patriot movement as essentially
fascist in the purest sense of the word', although his definition of fascism,
which emphasises 'phoenix-like societal rebirth, attained through a return to
"traditional values"', is perhaps rather vague. (Neiwert, 1999: 320) Berlet sees
it as 'proto-fascist', in that the ideology is in place and all that is required is for
a 'very charismatic leader to step forward. But it could happen at any time'.
(quoted in Neiwert, 1999: 322) Is the Patriot movement really fascistic? Mark
Neocleous's definition of fascism is worth bearing in mind:

[I]t is a form of reactionary modernism: responding to the alienation and
exploitation of modern society but unwilling to lay down any serious
challenge to the structure of private property central to modern capitalism,
fascism can only set its compass by the light of reaction, a mythic past to be
recaptured within the radically altered conditions of modernity. This politics
of reaction constitutes the ideological basis of a revolution from the right in
which war, nature and the nation become the central terms. (1997: xi–xii)

This definition would appear to exclude groups such as *Posse Comitatus* –
profoundly anti-statist, almost anarchistic in their belief that the only
legitimate form of power is that of the county sheriff. This is coupled with
unambiguous racism and anti-Semitism in which the federal state is regarded as
a tool of the Jewish enemies of America (as an organic, ethnically constituted
entity that pre-dates the nation-state). Such groups, rurally based and
favouring underground tactics (as opposed to the visibility of constitutionalist
militias), do not believe in nationalism in the modernist sense in which the
concept is closely tied to the nation-state. They represent a pre-modern
political formulation, but much of the energy from the rural heartland is
channelled into support for classically modernist nationalism. The liquidity of
the internet facilitates cross-fertilization and mutual reinforcement between
these variants of nationalism.

Aho identified two main types of 'Christian Patriot' – Christian Constitutionalists and Christian Identity believers. His distinction between these types, which is still valid today, hinges upon the identification of the enemies of America. Constitutionalists point the finger at 'insiders, Bilderbergers, Trilateralists' – the same enemies that are identified in the literature of the John Birch Society. Identity adherents see 'Jews' as the principle agents of evil in America. Aho's method of determining these positions was to ask individuals which publications they had read and then to follow this up with questions about the 'Jewish conspiracy'. By this means he identified Christian Identity adherents. By then asking for their definition of 'Jew' he was able to distinguish between two-seed and one-seed variants, the former believing that racial Jews are descendants of a different form of humanity – one literally spawned by the coupling of Satan and Eve in the Garden of Eden. Aho points out that there are racist as well as non-racist Identity strains of theology, but that 'it is important not to overlook the permeability of the boundary between them'. (Aho, 1990: 94) The defining characteristic of Identity Christianity is the centrality of race in the formation of a religious worldview. Thus racism, theology and conspiracism are blended to create a narrative of heroic struggle against the forces of evil, a struggle that will culminate in Armageddon.

The permeability of boundaries between ideological appeals emerges as a consistent theme when analysing the Patriot movement and the theocratic right (see Clarkson, 1997), especially on the internet. The contingent nature of the ideologies on offer and the habitual slippage between them points towards the formation of what Martin Jay (1993) tentatively suggested could be termed 'postmodern fascism'. He argued that the lack of a Marxist threat since the end of the 1980s, coupled with 'the near universalization of (...) bureaucratization, the expansion of the centralized state, the spread of the market, commodification, etc.', means that the resurgent fascism of the 1990s is 'not likely to be the real thing'. This is because we are well over the worst of the shock of the break from 'immanence' that was rendered by modernism and 'beyond the point of maximum anxiety about practical transcendence [modernization]'. That point occurred during the 1930s, when fascism was reacting against 'an aggressive and totalizing Marxism'. Jay acknowledges that 'we still have our share of "sovereign, martial, inwardly antagonistic groups", some of which will doubtless find it convenient to recycle the scapegoating appeals of fascism ... But by and large the postmodernization process is destined to engender new political forms, which will require still unimagined analytical categories and, alas, new strategies of defense'. The argument being presented in this chapter is that the militias fit into precisely this context, especially in cyberspace, and furthermore that the nature of computer mediated communication (CMC) lends itself to the construction of a postmodern fascism which is not 'the genuine thing'.

Christian Identity is an important factor when discussing the Patriot movement for it has played a key role in bringing together previously disparate racist right groupings both across and within North America and Europe.

69

Analysts such as Philip Lamy regard Identity-type belief systems as a common denominator, providing 'the most unifying theology for the diverse groups that compose the militant and survivalist right, including the Aryan Nations, the Ku Klux Klan, and many in the militia movement'. (Lamy, 1996: 130) The watchdog analysts enjoy virtual unanimity on the importance of racism within the Patriot movement, but there are dissenters such as Martin Durham (2000) and Paul de Armond who dispute this. De Armond (1995: 7, fn. 3) argues that the militias 'lack a clear and binding ideology. The leading militia organizers are predominantly white supremacists of the Christian Patriot variety, but racism is not a point of unity for militia followers'.

ZOG and the New World Order

Susan Zuskind (1997) draws attention to the vitally important role of The Protocols of the Learned Elders of Zion amongst racist extremists on the internet, quoting an individual on the newsgroup alt.politics.nationalism.white who called it 'a must-read for those interested in furthering their understanding of the New World Order'. The Protocols are purportedly the verbatim account of Jewish plans for global domination, to be carried out via such dastardly schemes as income tax, democracy, socialism, mass entertainment, and a wide variety of political front organizations. It was a forgery written in France in the early 1900s, created by the Tsar's advisors in order to discredit political opponents, and it has continued to be circulated by nationalists the world over – since 1945 it has been republished on average once every eight months (Pipes, 1997: fn. 27, 217). Abanes (1996: 137) comments, 'The Protocols continue to serve as a blueprint for most of today's conspiracy theories, including those being promoted by patriots'. Similarly, Ridgeway (1995: 13–14) is dismissive of those who think that the militias are in any way 'a welcome expression of working-class resistance', for their conspiracism, he argues, is unequivocally based upon the Protocols and upon racism.

The acceptance by the racist right of the veracity of Jewish conspiracy is ubiquitous. Sometimes it is presented within theological frames of reference – by Christian Identity sites – and sometimes in secular terms, for instance by the American Nazi Party. The discourse employed by anti-Semitic conspiracy theorists revolves around two key concepts: 'ZOG' and the 'New World Order'. ZOG refers to 'Zionist Occupational Government', that is, Western governments that have in effect become the tools of international Jewry. Ehud Sprinzak, highlighting the significance of this term, identified a process whereby racist groups regarded non-whites as illegitimate and so targeted members of minorities with violence and intimidation. They had an attitude of 'intense deligitimization' towards minorities but one of only 'diluted deligitimization' towards the state, a condition which he called 'split deligitimization' – 'where an uneven radicalization of a group of extremists develops against two separate entities'. Sprinzak argued that for many groups on the far right the split has disappeared as they now believe 'that the government has literally been taken over by the hated minority group and is no longer capable of reforming itself. It should therefore be destroyed with the same intensity as the original target group'. (1995: 20) Such an idea plainly would have been ridiculous in America of the 1920s, when the Ku Klux Klan was at its zenith, as the state was broadly supportive of its aims (at least locally and up to state level), but the term ZOG, which originated in the US in the late 1970s and 1980s, indicates a dramatic shift in the relationship between the radical right and the state since the success of the black civil rights movement in the 1960s. Christian Identity, Klan and neo-Nazi groups are far more willing to target state representatives now, and ZOG is, according to Sprinzak, 'the rhetorical device that seems to have made it possible'. Unsurprisingly, ZOG references are absent from Christian Patriot texts, both on the web and in published formats, since this would instantly alienate most Christian fundamentalists for who support for Israel and the Jews are central tenets of belief. However, the term New World Order, referring to the ultimate plan to enslave the world and destroy Christianity, is a term that is shared by both the racist right and the ostensibly non-racist Christian Patriots and militias. This particular overlap in the terminology of the discourses of conspiracism leads many commentators to assume that an ideological connection exists between 'hate groups' and 'Christian Patriots'. However, the assumption that anti-Semitism is at the root of all conspiracy theory is flawed. New World Order does not always equate with ZOG, and to assume otherwise only leads to the sort of demonising of the radical right that Fenster warns against. It ultimately assists the racist right in presenting 'common enemy' arguments to would-be allies in the Patriot movement.

The concern voiced by law enforcement agencies regarding Christian Identity is well founded. Aho (1994) stresses the importance of the theory of 'reification' in helping to understand the process by which people choose to carry out political violence. There is an increased propensity to act based on the assumption that a higher moral authority has sanctioned the acts, and that the actor is carrying out God's orders. Aho regards the notion of 'heroism' as central to an understanding of Christian Patriotism. He argues that Christian Patriots are motivated by the desire to 'save America' and because theirs is a crusade on behalf of God then they are willing to put up with vilification from mainstream society and to live with oppression from the forces of the state. The Christian Patriot actually requires the existence of an 'anti-Christian-constitutional-subverter', be it a 'Jew' (for Christian Identity adherents) or an 'insider' (for Christian Constitutionalists and the John Birch Society).

'[T]his symbolic antagonist is essential to the dialectic of heroic patriotism. Without it there would be nothing against which to struggle, nothing to give the patriot's life significance, nothing to justify his existence. What this implies, of course, is that if the 'Jew' or 'insider' did not exist he would have to be manufactured. (Aho, 1990: 79)'

71

The unique combination of theological and racial underpinnings to a belief system renders the believer more committed to the cause, less inclined to engage the mainstream and more likely to resort to acts of violence. For this reason the combination of race and religion is regarded as more worrying than regular bigotry, from a law enforcement perspective and indeed from a mainstream Christian one. Douglas Mitchell (1995), of the United Presbyterian Church in the USA, has analysed the history of extremism and the paramilitary movement. He regards Christian Identity as 'a system of lies about Christianity' which blends religion and racism whilst providing 'religious legitimation' for the racist right wing, resulting in 'the idolatry of the lesser gods of race, ethnicity, economic system, and nation'. This has led to the more widespread adoption of paramilitary tactics and the use of force amongst American extremists. There are other studies which point towards a distinct correlation between religious fundamentalism and right-wing authoritarianism (Hunsberger, 1995); indeed, that Nazism in its original formulation deliberately played on millenarian religious themes in order to mobilize a mass following.

Popular eschatology and conspiracism

Daniel Pipes, writing in the late 1990s, regards Pat Robertson as 'the single most influential conspiracy theorist' in the United States (1997: 10), and there is wide acknowledgement that the TV evangelist's 1991 bestseller, *The New World Order*, was instrumental in bringing conspiracism to a wider audience of Christian Americans. Fenster insists that in order to have an adequate understanding of the book (and indeed of the militia movement), one must be cognisant of the traditions of 'popular eschatology' – the practice of interpreting the past, the present, and the future in terms of biblical prophecy, as delivered to a mass market. This includes non-fictional works such as Hal Lindsey's *Late Great Planet Earth* (1970), as well as a range of fictional bestsellers, TV and radio shows broadcast by Christian media empires (including Robertson's own Christian Broadcasting Network). What they all deliver to their audience is an interpretation of world events in the context of the prophetic timetable outlined in the Bible, especially the Book of Revelations which counts down to the Second Coming of Christ, Tribulation, Armageddon, and the eventual Rapture of Christians to Heaven. Popular eschatology on television provides a metacommentary of current global events, summed up by the televangelist studio expert who declares: 'You can't have such an array of signs and not know the Lord is coming soon!' (Fenster, 1999: 165) A book by eschatology experts the LaLonde brothers promises on its cover that it 'will challenge you to live as if Christ were returning tomorrow'. This is the key to the function of popular eschatology – it serves to strengthen faith and belief. The narrative is built around the expectation of both 'horrific destruction' (Armageddon) and 'ecstatic rapture' (when Christians are taken up to heaven).

The attitude of conservative Christians towards secular politics is highly dependant upon whether they are pre- or post-millennialists. The former believe that Christ will come before Armageddon and the thousand-year kingdom of Heaven on Earth, whilst the latter believe that Christ will only come after all the prophetic events have taken place, including the millennium of godliness. Therefore a post-millennialist such as Pat Robertson believes that it is important for the church to grow strong and to involve itself in politics in order to make the conditions favourable for the eventual battle with the forces of darkness, which is some way off in the distant future. Taking part in popular eschatology offers a means of affecting the timetable of Prophecy or indeed of affecting the final outcome. If Christianity is destroyed in America (as a necessary part of the New World Order plan) then what chance will the forces of God have against those of Lucifer? Peter Doskoch makes this point in his article on 'The Mind of the Militias'. He notes the 'huge overlap between militias and fundamentalists' and points out that whereas most fundamentalists are 'pre-tribbers' (they believe that Jesus will come before Armageddon occurs) militia members tend to be mid- or post-tribbers, believing that He will come after violent apocalypse. Doskoch quotes Charles Strozier: 'That's an arcane point of theology, but it has enormous psychological significance because they want to be there during tribulation ... They want to take their Uzis and fight it out with the Beast. God needs their help'. (Doskoch, 1995: 12) It is perhaps understandable that, according to research cited by Fenster, 'working class believers tend to foresee the rapture occurring sooner than those of higher economic status'. (Fenster, 1999: 152) Post-millennialism does not necessarily imply political moderation, though. Christian Reconstructionists, who are post-millennial, believe that it is necessary to build a theocratic state in order to prepare for the coming of Christ – this belief leads to political militancy amongst conservative evangelicals.

Fenster argues that the conspiracism of popular eschatology is long established and is a separate tradition to that of anti-Semitic conspiracy theories. This is again not to imply, however, that slippage between the two does not occur. The furore over Robertson's *New World Order*, when his use of 1920s British anti-Semitic texts was pointed out four years after it was first published, is a case in point.[3] Not only does he employ such sources in his elaboration of a grand conspiracy against America and Christianity, he reveals his worldview when discussing the power of Wall Street bankers and the Eastern Seaboard establishment. Robertson asks plaintively, 'But why would the big money interests veer away from the goal of Anglo-Saxon world domination to flirt with radical Marxism?' (1991: 113) Although Robertson is apparently critical of both options, it nevertheless appears that there is a very stark choice facing global élites, from the perspective of theocrats and Dominionists; the purpose of Western capitalism is either to maintain white supremacy or to promote communism. The 'middle way' would be to fall back on Christian morality and the authority of the church to restore the natural order ordained by God. Both other options will lead to enslavement. This is the moral dichotomy that is echoed throughout the Patriot movement one way or another; and it reflects the Manichaean nature of their worldview. The key to understanding the ideological nature of conspiracism is to realize the importance of seeing fascism and socialism as similar aspects of élite manipulation. The long-established ideology of the right places 'middle America' between parasites above and below – unproductive and lazy 'poor people' and greedy élites who control economies. The notion of élites working with the poor at the expense of 'ordinary' citizens reflects an ideology that precludes a genuine understanding of the class nature of power. It is no accident that conspiracism precludes class-based analyses of power and it is this aspect that betrays its ideological functionality.

Within Christian Patriotism, direct references to ethnicity are very rare. Carolyn Gallaher notes that non-racist Patriot politics is 'realized through categories that are constituted for poor and working class whites but seldom reference the race of its adherents (eg, the category of the patriot) ... future research on the role of whiteness in the constitution of patriot identity is certainly desirable in order to provide a richer, more contextual understanding of its role'. However, she adds that this 'would require a deeper reading of the codes of whiteness in the [Patriot] organizations' because of their avoidance of overt mentions of race. (1998: 64–5; 215) Clarkson (1997) makes explicit the links between the theocratic right, committed to restoring government according to God's laws at the expense of democracy, and sections of the racist right. There have been cross-fertilizations between the myriad groups supported by the Unification Church of the Rev. Sung Myung Moon ('the Moonies') and those involved with the World Anti-Communist League, including fascist and Nazi groups. Clarkson also notes the anti-Semitism reflected in the material of Reconstructionists, such as R.J. Rushdoony, and points to clear links with Christian Identity theology, especially in the tendency to regard 'Israel' as the Church (or as America) rather than a place in the Middle East, and to see 'secular humanism' as a rival religion battling it out with Christianity to the death. (1997: 90)

John Birch Society

Ken Stern (1996: 139–141) highlights the role that has been played by the John Birch Society since the 1950s in helping to popularize non-racist nationalism and conspiracism. This well-funded and respectable organization, supported by big business donors from an array of industries across America, consistently portrays the United Nations as the central threat facing 'Christian America'. Its website is widely linked from militia ones and its articles are frequently circulated by Patriot mailing lists run by online activists. The John Birch Society is a key component of the theocratic right, unambiguously and lucidly supporting Christianity as the best framework for governing society, and channelling this into support for nationalism and anti-communism. In order to back up their claims to determine and enforce 'God's law' in America, the theocratic right tends to promote moral dualism. The John Birch Society monthly glossy magazine, *The New American*, asserts unambiguous differentiations between good and bad. They are offended by multiculturalism and 'political correctness', and also by moral relativism. For instance, J.K. Rowling's 'Harry Potter' books are regarded as immoral not only for the apparent acceptance of paganism that they promote, but also for the fact that the central characters are portrayed as problematic and complex, sometimes even switching sides in the conflicts narrated by the plot, making moral judgements less straightforward for the young readers they are aimed at. 'Good and evil are never clear-cut, it seems ... many of the supporting characters are confusingly two-sided' (Bonta, 2000).

Ideologically, moral dualism goes hand-in-hand with Manicheaism and the long tradition of secret society conspiracism – the enemy is motivated by absolute evil and so, therefore, it is the moral duty of every true American to resist the New World Order. This point bears repeating: conspiratorial dualism explicitly states that the motivation of enemies is not ideological – in the sense of having rational strategies and idealistic goals – irrespective of what they claim to represent they only seek to destroy what is good. For instance, when considering the motivations of those who seek to bring about the 'New World Order', Pat Robertson concludes, 'impulses of that sort do not spring from the human heart, or for that matter from God's heart. They spring, instead, from the depth of something that is evil, neither well intentioned nor benevolent'. (Robertson, 1991: 9) Karl Popper's explanation for this viewpoint is illuminating:

> The adoption of the conspiracy theory can hardly be avoided by those who believe that they know how to make heaven on earth. The only explanation for their failure to produce this heaven is the malevolence of the devil who has a vested interest in hell'. (quoted in Pipes, 1997: 178)

Christian Patriotism as a virtual community

The majority of the literature on the militias emphasizes the rural base of the movement, especially the farming heartland of the West and Midwest allied with 'nativist' forces in the South. Fenster describes the militia movement as a 'grassroots far-right movement emanating from the middle of the country'. (1999: 22) Manuel Castells, however, argues that it has grown beyond this base. He comments:

> It would be inaccurate to consider that the appeal of the movement is limited to a rural world phased out by technological modernization ... militia seem to be where people are, all over the country, not just in Montana ... it does not seem that the Patriots are a class-based or

territorially specific movement. Rather, they are, fundamentally, a cultural and political movement, defenders of the traditions of the country against cosmopolitan values, and of self-rule of local people against the imposition of global order'. (1997: 95–6)

The literature on the movement locates clusters of radical right activity, whilst Castells considers militias to be 'everywhere'. This is because Castells' research is heavily weighted towards the impact of new technologies, especially the internet. In the real world there are clusters of activists, but on the internet there are no clusters. Because analysts like Stern overlook the internet, or at least fail to adequately assess its impact as a 'recruiting tool', the parameters of the movement are mistaken.

In the same way that the internet has transformed the racist right across two continents, it is my contention that the internet has done much to promote unity between diverse groupings through the formation of a 'virtual community' of Christian Patriots, benefiting from the unique combination of public and private communication that is made possible by CMC. A major aspect of the construction of this community is based upon a shared mythology of resistance and what unity does exist is based upon the common enemy principle. Patriot movement activists continually refer to the federal government outrages at Ruby Ridge, Idaho (1992) and Waco, Texas (1993), the latter more so because it included scores of innocent black victims, as opposed to the victims at Ruby Ridge who were Identity adherents with ties to Aryan Nations. Martyrdom is an important aspect of communal spiritual unity, and even though the followers of David Koresh at Waco had no connections with Patriot organizations, their deaths are presented in terms of 'they died for us' by activists. The tragedies of Ruby Ridge and Waco exist in the mythology as tropes for state oppression.

The second central component of Patriot movement mythology, after that of state oppression, is the issue of gun control. With the passage of the Brady Handgun Bill (1994) and the ban on 'assault weapons', many perceived these increases in repressive state powers as a precursor to the final stage of the usurpation of constitutional government by elites in Washington, D.C. (Stern, 1996: ch. 10) The formation of armed response units served the dual purpose of preparing for physical confrontation with state forces whilst also demonstrating a literal commitment to the Second Amendment to the Constitution – the right to keep and bear arms. Morris Dees of the SPLC believes that the far right has effectively hijacked the pro-Second Amendment movement. He highlights the roles played by ex-Klan leaders in linking the passage of gun laws to the plan to create the 'New World Order'. (Dees and Corcoran, 1997: 75–67) They urged fellow Patriots to prepare to resist the coming round-up, and the resistance was likened to resisting fascism in Germany in the 1930s. Thus, liberal ('socialist') elites (including the Clintons) are often labelled 'fascists' by Patriots, who see no real difference between fascism and communism – they are both types of totalitarianism based on centralised state power. Only patriotic Americans stand in the way of the completion of this plan, hence the need for gun control. As Randy Trochmann (Militia of Montana) puts it,

> All other forms of government throughout the world must cease to function ... Because the Constitution is a document that safeguards [our] sovereignty it must be destroyed. Because of the genuine threat of the American militia, the American people must be disarmed, and become addicted to the government hand-outs and thus become "sheeple". (in Kaplan, 1995)

Resistance, it should be well noted, is always expressed in terms of the American Constitution, which is regarded as a God-given document that is inherently antithetical towards centralized state power. Thus the Constitution can only be 'restored' by reigning in (or destroying) the federal state, and vice versa.

To the central issues of state oppression and gun control can be added tax protest and 'religious freedom'. These are the entry points into the movement, for they are concerns that most conservative Christians across America would share. No one likes paying taxes, but what the Patriot movement tells Americans is that the IRS is an illegal organization, that income tax is unconstitutional, and that if you declare yourself a 'sovereign citizen' then you don't have to pay it. Income tax is presented as a crucial aspect of the communist plot to create the New World Order and it is highlighted within the Protocols as a central plank in Jewish plans for world domination through manipulation of the banking system. 'Religious freedom' includes the right to prevent abortions taking place, the right to form churches with 'unpopular views', the right to home school (in order to safeguard their children from dumbing down and liberal brainwashing), and, further along the extremist spectrum, the freedom to oppress (or kill) homosexuals. The movement also has a strong libertarian and free market aspect to it, with many militia websites providing links to the Libertarian Party.

Barkun (1996) argues that once individuals are exposed to the 'generic conspiracy theory ... treated as fact not hypothesis', then they are receptive to the full range of what Colin Campbell calls the 'rejected knowledge' of the 'cultic milieu'. This milieu is characterized by the powerful circular logic of conspiracism, as summarized by Barkun:

> The more seriously conspiracies are taken, the less trust can be placed in the centres of authority. If conspiracy is everywhere – embedded in the churches, universities, government, banks, the mass media – then no knowledge promulgated by such institutions can be trusted. Hence, seekers after knowledge must by default go to the cultic milieu, precisely that body of ideas condemned by the centres of authority ... if the conspiracy has co-opted authority, and if authority has rejected certain ideas, then those

rejected ideas must be the really true ones, for if they were not true, then why would the conspiracy have condemned them?' (1994: 249)

It is the internet that now plays a key role in introducing individuals to the cultic milieu and the body of rejected knowledge. As a result of recent developments, Barkun states: 'Beliefs once consigned to the outermost fringes of American political and religious life now seem less isolated and stigmatized than they once did'. This is because militias present themselves as 'representatives of patriotism and constitutional fidelity, open to all races and religions', which makes them attractive to people who wouldn't consider joining Klan-type or neo-Nazi organizations. However, Barkun argues that it is also because of the success that Pat Robertson has had as a 'popularizer, taking ideas widely shared on the radical right and bringing them to a much wider audience'. (Barkun, 1996: 61)[4]

The ideology of conspiracism

David Brion Davis, in his 1971 work on conspiracism, argued that the fear of conspiracy is sometimes reasonable and may serve important socio-psychological functions; that it's easier to handle the concept of hostile conspirators than to face the fact that no one is in control. He believed that there are some genuine conspiracies and hence that countersubversion movements could be ranked on a scale of realism and fantasy. 'Collective beliefs in conspiracy', he felt, 'have usually embodied or given expression to genuine social conflict'. (Davis, 1971: xiv) This raises the question of how we should regard conspiracism generally – on what basis can we make rational assessments of conspiracy theories? The argument that I am presenting in this chapter is that the ideological implications should be the key to such judgements.

Daniel Pipes (1997) appears to be wilfully blind to the ideological implications of conspiracism. For the most part his book is a comprehensive account of the history of the two basic strains of conspiracism: the first involving secret societies (Freemasons, Illuminati, or 'insiders'), the second featuring Jews at the centre of the plot to enslave the world. It is a useful and well-researched scholarly work for the first few chapters. However, it swiftly degenerates into a heavy-handed attempt not only to denigrate class-based analyses of power but also to discommend a whole range of conspiracy theories that implicate the US government in corrupt practices (such as drugs running by the CIA and various political assassinations). Pipes argues that 'American identity builds not on shared ancestry ... but on shared ideals'. (91) Thereafter, he abandons impartiality and open-mindedness in his desire to shore up the ideological consensus of mainstream American politics. He identifies two types of people who believe and promote conspiracy theories: the 'politically disaffected' and the 'culturally suspicious' (9); through these sweeping categories he lumps together the black community and the hard right, perhaps plausibly given that the Nation of Islam embraces anti-Semitism and sells the Protocols through their mail order service, but his account of conspiracism is ultimately highly misleading. To any researcher wishing to assess the validity of conspiracy theories Pipes puts forward a blueprint for a research method that includes 'common sense ... knowledge of history ... ability to recognize the distinct patterns of conspiracism ... [*and*] an understanding of the assumptions that lie behind this way of thinking'. (38) But because of his pluralist agenda his own study lacks these qualities.

He discusses the ideas of conspiracists as well as a range of 'petty' conspiracy theories, but he makes it clear that there exists a hard and fast distinction between conspiracies that are real and those that not: 'conspiracy theory', for Pipes, 'is that fear of a *non-existent* conspiracy ... a perception'. (21) Hence he approves of the German term, *verschworungsmythos* ('myth of conspiracy') 'for it more directly points to the *imaginary* content'. (fn. 3, 207 – emphasis added) This of course begs the question, what authority does Daniel Pipes have for deciding if a conspiracy is 'non-existent' or 'imaginary'? He seems to think he knows 'the truth' when declaring, 'conspiracism leads to a monumental lack of judgement; it is hard to imagine getting the story more wrong', as he sets out to separate reality from fantasy. 'Yet', he disclaims, 'no one can be sure in every case which is which, and I make no claim to certainty'. He quotes Nesta Webster (the British anti-Semite of the 1920s whose work was also cited by Pat Robertson) who claimed, 'a belief in widespread conspiracies is not always to be regarded as a sign of loss of mental balance'; but Pipes clearly believes otherwise. For him, those who believe in conspiracy theories inhabit the 'fringes of society'; their flawed thinking exhibits the 'paranoid style' or 'hidden hand mentality'; conspiracists such as Lenin (especially Lenin, in fact) become 'impervious to rational argument' and are 'filled with loathing and fear'. (23, 22, 26) For Pipes, 'conspiracy theories are a key element of extremism' (29) and he sees extremism of the right or left as much the same thing. Thus, for Pipes, 'political paranoia' is linked with 'personal paranoia ... often the two go together and mutually reinforce each other'. (24).

Pipes' main priority in his book is to discredit the left by associating it with the conspiracism of the right. For instance, in an assertion that lacks both common sense and knowledge of history, he argues, 'As the Nazi-Soviet non-aggression pact established ... extremists often find more in common with each other than with moderates'. (30) Pipes can make such claims because (and this is in no way a distortion of his argument) he believes that the analysis of 'imperialism' put forward by J.A. Hobson (1902) and Lenin (1916), which highlights the structural power of 'monopoly capitalists', is in fact a reworking of secret society conspiracism (ie, that featuring the Freemasons or the Illuminati). (82–83) His motivation for discrediting class-based analysis of power becomes clear when he laments the influence and credibility enjoyed by a variety of contemporary American leftists who put forward class-based analyses of power. For instance, Noam Chomsky's analysis of US foreign policy in Latin America centres on the role played by powerful corporations, 'especially', as Pipes puts it, 'the sinister arms merchants, responsible for duping the public with the cold war fantasy. This barrage of hairbrained ideas springs not form the mind of some ill-educated dreamer but from a leading scholar whose work has transformed the field of linguistics'.

> A right wing conspiratorial antisemite [sic] cranks out crude tracts with tiny circulation; his leftist equivalent, a writer like Gore Vidal, produces best-sellers. The Right distributes home-made videos; the Left has Oliver Stone making Hollywood feature films that win top awards. (160)

Just as he is distressed that contemporary leftists are not banished to the margins of political discourse, he is similarly dismayed that for many 'the Soviet Union appeared less bad than the Third Reich' (164); that Hitler is regarded as more evil than Lenin; and that 'even after its collapse, Lenin's state continues to enjoy much the better reputation'. (105) So he sets about convincing his readers that the Soviet Union 'without a doubt' did more to foster conspiracism around the world, 'both the anti-Semitic and secret society variants', (*ibid*) and that Lenin's theories about 'monopoly capitalism' can be compared to the Protocols as a classic exposition of conspiracism. (131).

Fear and hostility directed against Jews have been around since the first millennium, especially since the Crusades of 1096–99, whilst suspicion of secret societies has existed since the Knights' Templars of 1119. But, as Pipes points out, the notion that Jews or Freemasons had plans for global domination is certainly a more recent invention. Although he chides other historians for erroneously assuming the 'antiquity' of such beliefs, he totally fails to grasp the significance of *when* they became popular and widespread in the West. They only developed into all-encompassing belief systems following the French Revolution of 1789 and they subsequently received a massive boost following the Russian Revolution of 1917. This tells us a great deal about the logic and function of conspiracism. The immediate, élite-sponsored response to the French Revolution was the publication of *Memoirs Illustrating the History of Jacobinism* by Augustin de Barruel, written 1797–8, which linked the Jacobins to the Philosophes (anti-Christian), the Freemasons (anti-monarchy and anti-property) and the Illuminati (the ancient order who control the Freemasons). Pipes regards this book as 'the most influential conspiracist book of all time', noting that as a result of its publication 'belief in plots became part of mainstream political life'. (34) Although Pipes points out that the Memoirs 'met a widely felt need for a unifying explanation of the French Revolution'; he fails to identify whose need this was and what purpose it was designed to serve. It was, I believe, the powerful but precarious and insecure élites of Europe who required a belief system that would negate oppositional ideologies – that is, those based on class-consciousness.

Pipes quotes an early nineteenth century critic of those who argued that the Jacobins were manipulated by the Illuminati: 'To causes extremely complicated have been substituted simple causes, adapted to the capacity of the most indolent and superficial minds'. (Jean-Joseph Mourier, 1801, quoted in Pipes, 71) This 'cause substitution' effort was deemed necessary by the old order of Europe at the time because they were terrified by ideologies that threatened the legitimacy and viability of monarchic and aristocratic rule. The message that is spelt out time and again by conspiracists throughout modern history is not merely that these ideologies are dangerously wrong (this is regarded as self-evident) but also that they are deliberate lies. Thus, Nesta Webster insisted that Marx was not sincere in denouncing capitalism, as she argued in her evocatively titled, *World Revolution: The Plot Against Civilization*. Similarly, in the 1960s the John Birch Society saw the *Communist Manifesto* as an updated and codified version of Weishaupt's (the Illuminati founder's) principles; and it was quite serious in alleging that the Poor People's March on Washington in 1968 was directly linked with the storming of the Bastille in 1789, in that they were 'both planned by the same breed of conspirators'. (quoted in Lipset and Raab, 1970: 253) In 1966 the John Birch Society journal told subscribers that communism is categorically *not* about downtrodden masses rising up against ruling elites who exploit them, 'It is exactly the opposite'. (Quoted in Johnson, 1983: 134).

Almost as soon as secret society conspiracism became popularized it also became conflated with anti-Semitism. From 1806 Barruel was won over by the notion that the revolutionary forces he had identified were actually plotting on behalf of the Jews – 'the most dangerous conspirators'. Pipes concludes, 'de Barruel's associating Jews with Freemasons permanently and firmly linked these two groups together ... and so set the stage for their conflation'. (75–6) Pipes acknowledges that it was only after the Russian Revolution that, 'the two traditions perhaps became more merged than distinct'. (141) But he is blind to the significance of this connection. Through convoluted logic Pipes blames the left for putting 'the fear of conspiracy into an ideological context thereby magnifying it' (83) and later argues that the Holocaust was 'one of the many unanticipated and unintended consequences of the Russian Revolution' (94). Such assertions warrant no further attention, but they are indicative of the mainstream conservative mindset that seeks to discredit the left by associating it with the right, which is also the outlook shared by Christian Patriots. After the Russian Revolution, the Protocols of the Learned Elders of Zion became much more widely available, popularizing the message that leftist forces were really the agents of Jews. Hence, fascists such as William Dudley Pelley, who founded the Silver Shirts in 1930s USA, came to believe that 'Communism is world Jewry in action'. (94) The Protocols revolutionized the forces of reaction. It was a central component in an ideological assault on the notion of 'class', which was to be obliterated in the 1930s by those of race and nation, through the ideology of fascism.

Because of Pipes' anti-leftist agenda he fails to grasp the ideological ramifications of global conspiracy theories. The analytical problems of his work leads to a recognition of the need for an ideological approach to conspiracism. This point again arises when we consider the 'petty' conspiracies that Pipes wishes to dismiss as irrational and unfounded. These include the assassinations of John F. and Robert Kennedy, Martin Luther King, and Malcolm X; also the 'October Surprise' allegations concerning arms-for-hostages deals between Reagan aides and Iranian radicals; tales of CIA drugs-running into America; the notion that American anti-communism was used as a tool to restrict workers' power, etc., etc. Are all of these theories really false? If we choose to believe in a structural class-based analysis of power then does this mean that we must always reject all conspiracy theories? Michael Parenti addresses this question directly when considering the assassination of president Kennedy, which he regards as overwhelming evidence of the workings of a 'gangster state' in the US. (Parenti, 1996: 153–191) He believes that many on the left, including Noam Chomsky and Chip Berlet, refuse to deal in the currency of conspiracism because conspiracy theory is favoured by the right wing as an analysis that opposes structural analyses. Therefore they associate the failure to be aware of class forces or to have an adequate understanding of capitalism with belief in conspiracies. Parenti believes that a false dichotomy is being employed; it is not a straight choice between structuralism and conspiracy theory. Considering the JFK assassination itself, he argues, 'national security state conspiracies are components of our political structure, not deviations from it'. (188) And when we consider the allegations concerning CIA drugs-smuggling into America, the evidence seems overwhelming (see Department of State report 1992; Stich, 1998). These 'petty' conspiracies are significant because they strengthen the moralistic appeal of anti-government-alism and weaken the legitimacy of the state, but they are categorically not the same thing ideologically as global conspiracies and it is a mistake to dismiss them on that basis.

By way of an antidote to Pipes' book I should like to draw attention to a conspiracist book that puts ideology at the centre of its analysis. In *The Stargate Conspiracy* (2000) Picknett and Prince claim on the cover that they are 'Revealing the truth behind extraterrestrial contact, military intelligence and the mysteries of ancient Egypt'. The book at first glance appears little different to others from the vast canon of literature dealing with subject matter so esoteric that in some cases it becomes quasi-religious. The authors don't offer pat answers to the mind-boggling issues that they examine; they take a very sceptical approach to the claims of others and offer instead an exhaustive overview of the historical development of Egypt-related mythology. They note the influence of worldly ideologies in the pronouncements of a variety of psychics, scholars, Egyptologists and scientists since the late nineteenth century. A pattern emerges, they argue, of the involvement of key figures with close ties to the American intelligence community, often funded by maverick right wing millionaires. Those seeking answers to the problems of our destiny on earth outside of conventional religions or science are able to find thrilling solutions in the mystical and occultist teachings of figures such as Aleister Crowley, the psychic Alice Bailey, or even William Dudley Pelley – all of whom claimed to have made contact with 'The Nine' intelligences who rule the universe. When these teachings appear to be manipulated in such a way as to coincide with fundamentalist interpretations of human history, Picknett and Prince warn, we should be very wary. In particular, they highlight the role played by the fascist Pelley, whose 1950 *Star Guests* presents a collection of psychically 'channelled' material from extraterrestrials. According to Pelley, Jesus was a messenger from the rulers of the universe, sent to 'repair' the corruption amongst human life forms on earth. 'In Pelley's teaching', the authors inform us, 'everything is building up to the Second Coming with the advent of the Age of Aquarius'. They also describe the accounts of others in Pelley's élite circle who suggest that most human races are 'essentially part space-god', whilst black races are the earth's only indigenous ones. This is just one aspect of 'the apparently racist undercurrents in some of the teachings of the Nine'. (Picknett and Prince, 2000: 374, 193–6, 374) Just as it is surprising that these higher entities 'chose to make contact with a Fascist', it is also remarkable that calculations concerning the pyramids of ancient Egypt seem to coincide with Christian millenarian prophecies. The occultist/UFO/Egyptologist/quasi-religious vortex of belief systems, which is very much in evidence on the internet – never more than a few clicks away from a neo-Nazi or Christian Identity website – is an area of conspiracism worthy of attention. The *Stargate Conspiracy* heeds us to be aware of the ideological implications. And the same goes for any meaningful analysis of conspiracy theories in the modern world.

Conclusion

According to the right wing ideologues discussed in this chapter, the task of the shadowy élites behind the New World Order is the destruction of the very institutions that are the central components in the process of making life meaningful – the nation and the family. As Bauman points out, it is these supra-individual totalities that offer humans the psychological comfort that we require when we contemplate our own mortality. In pre-modern times the notion of a pre ordained order seemed logical when life was 'an apparently stagnant, repetitive and monotonous existence'. (1999: 34) The volatility of modernity brought all this into question. The meaning of our lives had to be created, whereas previously it was ascribed. For this reason, 'the membership of a durable totality ... was cast as giving sense to otherwise brief and meaningless individual life', (35) and the totalities on offer were primarily 'nation' and 'family'. The nation was cast as being immortal, thus belonging to it addressed 'the absurdity of individual mortality'. Bauman (1998: xxxiii–iv) emphasizes how the 'popular and populist medicine' of nationalism served the Enlightenment project's 'structure of domination in its new, modern form':

> In the course of modern history, nationalism played the role of the hinge fastening together state and society ... Indeed the élite-promoted alliance

between nationhood and statehood had become so close that by the end of the nineteenth century ... [*it was regarded as*] a product of the law of nature ...

The family has the same function as the nation in linking a human life with the past and the future: 'the links in a long chain of kinship/affinity'. Indeed, in modernist ideology the family is analogous to the nation. The uncertainty and lack of structure of postmodernity mean that we put ever more emphasis on the 'existential safety of larger totalities ... [*But*] the once rock-hard totalities now look as unsafe and death-bound as individual lives'. (1999: 39).

The Patriot movement is based upon these cherished institutions, evoking traditional beliefs as a defence against forces that are regarded as direct challenges to God. Much of the energy that is channelled into this religious movement comes from the yearning for the pre-modern times of 'heteronomy' – when the rules we followed were those legislated by God. Christian Patriotism can be seen as a 'cultural community': 'a site of cultural coercion' as Bauman puts it, whose 'preachers and defenders ... almost inevitably develop the mentality of a "besieged fortress" ... For its own spiritual security, cultural communities need many enemies – the more evil and scheming, the better'. (1998: xlii) Arjun Appadurai (1996: 15) coins the term 'culturalism' to refer to the process whereby 'identity politics [is] mobilized at the level of the nation-state'. He is referring to non-Western societies wherein culturalism 'is the conscious mobilization of cultural differences in the service of a larger national or transnational politics'. The contention of this essay is that culturalism is equally at work in contemporary America, being used strategically by élites but it is also self-generating and relatively autonomous of institutionalized power. Bauman (1998) argues that, 'freedom of self-determination is a blessing and a curse'; it can be exhilarating or frightening, depending on the psychology of the individual; and that 'freedom is a social relation': the freedom of others may not be welcome if it is considered threatening' (xii). Therefore, from the outset the notion of 'freedom' was closely allied with 'constraint', and the discourse of 'culture' 'necessarily' contains and reflects this ambivalence. It is because culture serves the dual functions of giving expression to the 'free-roaming spirit' as well as being a 'handmaiden of social order', that it is now 'as much an agent of disorder as it is the tool of order'. (xvi; xx) And it is because of this that postmodern political movements are cultural as much as anything else, and culture is both a tool and site of political struggle, as illustrated in the example of a Georgia militia leader (ex-Ku Klux Klan) who recounted the only occasion on which he thought that he might actually use the gun he took to work with him – he had a dispute with a (presumably black) work colleague over whether 'country and western' or 'rap' music should be played at their place of work. (Private e-mail, 2000).

Bauman believes that the notion of cultural 'systems' has been rendered obsolete by the postmodern condition and in particular by the 'end of geography', brought about by the mass availability of fast travel and the internet. (1998: xxiii) It is only now that we can fully comprehend how ' "distance" is a social product' and what a huge impact the end of geography has had on culture and society. Instead of 'cultural systems', we now have a cultural 'matrix' comprising 'practically uncountable permutations'. Instead of islands of cultural distinctiveness we have 'eddies' in which cultural identities can retain their shape 'only in so far as they go on ingesting and divesting cultural matter seldom of their own making'. (xlv) When speaking of 'communities', ' "inside" and "outside" have lost much of their once so clear meaning' and so the social cohesion that was once built around culture has been replaced by social flexibility. (xxiv) So, '[n]owadays, community is sought as a shelter from the gathering tides of global turbulence'. (2001: 142) The identification of communities that one can feel a sense of belonging with is intimately tied up with the task of identity construction, in respect of which culture is simultaneously 'the factory of identity and its shelter'. (xxix).

Bauman believes that 'freedom', as a social resource, is less equally distributed under postmodernity. It is experienced as 'exhilarating lightness of being for some, rebounding as an unbearable oppressiveness of fate for the rest' (1999: 26). 'The postmodern setting does not so much increase the total volume of individual freedom as redistribute it, in an increasingly polarized fashion'. (2001: 95) The relevance lies in the relationship between personal identity on the one hand and social identity on the other. The first gives meaning to the 'I', the second 'guarantees that meaning, and in addition allows one to speak of the "we", in which the otherwise precarious and insecure "I" may be lodged, rest safely and even wash out its anxieties'. (xxxi) In the quest for social capital the ethnic category can become a comforting refuge, built as it is upon the maintenance of a boundary, which excludes and indeed prevails over 'them' – the strangers, the adversaries, the hostile others – construed simultaneously with the 'we' in the process of self-assertion. ' "We" must be powerful, or the social identity won't be gratifying' (*ibid*). Being a part of the Patriot movement, taking part in the identifying of enemies and strangers, and sharing the language of righteous rebellion effectively delivers social cohesion instead of social flexibility and links the individual to 'supra-individual' totalities, to be enlisted in support of identity construction.

Bauman's analysis is valuable because it leads to an understanding of how the conditions of postmodernity render individuals more open to the appeals of nationalism as a means of bolstering identity constructions. He emphasizes the insecurity that is a result of 'the widening gap between the condition of "individuality *de jure*" and the task of acquiring "individuality *de facto*" '. (2001: 142–3) Inequality now means that those with the least social capital experience strangers as 'slimy' (Bauman borrows the term from Sartre) – their difference is experienced as threatening and challenging to identity boundaries. In contrast, the 'nomadic', cosmopolitan, transnational elites experience the strangers as 'purveyors of pleasures'. (1995: 211) Bauman has numerous analogies for social inequality: 'vagabonds and tourists'; those who experience 'the world as a trap, not an adventure park'. The point is that there is a relativity principle at work: 'the acuity of strangerhood, and the intensity of its resentment, grow up with relative powerlessness and diminish with the growth of relative freedom'. (*ibid.*) Thus we can better understand the distinction that Bauman draws between the 'benign patriotism [*of*] the contented and the secure [*who*] rejoice in a variety of guests and pride themselves on open minds and open doors' and the racist patriotism of 'the insecure and hounded [who] bewail the defilement and humiliation of the race'. (212) This presents opportunities for élites seeking to harness these emotions:

> [T]here is much energy boiling in this chaos; with a degree of skill and cunning it can be gathered and re-deployed to give the unruliness a direction ... They may try to condense the diffuse resentment of the weak into an assault against equally weak strangers, thus kneading it into the foundation of their own power ... while all the time claiming to defend the weak against their oppressors. (1995: 212)

Patrick Buchanan, the Reform Party presidential candidate in 2000, argues that by 2050 the United States 'will cease to be a Western nation, either in the composition of her population or in her culture'. In support of this he cites a demographic study that also suggests that non-white nations' populations will have grown hugely whilst European ones will have stagnated or declined. 'Christendom [meaning Europe as well as America]', he concludes, '... is marching merrily along toward civilizational suicide. God is not mocked'. (Buchanan, 1997) Similarly, William Pierce (2000) advocates the 'ethnic cleansing' of America as a survival strategy for the white race, which he presents as an endangered species, fighting for its survival. By presenting the nation, or the race, as threatened with extinction, subnational élites are able to mobilize support for protectionism and other more symbolic panaceas, such as school prayer or outlawing abortion. More strategically, opposition can be mobilized against perceived threats to sovereignty, represented by the United Nations, in order that America's comparative global advantage can be protected. It is a more long-term consideration that the demands for 'global democracy', wealth equality and environmental protection measures can be resisted; in the short-term tax cuts can be accomplished, to be welcomed by Patriots and conservatives alike.

'Your Country Needs You' is not a new slogan for enlisting the powerless behind nationalism, but for many the type of war now being waged is altogether different. It is being waged against the state, not by it. In this way the Patriot movement is both functional and dysfunctional in that on the one hand it is configured to support a pro-capitalist agenda of low taxation and minimal state intervention, whilst on the other it generates conspiracism that can lead to ideological extremism and violent tendencies. This is not to collapse the ideologies of Manichaeism and fascism together, merely to note the similarities in their respective belief systems. To conflate them, to assume that New World Order is the same as ZOG, undoubtedly pushes fundamentalists away from the mainstream and into the arms of genuine 'extremists'. It is noteworthy that Daniel Pipes, a relatively mainstream conservative, links a class-based analysis of power with the ideology of fascism. This linkage is a theme that is ubiquitous when considering Christian Patriotism on the internet; for whom 'socialists' are 'fascists'. The radical pro-gun group Jews for the Preservation of Firearms Ownership is premised upon the notion that it was only the enactment of gun controls that enabled the Holocaust to take place – it is literally 'the key to GENOCIDE'.

Such references to Nazism and the Holocaust proliferate within Patriot movement propaganda, not just in terms of gun control, but also as a general yardstick for gauging political evil in action. Law enforcement and federal agents are routinely likened to Gestapo officers or dehumanized as 'maggots ... like Hitler's pigs'. Raphael Ezekiel notes how 'White racists pay incessant attention to the Holocaust. Even denying, they must speak of it, perhaps because the appeal of the Nazi example is exactly that the Holocaust did happen, that the force one has joined is exactly a force that could do this and did do this'. (1996: 157) We should be wary of those who compare modern America with the Third Reich and speak of concentration camps, and therefore it is all the more alarming that such sentiments are not restricted to random, marginal individuals. WorldNetDaily, one of the most influential organizations in the Patriot-internet milieu, links the ideas advanced in the 'Socialist academic literature' of unspecified American intellectuals with those of the neo-Nazi Buford Furrow (who went on a murderous rampage across middle America in 1999, targeting Jews and non-whites). The article is entitled, 'Socialist Origins of Neo-Nazism' (Rockwell, 1999). Are we to assume, then, that these crass references to Nazi Germany are ironic double bluffs made by unreconstructed fascists? Although we cannot rule out this possibility in some cases, it is more generally the case that Nazism is referenced as the best example that modern history has to offer of absolute evil in action, along with Stalinism, of course. The comparison between the modern federal state in America and the Third Reich may be an analysis that lacks academic credibility, but it serves the purpose of presenting anti-governmentalism as a matter of good versus evil. Stalinism is equated with communism and socialism, and they are all equated with fascism – the common denominator is the creation of a strong, centralized state. Within this ideology, the state is always and forever a vehicle for evil.

The 'individualization' of society is illustrated by the centrality of the taxation issue for Patriots (many of whom began their journey from conservatism to 'extremism' via 'tax resistance', through which they came into contact with both conspiracist ideas as well as the IRS). This message comes from relatively mainstream conservative bodies such as the Heritage Foundation, for whom it is beneficial to depict redistributive strategies as part of the conspiracy against America, since they contradict free market values. It is a relatively short journey to the more hardline conspiracism of Patriotism that weaves a plot around taxation, the Federal Reserve and 'international bankers'/Jews. The Patriot movement is an incredibly diverse collection of disparate groups. In many ways 'movement' is a misnomer.[5] However, it can be considered a movement only because of the nature of the conspiracism with which all these groups are imbued. They are all opposed to the 'New World Order'; the fact that this can represent significantly different, albeit often overlapping, ideologies is testament to the slippery and functional nature of conspiracism. Secret society conspiracy theories regard powerful élites as motivated by evil, usually in a biblical sense, but without assigning them a racial identification, whilst anti-Semitic conspiracy theories are a vehicle for a racialized worldview. From their inception they have had blurred boundaries between them because, from a practical point of view, the only requirement is that the masses are mobilized against the forces of the left. Whether they do it in the name of race, God, or liberty (or all three) is not as important as the act of targeting enemies, which also serves to bind the 'imagined community' of the nation (Bauman, 1995). From the perspective of the forces of reaction, having a common enemy is far more important than having a common ideology.

The assault on ideology that conspiracism represents can be linked to the hegemonic triumph of the 'neo-liberal consensus', 'with its cult of the winner and its promotion of ethical cynicism' (Bauman, 1999: 127). Ideology has become merely an aspect of an individual world-view; in becoming individualized it has become devalued. Ideology in the era of modernity was 'a declaration of intent on the part of its preachers'. It represented a project to alter the status quo and to create a more ordered world. The 'neo-liberal' project, however, is characterized by 'the progressive separation of power from politics' (120), and it declares an opposite intent, a dis-engagement:

> What makes the neo-liberal world-view sharply different from other ideologies ... is precisely the absence of questioning; its surrender to what is seen as the implacable and irreversible logic of social reality. The difference between neo-liberal discourse and the classic ideologies of modernity is, one might say, the difference between the mentality of plankton and that of swimmers or sailors'. (1999: 127)

Neoliberalism is virtually synonymous with 'globalization', and a good deal of the rhetoric of the far right is directed at the damage that globalization is wreaking on America, to such a degree that for Patriots the word is also synonymous with 'New World Order'.

The Patriot movement is a response to this – offering the restoration of order through a 'phoenix-like societal rebirth, attained through a return to "traditional values" ... [*with the*] goal of creating a new nationalist state'. (Neiwert, 1999: 320–1) It is both the outcome and a continuation of conspiracist anti-communism, which has been used since the New Deal era to discredit the concessions made by the state at that time (eg, welfarism) and to marshal opposition to the enlarged role of the federal government. It also reflects the ideological divisions between subnational élites and what Sklair (1991) calls the 'transnational capitalist class'. They are divided over the fate of the nation-state and the erosion of sovereignty brought about by globalization. Nationalism offers those recoiling from postmodern anxiety the comfort of 'community', framed by subnational élites in such as way as to focus anger on 'strangers' and enemies, in whose interests the government is seen to be working. Thus it is traitors, and not market forces, who emerge as the scapegoats for America's decline.

Another conspiracy theory

Were I to acknowledge my role as the author of my research findings, with a privileged voice based in academia, attempting to convey a higher truth about the conspiracism of the subjects I am studying, then I could choose to play them at their own game ... I'll add to the body of conspiracy theories with one of my own: since the 1950s the American white working class has been conspired against by business élites and state authorities who have, through the efficacy of anti-communism, denied them a class-based analysis of how power operates in the global capitalist system. (Cook, 1962; Hofstadter, 1967: 72, 74, 81; Murphy, 1954.) The populist anti-governmentalism that has arisen since the late 1970s, which the Christian Right has benefited from and helped to promote, was also generated largely by mainstream business élites, not just marginal figures on the far right. (Jenkins and Shumate, 1985; Useem, 1984: 160–171; Edsall, 1984: 107–140; Burris, 1987; Saloma, 1984; Akard, 1992.) This is the real conspiracy, for me. For Patriots, of course, my analysis can be rejected because of my involvement with the Militia Watchdog website and mailing list, which I am here acknowledging publicly. This association discredits me as a part of the conspiracy and a dupe of the system. Within their dualistic worldview, you are either for the New World Order or against it. Only the enemies of America, or their dupes, would question the existence of the plot.

Notes

1 I am using this neologism advisedly since 'conspiratorialism' (the word used by academics such as Michael Barkun) refers to the deeds and actions of conspirators. 'Conspiracism' seems more fitting to refer to the style and substance of the discourses of those holding conspiracy-based worldviews. It has also been used by Mintz (1985: 243) to refer to the manner of use of 'conspiracy theory'.
2 Manichaeism is the view of human history as the site of struggle between the supernatural forces of good and evil. This will culminate in the final showdown, Armageddon, as foretold in Prophecy.
3 See Michael Lind, 'Rev. Robertson's Grand International Conspiracy Theory', *New York Review*, 2nd Feb, 1995, p. 23. For a full review of the exchange between Pat Robertson and his

critics see Gustav Niebuhr, 'Pat Robertson Says He Intended No Anti-Semitism in Book He Wrote Four Years Ago', *New York Times*, 4th March, 1995, A10.

4 It is noteworthy that Robertson's *New World Order* has just one endorsement on the back cover – from the John Birch Society's magazine, *The New American*.

5 'Forming armed paramilitary groups is no more a unifying ideology in the 1990s than having long hair, wearing bell bottoms and experimenting with sex and drugs was a unifying ideology in the 1960s. These are expressions of a culture, not a movement'. (Paul de Armond, of The Public Good watchdog organization, private email, 3rd September, 1998)

References

Abanes, R., (1996), *American Militias: Rebellion, Racism & Religion*. Illinois: InterVarsity Press.

Aho, J., (1990), *The Politics of Righteousness: Idaho Christian Patriotism*. University of Washington Press.

Aho, J., (1994), *This Thing of Darkness: A Sociology of the Enemy*. University of Washington Press.

Akard, P., (1992), 'Corporate Mobilization and Political Power: The Transformation of US Economic Policy in the 1970s', *American Sociological Review*, 57: 597–615.

Anti-Defamation League of B'nai B'rith (1995), *Hate Group Recruitment on the Internet*. New York: ADL.

Anti-Defamation League of B'nai B'rith (1996), *Web of Hate: Extremists Exploit the Internet*. New York: ADL.

Appadurai, A., (1996), *Modernity at Large: Cultural Dimensions of Globalization*. Minneapolis: University of Minnesota Press.

Barkun, M., (1994), *Religion and the Racist Right: The Origins of the Christian Identity Movement*. Chapel Hill, North Carolina: UNC Press.

Barkun, M (1996), 'Religion, Militias and Oklahoma City: The Mind of Conspiratorialists' *Terrorism and Political Violence*, 8/1.

Bauman, Z., (1989), *Modernity and the Holocaust*. Cambridge: Polity Press.

Bauman, Z., (1995), 'The Making and Unmaking of Strangers', *Thesis Eleven*, 43.

Bauman, Z., (1998), *Culture as Praxis*. London: Sage.

Bauman, Z., (1999), *In Search of Politics*. Cambridge: Polity Press.

Bauman, Z., (2001), *Community: Seeking Safety in an Insecure World*. Cambridge: Polity Press.

Berlet, C., (1994), 'Right Woos Left: Populist Party, LaRouchian, and Other Neo-fascist Overtures to Progressives, And Why They Must Be Rejected' *Political Research Associates*, February 22nd. http://www.publiceye.com/ghtist/rwooz6.html

Berlet, C. and Lyons, M., (1995), 'Militia Nation', *The Progressive*, June: 8–10, 22–25.

Bonta, S., (2000), 'Harry Potter's Hocus-Pocus' *The New American*, 16/18, August 28th.

Buchanan, P., (1997), 'The end of Western civilization' *Washington Times*, Nov 30th.

Burris, V., (1987), 'Business Support for the New Right ... the Most Reactionary Corporations' *Socialist Review*, 17: 33–63.

Castells, M., (1997), *The Power of Identity*. Oxford: Blackwell Publishers.

Clarkson, F., (1997), *Eternal Hostility: The Struggle Between Theocracy and Democracy*. Monroe, Maine: Common Courage Press.

Cook, F., (1962), 'The Ultras: Aims, Affiliations and Finances of the Radical Right', *The Nation*, June 30th.

Davis, D., (ed.), (1971), *The Fear of Conspiracy: Images of Un-American Subversion from the Revolution to the Present*. Ithaca and London: Cornell University Press.

de Armond, P., (1995), 'The Anti-democratic Movement: More than Militias', *The Public Good*, June/August.

Dees, M. and Corcoran, J., (1997), *Gathering Storm: America's Militia Threat*. Harper Collins.

Department of State report to Congress, (1992), BCCI Affair (Subcommittee on Terrorism, Narcotics, and International Operations 1991–92 investigation hearings). S382–9.

Doskoch, P., (1995), 'The Mind of the Militias' *Psychology Today*, July/Aug.

Durham, M., (2000), *The Christian Right, the far right and the boundaries of American conservatism*. Manchester University Press.

Edsall, T., (1984), *The New Politics of Inequality*. New York: Norton.

Ezekiel, R., (1995), *The Racist Mind: Portraits of American Neo-Nazis and Klansmen*. New York: Penguin Books.

Fenster, M., (1999), *Conspiracy Theories: Secrecy and Power in American Culture*. Minneapolis: University of Minnesota Press.

Gallaher, C., (1998), *America's New Patriots: Livelihood and the Politics of Identity*. Lexington: University of Kentucky, unpublished PhD thesis.

Hardisty, J., (1995), 'The Resurgent Right: Why Now?' *The Public Eye*, Fall/Winter.

Hofstadter, R., (1967), *The Paranoid Style in American Politics*. New York: Knopf.

Hunsberger, B., (1995), 'Religion and Prejudice: The Role of Religious Fundamentalism, Quest, and Right-Wing Authoritarianism', *Journal of Social Issues*, 51/2.

Jay, M., (1993), 'Postmodern Fascism? Reflections on the Return of the Oppressed' *TIKKUN* 8/6: Nov/Dec.

Jenkins, J. and Shumate, T., (1985), 'Cowboy Capitalists and the Rise of the "New Right": An Analysis of Contributors to Conservative Policy Formation Organisations', *Social Problems*, 33/2.

Jews for the Preservation of Firearms Ownership: http://www.jpfo.org/.

John Birch Society: www.jbs.org/ or www.thenewamerican.com/.

Johnson, G., (1983), *Architects of Fear: Conspiracy Theories and Paranoia in American Politics*. Los Angeles: Jeremy Tarcher.

Johnson, D., (1995), 'The Militia in Me'. *Esquire*, July.

Kaplan, J., (1995), 'Right Wing Violence in North America'. *Terrorism and Political Violence*, 7/1.

Lamy, P., (1996), *Millennium Rage: Survivalists, White Supremacists, and the Doomsday Prophecy*. New York: Plenum Press.

Lipset, S. and Raab, E., (1970), *The Politics of Unreason: Right-wing Extremism in America, 1790–1970*. New York: Harper & Row.

Militia Watchdog: http://www.militia-watchdog.org/.

Mintz, F., (1985), *The Liberty Lobby and the American Right: Race, Conspiracy, and Culture*. Westport, Connecticut: Greenwood Press.

Mitchell, D., (1985), 'Extremism and the Paramilitary Movement', in Stone, R. and Wilbanks, D. (eds), *The Peacemaking Struggle: Militarism and Resistance*. University Press of America.

Murphy, C., (1954), 'McCarthy and the Businessman'. *Fortune* 49, April: 156–158, 180–194.

Neiwert, D., (1999), *In God's Country: The Patriot movement and the Pacific Northwest*. Pullman, Washington: Washington State University.

Neocleous, M., (1997), *Fascism*. Buckingham, England: Open University Press.

Picknett, I. and Prince, C., (2000), *The Stargate Conspiracy*. London: Warner Books.

Pierce, W., (2000), 'Horror in Rhodesia' (American Dissident Voices broadcast, April 22.) Available on National Alliance website. www.natvan.com or www.natall.com

Pipes, D., (1997), *CONSPIRACY: How the Paranoid Style Flourishes and Where it Comes From*. New York: The Free Press.

Ridgeway, J., (1995), *Blood in the Face: The Ku Klux Klan, Aryan Nations, Nazi Skinheads, and the Rise of a New White Culture*. New York: Thunder's Mouth Press.

Robertson, P., (1991), *The New World Order*. Dallas: Word Publishing.

Rogin, M., (1967), *The Intellectuals and McCarthy: The Radical Specter*. Cambridge, Mass.: The MIT Press.

Rogin, M., (1987), *Ronald Reagan: The Movie, and Other Episodes in Political Demonology*. Los Angeles: University of California Press.

Saloma, J., (1984), *Ominous Politics: The New Conservative Labyrinth*. New York: Hill and Wang.

Sklair, L., (1991), *Sociology of the Global System*. Baltimore: Johns Hopkins University Press.

Sklar, H., (1995), *Chaos or Community? Seeking Solutions, Not Scapegoats for Bad Economics*. Boston: South End Press.

Sprinzak, E., (1995), 'Right-Wing Terrorism in a Comparative Perspective: The Case of Split Delegitimization', *Terrorism and Political Violence*, 7/1.

Stern, K., (1996), *A Force Upon the Plain: The American Militia Movement and the Politics of Hate*. New York: Simon and Schuster.

Stich, R., (1998), *Defrauding America: Encyclopedia of Secret Operations by the CIA, DEA, and Other Covert Agencies*. Alamo, California and Reno, Nevada: Diablo Western Press.

The Protocols of the Learned Elders of Zion: http://www.iahushua.com/BeWise/protocol.html

Useem, M., (1984), *The Inner Circle: Large Corporations and the Rise of Business Political Activity in the US and UK*. New York: Oxford University Press.

WorldNetDaily: www.worldnetdaily.com/.

Zuskind, S., (1997), 'Approaching the Radical Other: The Discursive Culture of Cyberhate', in Jones, S.J. (ed.), *Virtual Culture: Identity and Communication in Cybersociety*. London: Sage Publications.

Taking conspiracy seriously: fantastic narratives and Mr Grey the Pan-Afrikanist on Montserrat

Jonathan Skinner

> And it is their entire intent to reduce all of us back to the level where they perceive us in their minds. That is their intent because all we're supposed to be is servants.
>
> (interview with Mr Grey, 1995; Montserrat)

This is a chapter about Mr Grey's anxieties. It is a detailed account and examination of a conspiracy theorist who revels in revealing hidden political agendas, colonial conspiracies. It is about a man who is harassed by the British for proposing an alternative future to theirs, for protesting his present colonial condition under them, and for teaching a blackened history of his island's slave past. In telling his story, in particular a current broadcasting conspiracy he and others are struggling with, this chapter hopes to achieve several things, namely: to present conspiracy theories as fantastic narratives; to exemplify and evaluate conspiracy theorizings as a mode of reasoning; and to call for contemporary conspiracy theory research to be more interdisciplinary.

Fantastic narratives as conspiracy theory

After Kerby (cited in Rapport, 2000: 283), Rapport has written the following about narrative:

> Narrative can be conceived as the telling (in whatever medium, though especially language) of a series of temporal events so that a meaningful sequence is portrayed – the story or plot of the narrative. A narrative account involves a sequence of two or more units of information (concerning happenings, mental states, people, or whatever) such that if the order of the sequence were changed, the meaning of the account would alter. It is this sequentiality which is used to differentiate narrative from

various other forms of conveying and apprehending information about the world.

Roland Barthes (1973) has argued that these narratives are ubiquitous and translatable and may, as Rapport (1991) continues, have a beginning, middle and end within which the individual makes sense of their experiences, connects, frames, orders, recounts and makes meaning of their world, in an ever-emplotting fashion. As 'meta-codes' (White, 1987: 1), narratives are human universals, transcultural message transmitters. 'We may not be able fully to comprehend specific thought patterns of another culture, but we have relatively less difficulty understanding a story coming from another culture, however exotic that culture may appear to us', White suggests. Yet this universality at the narrative level is by no means shared at a narrative content level. Using White's vocabulary, the content is very different from the form. Narratives are used by historians to give their discipline the impression of objectivity and reality when in fact the historiography and the narrativity of historical discourse are less than scientific activities:

> ... this value attached to narrativity in the representation of real events arises out of a desire to have real events display the coherence, integrity, fullness, and closure of an image of life that is and can only be imaginary. The notion that sequences of real events possess the formal attributes of the stories we tell about imaginary events could only have its origin in wishes, day-dreams, reveries. (White, 1987: 24)

It would seem, then, that this narrative mode of representation, so natural to human consciousness, so resplendent in human action and reaction, is intrinsically connected with conspiracy theory when this texting of life takes a fantastic turn (see also Lilley, this volume).

It is in the world of conspiracy – where secret plans are suspected of hidden groups allying themselves to influence events by partly covert action (Pigden, 1995) – that what I would refer to as *fantastic narratives* appear. They are fantastic, not because they entirely belong to the realms of human fantasy, but because they are narratives composed from remote fragments, diverse nodes correlated and fitted together in unusual fashion. Like hyper-links stretching out on the World Wide Web, conspiracy narratives are hyper-narratives, weird and wonderfully interconnected spiders' web plots; Weberian meanings and theories of causation sharing affinities and extraordinary premises with the magic and divination logic of the Azande (cf Evans-Pritchard, 1987) and the Mambila (cf Zeitlyn, 1990). As such, these fantastic conspiracy narratives blur Jerome Bruner's (1990) distinction between a scientific mode of thought which involves representation of the world through propositional knowledge – *paradigmatic knowing*, and a story-telling mode of world-making – the perhaps more transparent portal into the telling person, one of *narrative knowing* (cf McLeod, 1997: 28–30, Goodman, 1978).

Conspiracy narratives, these fantastic traveller's tales through the mind, give us 'glimpses of the unmentionable' (Leach, 1984), insight as to how the mind works, thinks, processes the external, how a person narrates. 'There has recently been a good deal of interest in the assassination of President John Kennedy. Do you think it likely that President Kennedy was killed by an organized conspiracy, or do you think it more likely that he was killed by a lone gunman?', posed Ted Goertzel (1994: 732–3) in a random telephone survey in New Jersey, USA. 69% of the respondents thought it likely that Kennedy had been killed by a conspiracy. Goertzel also discovered the following: 15% of the respondents thought that 'the AIDS virus was created deliberately in a government laboratory'; 41% thought that 'the Air Force is hiding evidence that the United States has been visited by flying saucers'; 42% replied that the FBI was probably involved in the assassination of Martin Luther King; and 21% supposed that 'the American government deliberately put drugs into the inner city communities'. Aware of the relative prevalence of conspiracy theories in our postmodern age (where AIDS is perceived to be deliberate genocide from above, akin to the Tuskegee syphilis experiments conducted upon an unknowing black Alabama population 1932–1972), Goertzel sought to deconstruct his survey to identify psychological and sociological correlates of belief in conspiracies. Goertzel's (1994: 731) conclusions link belief in conspiracies with anomia, a lack of interpersonal trust and employment insecurity. Significantly, he also suggests that young people are more likely to believe in conspiracies than old, and blacks and hispanics more so than whites. Belief in conspiracy theories is linked, then, with people of minority status, people alienated, people marginalized, oppressed and impotent against the system.

Paranoia or persecution in popular conspiracy

Conspiracy theorizing may also be closely linked with paranoia, with 'self-referential delusions' (Harper, 1994: 95), yet conspiracy theories cannot be dismissed as just the ramblings of the crazed and jaded. The narrative of the paranoid can be more than the mental health syndrome carried by those who 'feel persecuted' as they have been characterized by British psychiatrists such as Aubrey Lewis (1970) in the past. For Freud (1976), paranoia was a pathology of defence, a way of fending off ideas incompatible with one's ego, conspiracy theory as projection, conspiracy theory as 'persecution mania' identified alongside expressions of megalomania. Perhaps paranoia has become a classic symptom of our world of internet inter-connectivity, the 'network society' (Castells, 2000) in which we now live and conspire. 'Paranoia with reason' is certainly how the anthropologist George Marcus (1999) describes the nature of conspiracy, a narrative of explanation where we desperately seek knowledge but do so 'in the absence of compass' (1999: 5). In describing it thus, as trajectory-less quest, Marcus indirectly acknowledges the delicate dividing line walked by so many conspiracy theorists: conspiracy with reason on the one side of the fence, and conspiracy without reason on the other ('a strategy of delegitimation' [Fenster, 1999: xii] common to political discourse).

Recognizing this flimsy mobile fence, but concerning ourselves with the semi-incredulous nature – and fantastic narratives – of conspiracy amongst the sane, we must also consider the political nature of conspiracy theories. Populist conspiracy theory is, for Fenster (1999: xiii, author's emphasis), 'the manifestation of a political life lived *in significence*'. This is perhaps a veiled reference to the post-structural and postmodern untying of the signifying chain with free-floating signifiers (*à la* Derrida) which results in a world of uncertain and arbitrary – if schizophrenic (after Jameson, 1984) – meaning-making. Is Marlboro affiliated with the Klu Klux Klan because of the K shapes on their cigarette packets; is the 'Masonic' eye in the centre of the American dollar a device for tracking currency; did the Animal Liberation Front introduce foot and mouth disease to British farms to further their revolutionary goals? Richard Hofstadter's (1966 [1952]) classic conspiracy essay, 'The Paranoid Style in American Politics', shows us that this 'paranoid social thought', this paranoid mentality, is one of marshalling facts to build coherent theses, quite often more coherent than those in the 'real' world of mistake, failure and ambiguity (36). Conspiracy theory has become a mode of cognition for those outside the pluralistic consensus, as conspiracy theory theorists convert singular events [*sic*] into larger frameworks, sometimes deliberately misreading or misinterpreting evidence and thereby rocking the boat of consensus history.

Mr Grey and 'the conspiracy theory of society' on Montserrat

The desire for the 'ur-text'; the 'texting of everyday life where everything is connected and the connections are uncanny' (Stewart, 1999: 17); the second-hand scavenging for bytes of knowledge for refashioning and emplotting: are all prevalent throughout contemporary media and political discourse – Cold War conspiracy babies grown up. Mr Grey is just one of these conspiracy theory theorists, whether he is right or wrong (and if there are – or could be – criteria for evaluation). Before presenting his conspiracies, however I would like to note the philosopher of science Sir Karl Popper's (1966: 94) inaccurate definition of the 'conspiracy theory of society':

> It is the view that an explanation of a social phenomenon consists in the discovery of the men or groups who are interested in the occurrence of this phenomenon (sometimes it is a hidden interest which has first to be revealed) and who have planned and conspired to bring it about.

Contra Popper, I would like to suggest that for there to be a conspiracy theory, there does not need to be an explanation of an event based upon the *discovery* of a group of interested plotters. Conspiracies can be perpetuated entirely in the ethereal; it is often precisely their intangibility, their unprovability, which contributes to their persuasiveness and longevity. The actual unmasking of the conspirators does not necessarily make the conspiracy. This is shown in the following profile and discussion of Mr Grey and his faceless foes with their *hidden agendas*.

Mr Grey is a controversial public figure on the small island of Montserrat in the Eastern Caribbean. Prior to a volcanic eruption in 1995, Mr Grey's island was a relatively quiet and intimate British Dependent Territory with a population of 10,000. Governed by His Excellency The Governor, a British Foreign and Commonwealth career diplomat, Montserrat was where the rich and famous idled away their retirement and winter vacations, or recorded albums in luxurious anonymity and solitude. A crown colony since her settlement in the seventeenth century, Montserrat rarely diverged from the traditional Caribbean plantation society pattern. Her historical chronology, documented by the resident historian on the island and adult education instructor Howard Fergus (1994), is one of British settlement – slave importation; 'sugar, cotton and lime' plantation exploitation and reactionary insurrection (St Patrick's Day is commemorated on Montserrat following Fergus's recent historical discovery of a failed 'slave conspiracy' [1994: 87] on 17th March 1768) slave emancipation in 1838; adult suffrage as a result of union protest as late as 1951; full secondary, technical and adult education by the late 1970s. But in over 300 years of British rule, there has never been a vote for independence such as that achieved by Montserrat's neighbours Antigua and Barbuda, St Kitts, Jamaica and Trinidad. The closest the island got to ending colonialism was the possibility of Statehood in Association with Britain in 1967 which was rejected by Chief Minister W.H. Bramble who felt that Britain's budgetary contribution was indispensable to Montserrat's financial survival.

'[W]edded to colonialism' (Mathurin, 1971: 147), 'the last English colony?' (Fergus, 1978), Montserrat is a place of curious developments, of black consciousness-raising and a rediscovery of folk traditions and tales in the 1970s, matched by an expansion of the Governor's powers in the 1980s with a new constitution (1989 Constitution Order) imposed from Britain giving him control of all financial matters on the island and the ability to introduce legislation even if it is not passed by the local-elected Legislative Council – this is on top of his normal responsibility for defence, external affairs, internal security and public service. Though these actions were taken in the context of the 1989 hurricane Hugo natural disaster and several instances of serious offshore banking financial irregularities, such acts and executive control over the island and the islanders – British Dependent Territory Citizens (BDTCs) without the right to abode in the motherland – are a cause for concern for those following Britain's political and strategic offshore activities, such as her UN commitment to decolonization of all territories by the year 2000. Mr Grey is one such follower, keenly aware of Britain's commitment and how Britain's stance has not facilitated any such transition but has instead deterred BDTCs from independence initiatives with her official line that a two-thirds majority vote for independence must come in a local referendum. Articulating his political outlook during an in-depth interview (approximately four hours long) after a large number of meetings during the course of my research year on Montserrat, Mr Grey pointed out to me that the islanders have not been prepared for such an event, there being no infrastructure in place to facilitate such a social and economic transition. His eloquence and convictions are self-evident:

> We are still a colony. And we're still being run and controlled as a colony, even more so now because it is more important for the British to maintain and hold onto the rest of its remaining colonies.

Why is that?

Because of what is going to happen in 1997. Because Hong Kong is going to go back to China in 1997 and Hong Kong is the most important colony for Britain right now. In its financial, in its financial offshore industry, Hong Kong plays a key hub. In that industry for Britain, Hong Kong plays a key hub period in the British financial empire, in the shifting of monies out to the Eastern hemisphere into Britain. When that, when that infrastructure is going to be impinged upon by Chinese, by Chinese legal laws, they cannot operate in the same manner as they used to operate when they only had to deal with a Governor. The entire, the entire financial structure of Hong Kong can only function under an atmosphere where a Governor is the sole head and control of the colony. So the whole entire financial infrastructure of Hong Kong has to be shifted and the only place it can be shifted is to places where there are remaining colonies and for this reason, and for no other reason, for the most overriding reason, Britain cannot afford to release any more of its colonies no matter what the Governor says, no matter what Britain pushes out diplomatically, Britain has all intentions of holding onto those remaining colonies because it is integral to its financial empire that it maintains them.

Taped back in 1995, Mr Grey's rhetorics and connections have, from the perspective of 2001, an uneasy fortune-telling quality about them: Montserrat is still a crown colony not undergoing any external decolonisation process; Hong Kong has been returned to the Chinese; and the British Foreign *Secret*ary is developing a White Paper on the status, identity and usefulness of Britain's remaining empire of small dependent territories (expected to change status to become 'overseas territories'). Mr Grey's suspicions and 'hidden agenda' suggestions would appear to be borne out. He demonstrates an acute and intense consciousness of the world and his place in it. In this acute – if not accurate – representation of the world, Montserrat and Mr Grey himself are components within an interactive system. This comes across as a lay expression of globalization as theorized by the likes of Appadurai (1990), Wallerstein (1990) and Holton (1998). Indeed, the world as flow of people, goods, meanings (Hannerz, 1990) and hidden agendas is a world of extremes for Barber (1992), one of either/ors: either globalism or tribalism; either homogeneity or heterogeneity; either MacWorld or Jihad. This fits with Mr Grey's understanding and representation of the world.

The colonization of the world, and the subsequent Coca-colonization of the world, is what Mr Grey has been fighting against, both mentally and physically, for most of his life whether as a Vietnam veteran, General Secretary of the Montserrat Seamen and Waterfront Workers' Union (MSWWU), local street politician, radio and classroom historian, radio presenter, night-class instructor, and Pan-Afrikanist and publisher of *The Pan-Afrikan Liberator*. The clandestine conspiracy is what Mr Grey considers himself to be pitched against, on an island where conspiracy is around every corner. The Governor and the local government, for example, illegally dismissed Mr Grey's trade union in an attempt to reduce labour handling costs at the capital's port, thereafter waging a propaganda war in the local media. That same media – local newspapers and government-run local radio – have banned Mr Grey's submissions, cancelling a very popular 'Conscious Connection' radio programme which was designed by Mr Grey to open people's minds to the interaction of local and global events around them. Equally, Mr Grey is no longer able to teach his occasional and sometimes voluntary history classes in the local schools because of his controversial politics. He is left to his own devices such as home tuition for the semi-literate, street politics around Plymouth (the capital), and the dissemination of his monthly newsletter.

'Collaborating with the enemy' runs the headline of one of Mr Grey's editions of *The Pan-Afrikan Liberator* (the unorthodox 'k' in 'Afrika' is 'reverse psychology', a 'tool for self-empowerment' to end the prevailing colonial realities; this is matched with a lower case 'b' when referring to 'britain' to foster a sense of equality between the oppressed reader and the oppressive colonists). The piece continues with an explicit rebuttal against Montserrat's Chief Minister:

In a speech given at the opening of the wharf for the police launch at Old Road Bay, Montserrat's chief minister said that there are some individuals and intellectuals in the community who are saying that the british have a secret agenda for Montserrat. He went on to say, 'I don't know why they have to be so negative, I wish that they would be more objective and write about the positive things that are happening'.

THE BRITISH AGENDA
The british do have an agenda for Montserrat. The political, social and economic implications of that agenda will carry the majority of the people in this country back into the MASSA days of our great grand parents.

(1994: 1, original emphasis)

In this quotation, Mr Grey is referring to the iniquities of the slavery plantation system and subsequent plantocracy of landowners which the unions fought to break up. These *Liberator* editions are published in runs of approximately 350. 200 are mailed out to subscribers, 100 are sold on the streets, and 50 are given to schoolchildren and libraries. The newsletter has been running for several years and often has contributions from like-minded island figures. Its intentions are clearly set out at the top of each edition's front page where on one side of the title is a picture of Montserrat and on the other is a picture of Africa. Below these are the following banners:

Agitate until we create a stable society that benefits all our people
Instigate the nation until we remedy the injustices of society
Motivate our people to set a meaningful path for the coming generations
Educate our people to free our minds and develop an Afrikan consciousness

The Official Publication of the **CARIBBEAN PAN-AFRIKAN MOVEMENT**
THE VOICE FOR AN INDEPENDENT MONTSERRAT

Mr Grey both speaks for Montserrat and argues for Montserrat. He promulgates his position, and fits in all developments and pieces of information into this worldview. His *life-world* is one of face-to-face relationships and impersonal – *they-relation* (Schutz, 1967) – relationships with a wary eye narrowed upon the latter. This is the conspiracy theorist as holder of a monolithic worldview as opposed to the variety and diversity of worldviews cognitively lived in the individuals in Rapport's (1993) study of life in an English village. There the 'loops of thought' worldviews were more varied and multiple – held simultaneously, but still 'self-enclosed and complete ... like a whole world of ideas around which its owner might cognitively travel' (Rapport, 1993: 80).

Discussing the possibility of corporate inventions such as the car that runs on water, the light bulb that last forever and no-snag panty hose, Stephen Demeo (1996: 211) introduces the reader to the idea of 'suppression narratives'. These are conspiracy stories of blocked technology because such developments are not in the interests of the organization employing the inventor. These narratives raise our conspiracy consciousness – that there are people and organizations out there who are in control; that 'we' are being ripped off and persecuted by 'them'. Conspiracy is thus more than just popular explanation in this light. Conspiracy is not simply the reduction of cognitive complexity and anxiety. Conspiracy is the antithesis of agency, as Keener (1997) concludes at the end of his biographical narrative analysis of President Kennedy's alleged assassin, Lee Harvey Oswald.

Paranoid within reason, persecuted without justice, Mr Grey's narrative during our interview certainly contained comments about Montserratian and British suppression, as though a calculated muting and editing of his voice was taking place against his choice. It had taken many months of casual interaction and ethnographic naivety to gain Mr Grey's confidence, to prove to him that I was too ignorant to be another spy for the British. And as a white man in a black world, I was lucky to get eye contact with Mr Grey whilst out on the streets of Plymouth. At his home, however, the story was very different, and I was able to see and feel the oppression and resistance which he always talked about. Some of this comes out of the interview, material complemented by the frightening rumours about town about Mr Grey's employer wearing a side-arm to work expressly to intimidate the union workforce, and how the Royal Montserratian Police Force persistently hassled him:

> A'right, those of us who are willing to stand up and suffer the brunt – brunt of the society, ok, to suffer the brunt of the system are used as prime examples of why you should not be against the system.

Uhuh

> We are not used as role models who have meaningful ideas for the benefit of the nation. We are used as people who are crazy, who are people you should not be like, and we're going to show you what we do with these people because we gonna magnify them in front of you and then we're gonna destroy them. What they do with us is turn us – from full walking prime people in our dignity, into shells of ourselves. What they would like to see a person like me become in this country is a person who would become a beggar.

Uhuh

> Understand, a person like me who has had the will and the audacity to stand up to them now that they have removed all my ability to live on the levels that I'm accustomed to live. They would assume at some point in time that they would break my spirit and, further on to that, they gonna drive me to drinking and drugs and, further on to that, they gonna destroy my entire ability to function in this society till I become an abject beggar; till I then become an object in the eyes of the people instead of a hero in the eyes of the people.

Uhuh

> And they have done this to us constantly from the days of slavery. In slavery days they just did it plain and simple: they just ripped you apart and quartered you, and lined up everybody to watch.

Right

> Or they beat you to death. Or they burned you to death. Or they hung you. Or they cut you up. They destroyed you physically in front of the people as a prime example of what you should not do in order to resist.

So in fact now it's more psychological?

Again yes. Right. Now it's, it's a psychological subtle type of approach but it has the same effect. Ok.

So

And it instils fear in the people.

For example, um, they cut off your means of support?

They've also suppressed my mail. They, they, they are attempting now to isolate me, Montserrat now already isolated as it is.

Uhuh

They are attempting further now to further heighten that isolation and put me in a psychological state of total isolation where I have no internal communications and I have no external communications. I have no financial base. I have five children to support and a wife. At some point in time I must become more concerned about how I am going to take care of my children than how I am going to show these people how you move a nation forward. Ok. My priorities must change once my ability to survive changes. And they are aware of this. They have used this – they have it down pat – they have used it time and time again.

Note the numbers of references to 'the system', 'they', 'them', the unknown and faceless antagonists frustrating and isolating Mr Grey. Mr Grey is referring to the British government and the British empire, looking upon them just as a mountain man in the western states of the US might view the FBI and the federal government (see James, this volume). Aware that he might appear to some to be crazed or deluded, conspiracy theorist Mr Grey offsets such potential and actual delegitimization by making it a deliberate part of 'their' persecution:

They have drawn a conclusion based on how they view us and they simply believe that our, I'm just a wild sheep, a lost wild cannon shooting shots that they can just suppress. But it's bigger than that – the same way that their empire is bigger than England: our empire is bigger than Montserrat.

Mr Grey is a Pan-Afrikanist because he wants to promote and develop an Afrikan consciousness – an awareness of colonial realities past and present, an independence of thought and action, and a close and productive affiliation with the continent of Afrika for Montserrat and all Montserratians. Pan-Afrikanism is more prevalent on other Caribbean islands than on Montserrat. Their ideology is underscored by the identification of oppressive divisions between themselves and 'the others': between Afrikans and Europeans. Pan-

Afrikanists believe that they are some of the subjects of a global conspiracy of racism continuing from the days of slavery, and that this racism is the natural predisposition of the European mind. Now, according to Mr Grey, the conspiracy against the Afrikan takes a more insidious line:

> Racism ... was invented by the European mind. It is a political tool, now, that the European capitalist system uses to keep us separated, to keep us divided, and to keep a small minority of them at the top of a class system that they have imposed upon the system of racism.

This hidden conspiracy of colour permeates the whole of Montserrat such that it has been internalized by the majority of Montserratians, many of whom cannot entertain the thought of a Montserrat independent of Britain; nor would they like to associate themselves with the dark continent, uncivilized and barbarian as they have been brought up to perceive it to be (conversely, many Africans no longer feel an affinity with the 'racially diluted' West Indians of the Caribbean). These Montserratians have been indoctrinated into the Western mythologies of Greek and Roman cradles of civilization when, according to Mr Grey, the Afrikan mind of the Afrikan people is superior in terms of creative inventiveness, and '[a]ll civilizations that are extant today got their foundations out of the continent of Afrika ... all creativity, all science, all medicine ... '. Further to this, as a victim of racism himself – sometimes from 'both sides' due to his light brown skin colour, the result of his parents' mixed race marriage – Mr Grey is now 'reintegrating [his] gene pool' into the original gene pool down his maternal side, towards the 'gene pool of the people who accepted [him] as a human being', consciously reversing what he considers to be his mother's mistaken belief that 'power lied in this [white] direction'.

Montserrat – centre of a global broadcasting conspiracy

One particular conspiracy discussed by Mr Grey during our interview, and one which I heard about repeatedly during my research with other Montserratians, was about the transmission broadcasts beamed out of Montserrat and their part in influencing international politics. Montserrat is a small volcanic island, only thirty nine square miles in size but in excess of 2–3,000 feet at its high points. Mount Chance, the summit of the principal mountain range, is a mystical place: it is approached through bamboo forests, shrouded in rain clouds which water the island, with a pond at the top rumoured to support a mermaid. Most notably, the summit is owned by Cable and Wireless (an offshoot of the former British government's telecommunications corporation, British Telecom) who maintain a radio transmitter at the top. Hardly the Caribbean equivalent to America's Area 51, Mount Chance is open to any public who wish to climb through jungle undergrowth in tropical temperatures.

Rumours and stories do, however, abound about this peak, and the interest of radio and telecommunication businesses in Montserrat.

Whilst I was on Montserrat, a topical issue with the local press and populace of Montserrat was the destruction of the local trade union branch of Cable and Wireless (C&W). The organization has a large Caribbean presence and was the recent target of Mr Grey's *Pan-Afrikan Liberator* for playing their part in breaking union labour on the island, thereby facilitating the island's slow change into a post-Hong Kong financial and telecommunications colonial centre – entrepreneurialism at the expense of the indigenous. The multinational refused to give the workers a 2% pay rise, a *total* amount far less than Chairman Lord Young's £798,000 bonus, and even less than the combined salary of the entire Caribbean C&W labour force. Furthermore, so Mr Grey notes, C&W have their headquarters in Hong Kong, presumably to avoid British tax levels. This interesting detail was followed up with his conspiratorial comment that though once 'a branch of British Telecom and British government foreign policy', their associations, connections and influence must continue in the same corridors. For Mr Grey, then, C&W belongs to 'them' that he was talking about above, and 'their' activities are part of the global governmental and multinational movements and machinations at work in our post-productive world. He is thus highly suspicious when they begin to lay fibre-optic cables from Montserrat. For Mr Grey, this is confirmation that something clandestine is taking place:

> So they, they are a humungous, multinational corporation at the leading edge of technology that continues to get better and better every day, and continues to get more lucrative for them. They are *just* putting a fibre-optic line here which is connecting the whole world when you can carry the entire population of Montserrat on one single strand of that fibre-optic line ... So you can imagine the huge amounts of communication and as you said again, we are a key link in the world. That is a national secret. That is an international secret. That is a secret that nobody in the world knows other than the British government and the few of us that have cared to investigate it.

C&W actions thus become confirmation of Mr Grey's conspiracy theory worldview. The pieces of information which come to him are like jig-saw pieces which *always* fit together. I would even go so far as to suggest that they conveniently come together to confirm Mr Grey's suspicions rather like the cognitive pathways taken by those devoted to a particular religious belief system.

Conspiracy beliefs force one to apprehend the world differently; curiosity merges into suspicion if not paranoia. Secret knowledge becomes the currency as conspiracy theory purveyors narrate a struggle which we are all embroiled in but cannot all see. There is an evangelical religious streak, then, associated with the passing and communication of conspiracy theories as everything feeds into the conspiracy theory ecumene. The way in which conspiracy beliefs are held onto are, perhaps, also similar to the convictions of the Marxist zealot seeking to raise the consciousness of the proletariat, to open their eyes to the reality of their oppression – colonial in this case. Continuing this communications conspiracy, Mr Grey notes that Montserrat holds a very strategic place in the globe, a place of critical interest for the British:

The communication link that Montserrat has ties it to the entire globe. There's only two places in the world that occupy that. One place is a mountain in Peru which is also on the same ehm, longitude and latitude and alignment as Montserrat and other places as Montserrat. From those two places in the world you can touch through the link communication anywhere in the world. It is a huge, humungous national secret, ok.

Mr Grey is referring to the use of short wave radio signals which, transmitted from Montserrat, can ostensibly be received throughout the world. This national/British secret provides Mr Grey with some context with which to comprehend the British governorship of Montserrat, aspects of British foreign policy, as well as the curious history of Radio Antilles on Montserrat. Furthermore, this all places Mr Grey's Montserrat at the centre of the world:

Radio Antilles was the reason for um, bringing down the Berlin wall, for breaking up Eastern Europe, ok. Radio Antilles was a subsidiary of Deutsche Welle.

Uhuh

And Deutsche Welle subsidized Radio Antilles for 25 years and Radio Antilles broadcast 24 hours a day on a short-wave station for 25 years in 6 different languages non-stop. Ok.

Uhuh

The day the Berlin wall came down, Radio Deutsche Welle cut off its subsidy to Radio Antilles. Radio Antilles ceased to operate the same point in time and day that the Berlin wall came down. So the whole objective for Deutsche Welle and Radio Antilles and the German government was to propagandize Eastern Europe, to destroy the communist empire – the Russian empire, and to reunite Germany. Major, their major priority was the reunification of Germany. Everything else was secondary, but they got all of it in one bag anyway because a few years after the reunified Germany, the Russian empire fell apart. And the main reason for the Russian empire falling apart was the huge amounts of propaganda that they were able to pump into Eastern Europe, attempting to convince the Eastern European population that all they had to do was to turn over their governments from a communist government to a capitalist government and the western hemisphere would funnel all the money in the world into their industries to help them to, um, become western capitalist, um, free-enterprise systems.

The thought behind conspiracy

Though no longer on Montserrat, I am still able to keep up with island events and gossip through the internet. Daily there are messages exploring and commenting upon the British handling of the volcano crisis on the island, and their colonial development policies and practices. Recently there was a message about a party of ham radio enthusiasts visiting Montserrat to set up radio links around the world, impressed by the extraordinary reception and transmission qualities on the island. In other words, the above extracts from my interview with Mr Grey are another example of a conspiracy – fantastic and incredible at first, but increasingly fashionable and credible over time. 'Their' global machinations – whether British government, multinational, or other white supremacists – are all fitted into Mr Grey's conspiracy theory of society (Popper), paranoia (Freud, Marcus), suppression narratives (Demeo). COINTELPRO was an FBI programme, run in the 1950s and 1960s to harass communists and other alleged subversives in the United States, which went so far as to use devious techniques to sow suspicions between marital partners, so why couldn't Mr Grey be the recipient of an equivalent British campaign?

Taking conspiracy seriously means that we can look first at Mr Grey's lived reality, his worldviews and the context for their formation as evinced above. We can also look, second, as we have done at the start of this chapter and in subsequent comments, at the nature of belief in conspiracy theories, as to who and how many are susceptible and for how long. Here, conspiracy theories can be linked to religious beliefs in that conspiracies are difficult to prove or disprove, relying upon conviction and worldview with evidence to support the beliefs, though evidence cannot be gleaned to refute the beliefs (ie, failure to prove a conspiracy does little to disprove a conspiracy). In her light-hearted introduction to conspiracy, Tuckett (1998: 11) makes some more profound points than she realizes when she wrote the following:

> Belief in conspiracy theories is more than just the belief in an occasional conspiracy. It is a belief system that asserts that world events are being governed in secret by a group of ultra-powerful puppeteers behind the scenes. While little may be able to be done about this sorry state of affairs, at least we can have the satisfaction of having worked out what is going on.

From this quotation, we might assert that subscribing to a conspiracy, taking on board a fantastic narrative, is like converting to a new faith, adopting a belief system. It is more than a way of making the complex world simple: conspiracy theories do more than – as Hollander (1999: 88) nicely delimits them – 'simplify the world and the chains of causation, while providing emotionally satisfactory identifications and explanations'. Taking conspiracy seriously is about taking on board distinctive and self-enclosed explanatory resources and devices. In doing this, critics argue that history becomes travesty as complex events are reduced to superstitious plots. With this, the historicities of events are turned into 'hystories' (Showalter, 1997), epidemics of the imagination – Mr Grey's broadcasting conspiracy on a par with alien abductions and satanic ritual abuse (cf La Fontaine, 1998). Yet Mr Grey's hermeneutics of conspiracy highlight connections between events which do in fact bear out the test of time. Whilst on Montserrat, when I did chance upon the Governor at a social gathering, out of the blue came this unsolicited comment – 'now we've got him and he won't be able to publish his silly little magazine'.

Evidently Mr Grey is not a consensus historian like Dr Fergus who holds the position of Deputy Governor on the island as well as Speaker in the local government and has published a mainstream history of Montserrat. Because of his less than orthodox historical representations, Mr Grey is more of a Marcus Garvey revolutionary figure than the academic-like Du Bois. Mr Grey publicizes conspiracies in his newsletter and in his street-speeches, using whatever medium available to mobilize resistance on the island. Passages in *The Liberator* have even been written expressly for consumption by the Foreign and Commonwealth Office in Great Britain. This alienation and dissatisfaction with 'the system', and his attempts to identify and change it, are held alongside a conviction, a belief system, which is flexible and adaptable to the synthesis and absorption of new information, but rigid and indomitable to the possibility of reversion to mainstream consensus opinion. Writing specifically about the logic in witchcraft and its persistence in modern Africa in the social anthropological debates between the 1950s and 1970s, Max Gluckman (*Custom and Conflict in Africa*, 1966 [1956]) and E.E. Evans-Pritchard (*Witchcraft, Oracles, and Magic among the Azande*, 1987 [1976]) made some general points about the nature of belief systems which are directly relevant to our examination of conspiratorial thought and the thoughts of Mr Grey. 'The difficulty of destroying beliefs in witchcraft is that they form a system which can absorb and explain many failures and apparently contradictory evidence' (Gluckman, 1966. 102). By this, Gluckman means that the result of a Zulu warrior being killed by a colonizer's bullet when their magic charms and chants were reputed to have made them invulnerable to harm does not necessitate the collapse or failure of the belief system; neither does a house being struck by lightning after the rain-magicians' treatment of villages against lightning necessarily result in the loss of confidence in the rain-magicians' abilities. Instead, the believers present a 'secondary elaboration' (Evans-Pritchard, 1976: 150) of the belief system to excuse the failure; reasoning circuitously to explain away events; integrating all into the resolute worldview (see Parker, this volume).

'Direct assault on a closed system of ideas is not easy, since the system absorbs the attacks and converts them to strengthen itself', Gluckman (1966: 105) continues, bringing home these fundamental principles derived from exotic examples. In effect, systems of thought have a circular nature of reasoning about them. It would appear that this 'conscious ratiocination' (Gluckman, 1966: 105) involving 'secondary elaboration' can be found in belief systems, not least in conspiracy theory belief systems. These anthropological theories, though not acknowledged, do manifest themselves in more contemporary behavioural science research. Kruglanski's (1989) theory of 'lay epistemics' has been applied to the conspiracy and cover-up context by Harrison and Thomas (1997) in their recent cognitive systems research at the University of California, for instance. Lay epistemology, or lay epistemics, is a general theory about how people acquire knowledge about themselves and the world as an overarching paradigm, taking on board social cognition topics such as attribution theory, cognitive consistency theory and the many psychodynamic variables. Applied to conspiracy theories, the subject passes through phases of hypothesis generation and hypothesis testing or evaluation. Approximating an if-then relationship with information, a lay epistemic approach to Mr Grey's conspiracy theorizings would be to consider them 'pet theories' which Mr Grey is seeking consistency over, to the point that he operates a selective perception – assimilating, interpreting and remembering information and knowledge which supports his ontological base; equating examples of slave oppression with examples of present-day colonial practices. According to this approach, Mr Grey is more than likely to 'confirm' evidence at face value whilst subjecting any 'disconfirming' evidence to a great deal of critical evaluation. This would go some way towards explaining Sasson's (1995) suggestion that African Americans (and West Indians) are more receptive to conspiracy theories because of their age-old folk knowledge of racial oppression.

An investigation into the truth behind Mr Grey's conspiracies – as to whether or not there is a global hidden agenda held by the British, that there are world-wide broadcasting machinations afoot atop Mount Chance – is perhaps not the way forward from this point in a social anthropological or sociological approach to conspiracy theories. Mr Grey is not going to be dissuaded from his worldview, for a conspiracy theory can only be reiterated. To a certain extent, it is not possible to dissemble a conspiracy, bar make it common knowledge and thus no longer secret. A more productive line of inquiry to take with conspiracies is to continue by looking at their connection with belief systems, and – to return to Ted Goertzel (1994: 740) – to explore the logical processes which lead to, and are used to substantiate, the beliefs. Of note, here, is Ted Goertzel's adoption of Benjamin Goertzel's (1994) mathematical models of belief systems – despite its blind repetition of what Gluckman had been indicating several decades earlier – in his political psychology analyses of belief in conspiracy theories. The Goertzels distinguish between *dialogical* and *monological* belief systems, the former engaging with their context, the latter only speaking to themselves – this codification being a mathematical model of the philosophical distinction between the 'open' and the 'closed' mind (cf Gluckman, 1964). The conspiratorial belief, according to the

Goertzels, is associated with the monological belief system in that it allows the believer to easily integrate new information which has the potential to threaten the belief system. In the end, the belief components, bytes of information and the minor narratives which link them, all come to serve each other, creating and binding all in the wider fantastic narrative, the grand plot or conspiracy.

Conclusion

My representation above of Mr Grey the Pan-Akrikanist and his fantastic conspiracies gives us a detailed example of a man and his belief system, and how this affects and is affected by his interaction with the world. T. Goertzel (1994) goes on to conclude his article with a call for a qualitative testing of tl.eir monological hypotheses, one which would have to be gleaned from examples in published literature and/or in-depth interviews. This chapter is just one such answer to this call, one which hopefully substantiates in part the work of the Goertzels but one which, in doing so, brings the topic of narrativity into the equation, and makes the point that these theories and ideas about the nature of belief, and systems of thought, have already been tentatively worked at by sociologists and anthropologists evaluating their own fieldwork materials. Perhaps, after all, conspiracies do share White's narrative forms if not Grey's conspiracy contents. As many of the chapters in this book argue, the fantastic narratives of conspiracy do appear to be growing in presence in the world as the traditional footholds of modernity – with the maxims of continuing certainty, increasing safety and omniscient history – erode away. For continuity though, we have the unorthodox, controversial and pioneering work of Gluckman and Evans-Pritchard which show remarkable prescience from the point of view of our new age of anxiety, risk and fantasy.

Acknowledgements

Acknowledgements are made to Mr Grey (name changed) and the people of Montserrat who assisted me during my fieldwork on Montserrat; to Jane Parish, Martin Parker and JS for helping me to frame this piece; and to Mils Hills for an ever-suspicious mind.

References

Appadurai, A., (1990), 'Disjuncture and Difference in the Global Cultural Economy', *Public Culture*, 2 (2): pp. 1–23.
Barber, J., (1992), 'Jihad Vs. McWorld', *Atlantic*, 269 (3): pp. 53–63.
Barthes, R., (1973), 'Introduction to the Structural Analysis of Narratives', in Sontag, S. (ed.), *A Barthes Reader*, London: Cape.
Bruner, J., (1990), *Acts of Meaning*, Cambridge, MA: Harvard University Press.
Castells, M., (2000), *The Rise of the Network Society*, London: Blackwells.

Demeo, S., (1996), 'The corporate suppression of inventions, conspiracy theories, and an ambivalent American Dream', *Science as Culture*, 6/2 (27): pp. 194–219.

Evans-Pritchard, E., (1987 [1976]), *Witchcraft, Oracles and Magic among the Azande*, Oxford: Oxford University Press.

Fenster, M., (1999), *Conspiracy Theories: Secrecy and Power in American Culture*, Chicago: University of Minnesota Press.

Fergus, H., (1978), *Montserrat – The Last English Colony? Prospects for Independence: Two essays on Montserrat*, University of the West Indies Department of Extra-Mural Studies, Montserrat.

Fergus, H., (1994), *Montserrat – History of a Caribbean Colony*, London: The Macmillan Press Ltd..

Freud, S., (1976), *Introductory Lectures on Psychoanalysis*, Harmondsworth: Penguin.

Gluckman, M. and Devons, E., (1964), *Closed Systems and Open Minds: The Limits of Naivety in Social Anthropology*, Chicago: Aldine.

Gluckman, M. (1966 [1956]), *Custom and Conflict in Africa*, Oxford: Basil Blackwell.

Goertzel, B., (1994), *Chaotic Logic*, New York: Plenum Press.

Goertzel, T., (1994), 'Belief in Conspiracy Theories', *Political Psychology*, 15 (4): pp. 730–742.

Goodman, N., (1978), *Ways of Worldmaking*, Indianapolis, Indiana: Hackett Publishing Company, Inc.

Grey, C., (1994), 'Collaborating with the enemy', *The Pan-Afrikan Liberator*, 2 (7): pp. 1–2.

Hannerz, U., (1990), 'Cosmopolitans and Locals in World Culture', in Featherstone, M. (ed.), *Global Culture: Nationalism, Globalization and Modernity*, London: Sage Publications, pp. 237–251.

Harper, D., (1994), 'Histories of suspicion in a time of conspiracy: a reflection on Aubrey Lewis's history of paranoia', *History of the Human Sciences*, 7 (3): pp. 89–109.

Harrison, A. and Thomas, J., (1997), 'The Kennedy Assassination, Unidentified Flying Objects, and Other Conspiracies: Psychological and Organizational Factors in the Perception of 'Cover-up', *Systems Research and Behavioural Science*, 14 (2): pp. 113–128.

Hofstadter, R. (1966 [1952]), *The Paranoid Style in American Politics and Other Essays*, London: Jonathan Cape.

Hollander, P., (1999), 'review of *Conspiracy: How the Paranoid Style Flourishes and Where It Comes From* by D. Pipes [1997]', *Society*, January/February, pp. 88–90.

Holton, H., (1998), *Globalization and the Nation-State*, Basingstoke: Macmillan Press Ltd..

Horton, R., (1991), 'African Traditional Thought and Western Science', in Wilson, B. (ed.), *Rationality*, Oxford: Blackwell, pp. 131–171.

Jameson, F., (1984), 'Postmodernism, Or, The Logic of Late Capitalism', *New Left Review*, 146, pp. 53–93.

Keener, J., (1997), 'Biography, Conspiracy, and the Oswald Enigma', *Biography*, 20 (3): pp. 302–330.

Kerby, A., (1991), *Narrative and the Self*, Bloomington: Indiana University Press.

Kruglanski, A., (1989), *Lay Epistemics and Human Knowledge: Cognitive and Motivational Bases*, New York: Plenum Press.

La Fontaine, J., (1998), *Shout at the Devil: Tales of Satanic Abuse in Contemporary England*, Cambridge: Cambridge University Press.

Leach, E., (1984), 'Glimpses of the Unmentionable in the History of British Social Anthropology', *Annual Review of Anthropology*, 13, pp. 1–23.

Lewis, A., (1970), 'Paranoia and the Paranoid: A Historical Perspective', *Psychological Medicine*, 1, pp. 2–12.

McLeod, J., (1997), *Narrative and Psychotherapy*, London: Sage.

Marcus, G. (ed.) (1999), *Paranoia within Reason: A Casebook on Conspiracy as Explanation*, Chicago: University of Chicago Press.

Mathurin, O., (1971), 'Electoral change in Montserrat and Antigua', in Monroe, T. and Lewis, R. (eds), *Readings in the Government and Politics of the West Indies*, no other references available.

Pigden, C., (1995), 'Popper revisited, or What Is Wrong With Conspiracy Theories', *Philosophy of the Social Sciences*, 25 (1): pp. 3–34.

Popper, K., (1966), *The open society and its enemies, volume 2: The high tide of prophecy: Hegel, Marx and the aftermath*, London: Routledge and Kegan Paul.

Rapport, N., (1993), *Diverse World-Views in an English Village*, Edinburgh: Edinburgh University Press.

Rapport, N., (2000), 'Narrative', in Rapport, N. and Overing, J. (eds), *Social and Cultural Anthropology: The Key Concepts*, London: Routledge, pp. 283–290.

Schutz, A., (1967), *The Phenomenology of the Social World*, Evanston, Illinois: Northwestern University Press.

Showalter, E., (1997), *Hystories: Hysterical Epidemics and Modern Culture*, London: Picador.

Skinner, J., (2000), 'The eruption of Chances Peak, Montserrat, and the narrative containment of risk', in Caplan, P. (ed.), *Risk Revisited*, London: Pluto Press, pp. 156–183.

Stewart, K., (1999), 'Conspiracy Theory's Worlds', in Marcus, G. (ed.) (1999), *Paranoia within Reason: A Casebook on Conspiracy as Explanation*, Chicago: University of Chicago Press, pp. 13–19.

Tuckett, K. (ed.) (1998), *The A-Z of Conspiracy Theories*, Chichester: Summersdale.

Wallerstein, I., (1990), 'Culture as the Ideological Battleground of the Modern World-System', in Featherstone, M. (ed.), *Global Culture: Nationalism, Globalization and Modernity*, London: Sage Publications, pp. 31–55.

Zeitlyn, D., (1990), 'Professor Garfinkel visits the Soothsayers: Ethnomethodology and Mambila divination', *Man*, Volume 25, pp. 654–666.

Tout est lié: the Front National and media conspiracy theories

Adrian Quinn

The *Times Higher Education Supplement*, mandatory Friday reading for British academics, celebrated Christmas day 1998 with a review of five books about a modern obsession: the conspiracy. Coincidentally, just across the English Channel, the Front National in France was in the heat of a major internal crisis; a power struggle that was quite possibly the most serious threat ever experienced by the Front since its leader, Jean-Marie Le Pen, founded it in 1972. In keeping with his ideology, Le Pen attributed the crisis to a conspiracy, but for the first time, he identified the source of the conspiracy within the very ranks of a Right wing movement of which he is father figure, guardian and focal point. Conspiracy theory is seminal to the Front's ideology; especially the belief that the media conspire with political élites to destabilize the Front en route to destroying true nationalism in France. The *THES* piece, 'Plots all over the landscape', critiqued five recently published books on conspiracy theories. In it, Peter Knight and Alasdair Spark argued that the five books they reviewed, 'though wearing the colours of different disciplines, all agree that the real dispute is not so much between academic disciplines as between scholarship and pseudo-scholarship'. Theirs was a well-timed reminder of the dominant, dismissive view that conspiracy is not to be taken seriously.

This chapter re-examines the role of conspiracy theory as a model for the analysis of the communications process, taking the Front National as its focus. Conspiracy is widely rejected by scholars – indeed it is employed as a term of abuse – and, granted, there are some spectacularly crude uses of conspiracy in publication which invite abuse. Still, a serious scholar cannot dodge the fact that the conspiracy model has helped the Front win the support of over four million French voters; a significant minority (15%) of the French electorate.[1] Accordingly, this chapter also considers whether the conspiracy model can be used for genuine media scholarship, providing one with a model that can usefully tease out the nuances of mass political communication. It offers a rethink on the conspiracy model of mass communication by focusing on the Front National (hereafter the Front or FN), a political entity that holds the conspiracy at the absolute centre of its thinking. In offering a British perspective on the use of the conspiracy model by the Front I will also try to resituate the model within the context of existing theoretical models for the analysis of mass communications, showing the conspiracy model to be at least as sophisticated as some of the less lampooned communications models that have thus far been forwarded.

Kevin Williams (1998) has observed a reluctance among researchers in the more traditional areas of the humanities to treat film and television sources on par with written ones. In their work on the Front, Tévanian and Tissot elected to concentrate exclusively on French press coverage and not that of the broadcast media, arguing that, due to their proximity, broadcasting in France has 'basically ... nothing special about it' (1998: 15 *my translation*). In recognition of Williams's criticism, this chapter makes considerable use of visual media sources in offering, as it does, to provide an account for the Front's conspiratorial reading of its relationship with the media. To do this, I have drawn from a representative sample of current affairs programmes from the French television broadcasters TF1, France 2, La cinquième, ARTE and TV5 as well as the official websites of Le Pen and Bruno Mégret, the two main players of the far Right. Conspiracy has outgrown its once marginal influence on western culture (French included). For precisely that reason this chapter looks into the communications aspect of conspiracy theory to account for its appeal since, as two other contributors to this volume have elsewhere noted, for Le Pen and the likeminded, 'the plot-line for history is conspiracy' (Knight and Spark). I have adopted an interdisciplinary approach for this chapter in which I build upon the existing work in this area by historians, sociologists, print journalists and broadcasters working in English and in French.

Mass society theory

Since 1995, the FN has successfully cast itself as a party of ideas. This, according to some observers, is where the power and danger of the French extreme Right resides. Drawing on C. Wright Mills's idea that society is 'shifting from a democratic base to a mass society', John Eldridge has observed that 'one sociological sign of such a trend is when individuals are not able to connect their private troubles with public issues' (1993: 17). Transposing this observation to the French example, one finds that the Front is able to seize on the void created by this disconnectedness and fill it with a long standing myth: the conspiracy. On the basis of the one year that Mark Hunter spent doing participant observation on the Front in 1995–96, he affirms that this aspect of Mills's idea corresponds perfectly to what he observed there.[2] To remain with the 'mass society' notion – cognisant of what McNair calls its 'conspiratorial presuppositions' (1999: 24) – Hunter identifies two levels on which this search for connectedness finds expression. The first level is practical and is reflected in the familial structure of the Front. Life in the Front is very complete and its leaders recognize that for new entrants who are not structured politically in any way, the Front is able to offer them its very own rituals, music and culture. Belonging to this family is very absorbing, especially for those who might not have had much in life prior to joining the Front. The second level is ideological and is where the conspiracy theory resides. Mary Anne Sieghart of *The Times* says that the French feel 'alienated from government ... Indeed, the French hardly ever talk of *le gouvernement*: they refer to *l'Etat* (the State) or *le pouvoir* (the power). Both words have slightly malevolent connotations: these are seen as mysterious forces that conspire against the citizen' (1 September, 2000).

One of the most striking characteristics of the Front's particular take on conspiracy theory is that it explains *Everything* in life. It provides 'the citizen' with a reading of politics that sees the immigrant, the corrupt government, the media, the lack of rigour in academic texts *et cetera* as nothing more than different facets of a single interlocking plot in which the detail proves the whole, just as the whole gives meaning to the detail. This is the reasoning underlying the Front's central tenet or theme that *tout est lié* (everything is connected). The conspiracy theory was a pillar of the Front's ideology, and necessary for assuring (at least prior to Christmas 1998) the internal unity of the far Right. The idea that 'everything is connected' provided an intellectual path for the Front, and its constituents, to make sense of French society; a society which is in a state of civil war in their eyes. This expression, *tout est lié*, punctuates and reinforces the Front's discourse and is one of the most effective applications of its conspiracy theory. Though one would be quick to point out that the conspiracy theory is not particular to the Front, what is unique is the success with which the party has used the media to spread its theories. Stéphane Wahnich says that the idea of conspiracy has always provided a structure for Le Pen's 'obsessive discourse' (in Perraud, *Télérama* 23 December 1998 *my translation*). However, what was unique, and of particular relevance for this chapter, is that Christmas 1998 saw the conspiracy-driven attack mechanism usually reserved for the Front's traditional enemies (Jews, Leftists, *et al.*) suddenly wrenched inward and aimed at the Mégretists (*ibid*). If one can gauge the seriousness of a political crisis by the type of ammunition used, then Le Pen was clearly in jeopardy. The tactics of other political figures like Hillary Clinton – who risked her credibility on television by alluding to a 'vast Right-wing conspiracy' to bring down her husband – show that playing the conspiracy card is not something a political figure does lightly.

The Christmas divorce

What France witnessed at the tail end of 1998 was a festive season power struggle between Jean-Marie Le Pen, and the then-deputy leader of the Front, Bruno Mégret. Le Pen expelled the Mégretists from the party thereby splitting the Front in two; a split that followed the lines of its two main camps. The Catholics in the Front remained loyal to the leader while the neo-pagan[3] faction sided with Mégret. Michaël Darmon who had for three years covered the Front for France 2 television sketched the essential differences between the two factions. Those loyal to Le Pen gather around a paternal and old-fashioned, colonial vision of France. Modelled on Le Pen the brawler, their Front pines for Vichy and Algeria; a party whose roots lie in battles lost. Conversely, Mégret and his followers have an altogether different idea about France and the strategic way forward for the far Right. Mégret holds an essentially biological view of the French race, once declaring it an endangered species (*Envoyé Spécial*, TV5, 17 December 1998). In short, the hardest core of far Right ideology resides with Mégret and many observers find him by far the more dangerous and disturbing political figure. Where Le Pen the autodidact politician has survived on improvisation (even outright transgression) and soft populist racism, Mégret is firmly anchored in his ideological views. His camp generated the Front's propaganda and was responsible for bringing a structured platform to the far Right which Le Pen could not. The Mégretists cultivate an admiration for Nazi paganism and inherit their world view from the Mussolinian fascist thinker Baron Julius Evola (1898–1974), a figure who has been especially influential in the pagan new Right since the 1970s. However, what brought Le Pen and Mégret together in the heterogeneous family of the Front was the far Right's characteristic inclination 'to adopt a conspiracy theory of politics' (Vaughan, 1995: 216). They also share a common appetite for revisionist theories of history and a quasi-theorized suspicion that the mass media are agents of this global plot operating against the French republic. But most significantly (and for Le Pen the most threateningly) for many in the Front Le Pen represented the past and Mégret the future.

Public, arrêt sur images and envoyé spécial

According to Paris-based, American investigative journalist Mark Hunter – author of *An American in the Front* (1998) an account of the year he spent observing the Front from the inside – the Front is now finished as an electoral force. Le Pen believes that since the Front could not be destroyed from the outside, its opponents resolved to try to destroy it from the inside. 'Who could have wanted this?' Le Pen asked Michel Field, presenter of TF1's programme *Public* (13 December 1998). On his major television appearance on the Sunday evening following the split with Mégret, Le Pen suggested that the answer to that question could be found by looking among the Front's traditional enemies. The first culprit was the Freemasons, the second was the Leftist press. But with many of his remaining lead supporters in attendance (most visibly secretary general Bruno Golnisch who would succeed Mégret as deputy leader) Le Pen would not admit that his Front was in any way compromised. With one hour (less commercials) in prime time to give his account of the divorce with Mégret, Le Pen tried to ride a difficult balance between two contradictory positions. He attributed the troubles within the Front to the difficulties attendant to creating a united Right wing movement, and of keeping it united, rather than to any leadership failing on his part. He insisted that the Front was not damaged, despite the efforts of the media and the anti-Front lobbies to destroy it. But if there was any damage it was all Mégret's doing.

Nick Fraser and Mark Hunter, two Anglophone journalists who have observed the Front at close ranks, have perceived that their basic journalistic tenets, British and American respectively, do not work in France. This is partly to do with the fact that investigative methods are very culture specific, but more centrally to do with the fact that the extreme Right in France occupies a political space unlike anything which exists in the English-speaking world.[4] Fraser's documentary *Journey to the Far Right* (BBC2, 20 March 1999/ARTE, 25 March 1999)[5] one of a series of programmes broadcast during the BBC's *Fear and Loathing* season, is an example of the issues surrounding French nationalism and the dynamics that make that movement distinct from nationalist movements in the other EU states that Fraser visited while making his film. In simple terms (and his French background notwithstanding) the strength of Fraser's material on France – compared with markedly weaker material on neighbouring and ostensibly similar nationalist movements in western Europe – derives from the political legitimacy that the Front has come to enjoy. A good measure of the Front's mainstream success, as compared to the still marginal status of similar Right wing parties, is rooted in a long-standing popular concern. The Front has been able to seize on the issue of national security, principally immigration, which it refers to as an 'invasion', and – in times of high unemployment – appropriate some of the electoral ground normally occupied by the main parties of the centre Right.

However, despite the Front's contention that it is the victim of a media conspiracy, Nigel Copsey (1997) has argued that unlike the UK, whose media did work to bring down the British National Front in the 1970s, the French media have actually assisted the Front's politics in fundamental ways. At FN rallies, Le Pen has claimed that the 'populace' or mob, 'incited by the Leftist, Masonic press', has lined-up against the Front in an attempt to bring it down and thereby kill nationalism in France. Copsey says that, in reality, 'Le Pen was given credence by a benevolent national and local media that did not actively seek to de-legitimize the FN' (1997: 108). Copsey's observation can be re-visited by looking at French broadcasters' coverage of what was being called the Christmas divorce. On the Sunday lunchtime discussion programme *Arrêt sur Images*[6] which brings together journalists from various media, Eric Zemmour of *Le Figaro* newspaper said that Le Pen's observations had convinced him that a vast, triangulated conspiracy was operating involving the Mégretists, the media and the Gaullist party Rassemblement pour la République (RPR); one of the two main parties of the centre Right (La cinquième, 11 December 1998).[7] The objective of this conspiracy was obviously to divide and thereby destroy the far Right, or as Le Pen calls it, the true Right.

Later that evening Le Pen himself appeared on *Public* on TF1 television. Arguably, TF1 might have been one of the major contributors to the Front's credibility. Years earlier, the major French broadcasters had, at the behest of former President François Mitterand, been encouraged to give Le Pen broadcast time (Mayer, 1998: 21) and in response to the growing split in the Front, *Public* subsequently offered a half hour's airtime to both the Le Penistes and the Mégrétistes (*Le Monde* 13 May 1999). In quantitative terms, Le Pen's contention that he is the victim of a media conspiracy designed to exclude his party from mainstream politics is obviously difficult to sustain. In fact, whereas the British media arguably did conspire to bring down the UK National Front, the French media have aided the Front both in terms of credibility and exposure. Michel Wieviorka maintains that the 'British National Front ... never got the support that the French National Front has obtained' (1993: 63). In fact, some scholars have (not always reasonably) damned the media for aiding the Front. Nonna Mayer explains that

> as early as June 1982, François Mitterrand had extended his *help* to the leader of the Front National, who complained to him that the media were boycotting his party congress. Mitterrand *urged* the presidents of the three public television chains to invite Le Pen more often (1998: 21 emphasis added).

While the late French president's motives for this may be suspect (it is said that he saw this additional television coverage as an historic chance to divide the far Right and expel it from power once and for all (Hunter, 1998: 26) – offering some room to follow a conspiracy line) the result was that it 'not only considerably increased the party's visibility but also gave it legitimacy' (Mayer, 1998: 22). French sociologist Pierre Bourdieu also suspects the media for their part in the equation. He says that even when the media do attack Le Pen, they make themselves 'appear virtuous and humane for denouncing the racist moves of the very figure they helped create and to whom they continue to offer his most effective instruments of manipulation' (1998: 64).

Nevertheless, Le Pen maintained in his interview on *Public* that since the Front's opponents had been unsuccessful in bringing down the Front from the outside, they designed to do so from the inside of the party. Le Pen wondered aloud who could have wanted this? He made the ironic claim that he had observed the Leftist press exploiting the divorce as an occasion to publish biased stories; stories that were published on the condition that they had to be either pro-Mégret or anti-Le Pen. An outstanding exception to this arguably benign media treatment of the Front has appeared on the terrestrial television channel France 2, second only to the BBC as the largest public service broadcaster in Europe (OU, 1996). In 1992[8] and 1997, France 2's current affairs programme *Envoyé Spécial* engaged in extensive investigations into the politics and origins of the Front. For the second of the two, *Le Pen dans le texte*,[9] the Envoyé Spécial journalists obtained access to a range of specialists on the Front including Pierre-André Taguieff, an acknowledged authority on the Front, and Lorrain De Saint-Affrique, who was for ten years the Communications Advisor to Jean-Marie Le Pen, leaving the Front in 1994. De Saint-Affrique explains that the conspiracy is interpreted by the Front's members in a very individual, even egocentric way. During his ten years in the Front, he was among the ranks of many of the Front's lead players who believed that they were in the direct firing line of a massive conspiracy based in New York or Tel Aviv which occupies itself daily with the routine task of destroying individuals within the Front. This has the added effect of making a marginal party seem more important; cementing in its members the conviction that they must have put their finger on something essential. For while the conspiracy is global, its main target is France, its sole defender the Front National (*Envoyé Spécial*, France 2, 20 February 1997).

What is a conspiracy theory?

Conspiracy theory is something of a contradiction in terms. For analysis of the communications process, a *theory* of the media is 'a body of principles that attempt to develop clear, logical explanations for things' (Downing *et al.*, 1995: 492). But for examining this process – one which scholars like Greg Philo say needs to be treated 'as a totality' (1996: xi) – the conspiracy is necessarily a highly selective and convoluted model finding evidence anywhere, even in the very lack of evidence. Since it lacks both clarity and logic, one could reasonably argue, as scholars like Watson and Hill have, that the conspiracy is hardly a theory but 'more of a hunch or a suspicion' (1997: 49–50). Yet, traditional media theory has also failed us, lacking, as Ralph Negrine has observed, in 'intellectual coherence' (1994: 31). In the academy, as in politics, the term conspiratorial is a term of abuse used to dismiss fellow scholars' work.[10] It often seems as though the word conspiracy, like romantic or realistic, has been bandied about to the point where it has ceased to have any meaning.

This is compounded by the serious press's use of the term which is seldom serious. Below is a scatter-shot of headlines from British broadsheet newspapers to illustrate this. In late 1999, *The Guardian* reported on 'The Livingstone conspiracy: Truth or bluff' (18 November) about the London mayoral contest, and on 'HMV's annual conspiracy to frighten the horses (and Auntie Doris)' (7 December) about Christmas shopping. In the new year, the same issue of *The Times* carried Paul McCann's story about Mohamad Al Fayed's successful legal action against *The Sun*, reporting that he 'told the High Court that the Duke of Edinburgh was involved in a conspiracy to kill the Princess [of Wales] and Dodi [Al Fayed]' (11 February 2000) along with a story by someone identified mysteriously as 'A Correspondent' about revisionist British Historian David Irving and the 'theory that there was a "worldwide Jewish conspiracy" to supress Mr Irving's works ...' (*ibid*). *The Independent* followed a similarly light-hearted path with Susannah Frankel's comment piece on 'The Great Male Fashion Conspiracy' (25 February 2000) and, in the same vein, comedian Alexei Sayle writing about 'The Great dot.com paper bag conspiracy' (6 June 2000). Admist all this, one could be pardoned for forgetting that a true conspiracy does have certain criteria, however loose, involving interaction and criminal intent and is punishable by law in Britain under the Criminal Justice Act 1998 (Terrorism and Conspiracy). Still, populist conspiracy theory makes a nonsense of scholarly attempts to theorize media (in the way that media scholars associate with Fred Siebert *et al's Four Theories of the Press* and all four editions of Denis McQuail's *Mass Communication Theory*) as endlessly 'reinventing the firm'.[11] In that respect, the conspiracy constitutes an anti-theory; a way for those who believe in conspiracies to express their distinctiveness. They are not like the lumpen dupes who are content to adhere to conventional, textbook readings of the media/state relationship. For the initiated, the conspiracy model provides a comprehensive way of understanding the nature of power in society including (indeed especially) the power of the media. This makes them distinct from those who simply recognize that isolated conspiracies do operate.[12]

With the current academic appetite for analysing the minutiae of media operation, the most dismissive observation about research with which one might disagree is to say that it is 'simplistic'. Watson and Hill (1997) cite Richard Hoggart's Foreward to *Bad News* (1976) as a useful classification of conspiracies into two categories: high and low. To illustrate the low end, Hoggart seized on the idea of a 'direct order from Downing Street' (xi) as a rather fanciful setting for a media conspiracy, the kind of cover up one might find narrated in an Ian Fleming novel:

'Will the Press wear the story?' asked Bond dubiously. M. shrugged his shoulders. 'The Prime Minister saw the editors this morning', he said, putting another match to his pipe, 'and I gather he's got away with it so far. If the rumours get bad later on, he'll probably have to see them again and tell them some of the truth. Then they'll play all right. They always do when it's important enough ... ' (1955: 184).

Closer to reality, we do know of phone calls 'from Downing street' being made to newspapers editors, but as Andrew Neil narrates it, such calls are likely to take the form of inquiries rather than direct orders. Following Black Wednesday in 1992 which led Britain to devalue the pound and withdraw humiliated from the Exchange Rate Mechanism (ERM), Prime Minister John Major telephoned Kelvin MacKenzie, then-editor of *The Sun*, to ask him what angle his paper was going to take on the debacle. MacKenzie is said to have replied 'Well, John ... let me put it this way: I've got a large bucket of shit lying on my desk and tomorrow morning I'm going to pour it all over your head' (Neil, 1996: 9). Moving on to high conspiracy theory; it promises a more sophisticated reading of media control, one that allows more room for movement. Neither Hoggart nor the Glasgow Media Group advocates this as general theory of the media, though Hoggart recognizes that the conspiracy 'is a line which can be usefully followed a long way' (1976: xi). Accordingly, in analysing the *Front's* relationship with the media, it is perhaps more constructive actually to engage with the conspiracy model – to see just how long a scholar can follow it and identify the point at which it breaks down and fails – rather than dismiss it as is customary in academic work.

A common denominator

'Above all, the media are always against us', Bruno Mégret told Nick Fraser at an FN rally in the south of France, what Vaughan calls its 'neo-Fascist heartland' (1995: 227). The media are the common denominator in the Front's conspiracy theory. While in any given plot the secondary players may change, the Front sees the media as always there, ready and willing to play the stooge when the Front's enemies mount an attack on the true Right. However, one of the things that Mégret actively dissuaded in the Front was its members' impulse to make the kind of gratuitous and spontaneous made-for-TV remarks that characterize the figure of Jean-Marie Le Pen. The one most often cited came in 1987 when Le Pen called the Nazi gas chambers 'only a detail' in the history of the Second World War. Eric Zemmour of *Le Figaro* newspaper said that there was a 'thirst for credibility' among the Front's cadres and supporters that was steadily worsened by Le Pen's outbursts (*Arrêt sur Images*, La cinquième, 11 December 1998). One of Le Pen's more spectacular moments came in an interview with Christine Okrent on France 3 television in September 1996. Feeling that he was being bested by her, Le Pen lashed out at Ockrent claiming she was interrogating him without letting him respond and that her interview technique must be one of the weapons in the conspiracy against the Front – a conspiracy in which she and her husband (Leftist politician and United Nations representative Bernard Kouchner) were probably involved (*Envoyé Spécial*, France 2, 20 February 1997). Unlike Mégret who is measured and unshakable on television, Le Pen seems to take his lead from his interviewer. Half way through his appearance on *Public*, discussed earlier, Le Pen had yet to refer to Mégret and his supporters as 'les comploteurs' (conspirators). It was actually the show's host Michel Field who was the first to refer to Le Pen's rivals (rather off-handedly) as 'un petit group de comploteurs'. Three minutes later, an agitated Le Pen used that exact phrase having avoided doing so until that point in the programme. The common denominator also showed itself during the phone-in segment of the show when Le Pen protested to Michel Field that 'all the callers thus far have been hostile to my position', suggesting that the calls were being screened so as to wrong-foot the leader of the true Right (TF1, 13 December 1998).

Rethinking the model

Tim O'Sullivan notes that for serious study of mass communications, the conspiracy model, in which 'the mass media are conceived as powerful automatic relay mechanisms, directly controlled by certain powerful members of a conspiratorial group ... is a theory with little or no credibility' (1994: 61). Though correct, this reading does not do justice to a model which, credible or otherwise, is a highly effective political tool. Therein lies the paradox. Though it is the most porous of all the post-Siebert models that have been assembled to account for the media's role in society, the conspiracy theory 'works' within the political space it occupies in ways that it (or any other model) never would on paper. For instance, though the idea that the media are conspiratorial by disposition is dismissed by the academy (a notable exception being the Centre for Conspiracy Culture, a collaboration between academics from two British universities)[13] this myth is the life blood of the Front. It constitutes their reality, and their actions, including violent attacks on journalists, show that the Front, as expressed through its publication *Présent* 'believes that the media are all powerful and have no other objective than the total destruction of France' (Hunter, 1998: 61). This myth is a large part of the Front's overall message, but it is important to consider that this myth (what Vaughan (1995) calls an organizing myth) whereby the media take their lead from the political élite is not simply something which is untrue. This myth is consistent with Roland Barthes's idea that 'a myth is a story by which a culture explains or understands some aspect of reality or nature. A myth, for Barthes, is a culture's way of thinking about something, a way of conceptualizing or understanding it' (Fiske, 1990: 88). Thus, the academic tendency to scorn and ridicule the myth of the conspiracy as naive and simplistic (though an altogether natural impulse) is misplaced. For despite 'all its inconsistencies, the message is powerful, precisely to the extent that it is simplistic' (Vaughan, 1995: 225).

Anti-France (La décadence)

In his book on journalism, modernity and popular culture, John Hartley fixes the revolutionary date 1789 as 'the most decisive political development of modernity' (1996: 2). It is a measure of the difference of the Front's perspective that for its major players (especially its royalists) 1789 signals the point at which the natural order of society was turned on its head and corruption inevitably followed. The cadres trained in accordance with this ideology reject at least one of the three pillars of the French Revolution: liberté, égalité, fraternité. Le Pen says that 'the theme of equality strikes us as decadent' (in Vaughan, 1995: 223). Some royalist members of the Front have claimed that their party was the only one willing to admit that 1789 'was a disaster' (Hunter, 1998: 24).

The decadence in French society has been an obsession of the far Right in France for over one hundred years. The Front National under Jean-Marie Le Pen portrayed itself as a space of purity where one was safe from that decadence and its sinister conspiracies. By accessing the party's official website, one can bypass 'the media's censorship and boycott' of the Front's politics. Once on the website one has access to ideas and photos of the kind 'we rarely see in the media'.[14] The Front's image of itself as a space of nationalist purity, a haven from the decadence which has infected contemporary life in Europe, was shattered when Le Pen admitted that the conspiracy had entered his house. Hunter says that Le Pen 'shot his movement in the face' with this admission.[15] He totally inverted his usual line and identified a conspiracy within the ranks of his own movement. It is also a measure of the adaptability of the Front's approach to conspiracy theory that when his movement was threatened from the inside, Le Pen was able to shift his sights away from the usual suspects in the media conspiracy and lay the blame for the dissension within his party at the feet of nearby political players. The Front's model of choice is the only one malleable enough to allow Le Pen to play both sides so fluidly. Since it was clear that the Front was in crisis, Le Pen had to concede that the Mégretists had mounted a serious challenge to Le Pen's leadership, but he insisted that he was in charge and had rescued the movement with an act of redeeming discipline (*Public*, TF1, 13 December, 1998). Close observers of Le Pen recognized the need for his tactics, but also recognized that Le Pen had invited a sort of 'live by the sword, die by the sword', reading of the Front's relationship with the news media. If one charts Le Pen's reasoning, one finds that the media are precisely the problem in the Front's conspiracy theory (in as much as it has been problematized). They court the media's attention, but at the same time, use the space granted to them to promote the absolutist view that there is a conspiracy in place that alternately excludes the Front from mainstream channels of mass communication, and falsifies the party's image.

For practical purposes, the catalyst for Le Pen's politics is this notion that French society is suffering from an insidious form of cultural decadence. While this equation – 'modernity, construed as decadence' (Vaughan, 1995: 217) – is by no means a new one for the extreme Right, and pre-dates the collaborationist Vichy government of Marshal Philippe Pétain, his legacy can be seen as the Front's most obvious ideological antecedent.[16] The ideological platform of Pétain during the German occupation of France during World War Two, required a culprit on whom to hang the ultimate responsibility for France's capitulation to Germany in 1940. Historian Denis Peschanski explains that for Pétain, and those who came after him, that capitulation was the direct result of the decadence of the third republic, imported into France as part of a conspiracy by the forces of 'anti-France'; a label which the Front continues to apply to its adversaries. These forces were: Jews, communists, foreigners and Freemasons (*Envoyé Spécial*, France 2, 20 February 1997). This very inclusive list fashioned a broad-based conspiracy theory that the far Right continues to invoke at regular intervals. Patrick Bishop of *The Telegraph* says that Vichy remains associated 'with defeat, collaboration and a dark phase of French history ... The word Vichy is a shorthand for everything the French want to forget ... The name of the Auvergne town is redolent of anti-Semitism, fascism and defeatism' (28 October 1999).

Yet, while it is clearly a myth that attributes defeat to a 'conspiracy of decadence', the importance of this myth cannot be overstated for it constitutes not only the very basis of the Front's ideology – but also, argues De Saint-Affrique, adherence to that myth is the *sine qua non* for admission to the party's revisionist polit bureau. Just as Gouldner believed that 'ideologies are the connecting link between the so called "facts" of the news and the background assumptions which enable us, the audience to, to understand those facts' (Glasgow Media Group, 1995: 368) – in ideological terms, the Front's lead players must believe that the messages carried by the global media, and owned by Zionist conspirators, are designed to destroy France. De Saint Affrique says 'the cement is there. If you don't believe in it, then you are not admitted to the polit bureau' (*Envoyé Spécial*, France 2, 20 February 1997).

Evidence

The notion of evidence, and the validity of evidence, is one of the most nebulous areas of Right wing conspiracy thinking. The Nick Fraser documentary cited earlier concentrated solely on fascism on the continent; specifically in France, Denmark, Germany, Italy and Austria. Other programmes in the *Fear and Loathing* season like *The Lost Race* (BBC2, 24 March 1999) treated British fascism and the British National Party (BNP) specifically. Appropriately, though, the only British conspiracy theorist to appear in Fraser's film was revisionist historian David Irving, whom Fraser interviewed at Speaker's Corner in London's Hyde Park. While this chapter is not about Irving, the issues that have gathered around him allow for useful parallels to be made which illustrate the conspiracy thinking that one also finds in the Front National. Earlier, I mentioned that the research methodology of the conspiracy theorist sees detail giving meaning to the whole; and in return the whole imparting meaning to the detail. Jonathan Freedland describes as 'maddeningly frustrating' the experience of observing David Irving employ just such a strategy of argumentation in court during his failed libel action against Penguin Books (*The Guardian* 5 February 2000). Freedland writes,

> the problem with Irving is that he refuses to accept the basic rules of evidence ... This is how he approaches the entire topic. He dismisses the evidence of the witnesses' own eyes: whether Jew or Nazi: they made it all up ... It is history itself which is on trial here, the whole business of drawing conclusions from evidence. If Irving is able to dismiss the testimony of thousands of witnesses, where does that leave history? If we start to doubt corroborated facts, how can we prevent ourselves being swallowed up in doubt, unable to trust anything we see? It might all be a conspiracy ... This is the bizarre never-never world inhabited by Irving (*ibid*).

It is also the world inhabited by the Front. The fact that Irving, like Le Pen and Mégret, refuses to be bound by the rules of evidence is precisely the point. The conspiracy theorist is empowered by this refusal. It keeps an all-purpose get out clause at the ready. While the competent scholar knows that a theory can never be established by example alone, this runs directly contrary to the Front's preferred mode of analysis, one that strings together a series of anecdotes and examples and binds them together with received wisdom, thereby producing meaning. However, invoking the conventions of scholarship to reveal the shortcomings of the Front's thinking does miss the point somewhat, since it is the imaginative limitations of such mainstream scholarship in opposition to which the Front defines itself.

A correspondence with reality (something comprehensible)

In *The Media in France*, Raymond Kuhn observed something of a quantitative paradox in the Front's relationship with the press. He notes that

> Jean-Marie Le Pen's electoral score of 14.38%[17] of the vote in the first ballot of the 1988 presidential election was not reflected in favourable editorial columns (though, paradoxically, the amount of space given the party in newspaper articles in the 1980s may have overstated its electoral importance) (1995: 76).

However exaggerated, the Front's electoral importance does not tell the whole story and Kuhn's supposition does not discount the potential impact of the Front's political message. For by the year Kuhn's book appeared, the Front had successfully graduated from being merely a party of reaction to being a party of ideas. Some have identified the true danger of the Front as exactly that: that once it had graduated to its present status as a party of ideas, those ideas began to spread more rapidly than its electoral influence. Tévanian and Tissot (1998) find evidence of this by observing other political parties, and the media, picking-up on the ideas of the Front; not unlike the way the Conservative Party appropriated the race issue in its first term back in office under Margaret Thatcher, thereby undermining the British National Front's electoral platform in Britain. This is not surprising since, as Paul Webster, *The Guardian's* Paris correspondent has noted, the Front 'has an unambiguous nationalist platform admired by a large section of traditional Gaullists' (22 April 1997). This admiration would become increasingly evident with the arrival in 1999 of the Rassemblement pour la France (RPF),[18] a splinter party lead by two well-known dissidents: Charles Pasqua from the RPR and (briefly) Phillipe de Villiers from the UDF. Paul Webster says that when one factors in the new option of the RPF, with its eurosceptic, anti-immigration platform, Le Pen's post-divorce troubles can only be 'compounded by the drift of far-right voters towards [this] breakaway Gaullist movement' (*The Guardian* 25 April 2000). These developments confirm that as the Front's message was not cellularized, its influence was able to spread faster than its electoral gain, and they confirm what Tévanian and Tissot have argued; that although France has yet to become fully *Lepenised*, it is rapidly *Lepenising* (1998: 12). Webster has also reported that Pasqua 'once said that his political views were close to those of Le Pen' (*The Guardian* 25 April 2000). Le Pen would certainly read the RPF's attempt to appropriate the softer end of the Front's electoral turf as part of the conspiracy against him and a vindication of his political message. He would not be entirely mistaken.

But if the media are not involved in an outright *conspiracy*, how then should one characterize their role in influencing those who receive media messages? Taking *Le Monde* as an example of the micro level, Kuhn points outs that that newspaper, 'does not operate in either an ethical or an ideological vacuum, as can be seen from its critical coverage of Le Pen and the National Front in the 1980s' (1995: 730). Bringing the discussion back to the macro level, though a definitive articulation of the nature of media power and ideology continues to elude us, for the purposes of the argument offered by this chapter, Jenny Kitzinger's reading is helpful. In *The Circuit of Mass Communication*, she notes that

> Media power is certainly not absolute, nor does it exist in a vacuum ... The media do not operate as single force in a hermetically sealed ideological conspiracy. However, there can be a powerful interaction between media messages and broader contextual assumptions and the media still influence the way we think (1998: 211).

In the end, the Front's conspiracy theory fails because, while those with access to the media certainly exert a certain degree of control over the media, those 'controls are not complete' (Eldridge, 1995: 9). Hence, Kitzinger speaks of 'influence' rather than 'control'. The conspiracy model, sometimes very successfully, gets us half the way there and one's imagination completes the picture. So where conventional media *theory* comes about by 'synthesising what is *known* about influences on media content into a more systematic set of inter-related statements about the relationships between media content and the influences on it' (Shoemaker and Reese, 1996: 261 emphasis added) – a media conspiracy theory may have enough room to germinate in the space left by what is *unknown*. For the Front, the circuit of mass communication is a closed circuit. Its model of choice, the all-purpose media conspiracy theory should be seen as a hermetic intellectual construct. Any outside evidence introduced into it will either be taken as confirmation of that construct or will be rejected out of hand.

Far from being completely imagined, however, Noam Chomsky says that a successful conspiracy theory must be based on 'something comprehensible'.[19] Bruno Mégret did constitute a real and mounting threat to Le Pen's leadership of the Front. He had a more proficient TV technique and he and his fellow expulsees had secured the support of major factions within the far Right. Though Le Pen exaggerated the vastness of the plot against him (especially the media's role in that plot), those who had been observing the Front closely recognized that important aspects of Le Pen's conspiratorial reading of the situation did correspond to reality. The Institut de Formation Nationale (IFN), which trains the Front's cadres, was dominated by Mégret and the pagan movement within the Front, which in turn dominated the Front's ideological apparatus. Le Pen was also aware that other sources of support within the new Right – pagan intellectual circles like Club de l'horloge and GRECE – were also firmly behind the Mégretists whose domination of the Front had become especially conspicuous within the Front's general delegation. Thus, there is a need for a theoretical middle ground between rejecting conspiracy theory as nonsense and embracing it as an answer to all one's questions about how the media can be influenced. This middle ground, however, can be occupied only once academics get past the prejudice against conspiracy that either it deems unworthy of scholarly investigation or, a bit more generously, insists that conspiracy cannot be treated academically because any conspiracy worthy of the name could not, by definition, be accessed by the scholar. Our *understanding* of a movement like the Front National (understanding is, after all, the reason for making theory) requires that we engage with this middle ground as almost a prerequisite for grasping contemporary political communication. The middle ground makes provision for the acknowledgement of genuine conspiracies (calling a spade a spade) and in the case of the Front – where there is no outright conspiracy – allows us to account for cultural conditions that incite conspiracy thinking. Finally, and for this present argument most importantly, it also provides the facility to identify what, if any, aspects of a political conflict (like between the far Right and the media if one accepts this present example) do contain authentic traces of conspiracy.

The Front now – concluding remarks

The Front National is no longer the party it was. Without Mégret, who has now formed his own party, Le Pen's Front does not have a structured platform. Without Le Pen, Mégret's new splinter party, the Mouvement National Républicain (MNR)[20] will not enjoy popular support. Purged of its pagan element, in June 1999's Euroelections Le Pen's Front attracted the support of nearly six percent of French electorate gaining the Front five MEPs. In April 2000, however, Le Pen would be banned from sitting in the EU parliament, where he was a member since 1984, the cumulative result of attacking a socialist woman candidate during a local election campaign in 1997 and of repeating his revisionist views on the Holocaust during a visit to Munich, Germany in December 1997.[21] Most observers are looking to the 2002 presidential elections to ascertain how much of a setback the far Right has suffered since Christmas 1998. Its media campaign should provide clues as to how well Mégret's new party deals with the media and, perhaps conversely, how badly Le Pen's Front deals with the media post-Bruno

Mégret. Present indications are that, while a potential electorate still exists for the far Right, even when combined, the pair's electoral success does not match their pre-divorce heights (Pognon, *Le Figaro* 7 February 2000). This is a setback for the far Right and should be read as such. Meanwhile, unemployment in France has fallen and that may further diminish support for the Front's platform. But in an article on tendencies to racism in Europe (one that now reads prophetically) Michel Wierviorka (1993) asks 'Does France Represent a Unique Case, or is it Representative of a Trend?' He says that the far Right has come to exert pressure through 'the extension to a popular level of a renewed set of racist discourse' and 'even if the Front National did not exist, or were to disappear, this pressure would still exist, and be quite impressive' (1993: 56). As one would expect, Wierviorka's answer is that there is indeed such a trend in Europe, though France displays clear differences where 'political expressions of racism' are concerned (*ibid*: 63). Those are the sort of expressions I am ultimately concerned with here. In his film on the far Right in Europe that I have used for this chapter, Nick Fraser said that 'again and again' he returned to Le Pen and the French example. Though, admittedly, his is a personalized documentary, Fraser recognized that for a broadcaster, there was something compelling and unusual about the Front.

To conclude, one would note that in some important ways the France of 1995, when the Front seemed at its strongest, feels like a very long time ago. A few years after filming his documentary, Fraser noticed that 'there were fewer Le Pen posters, and the FN graffiti on the autoroute bridges was faded' (*The Guardian* 26 August 2000). Writing for the same newspaper, Jon Henley says that 'France can be rightly proud that, with the demise of Jean-Marie Le Pen's anti-foreigner National Front, racism no longer has a voice on the national political scene', but cautions that in France, 'racism has never really been about grand public gestures ... it emerges in small everyday incidents, in coy linguistic double-thinks. It is, in a way, genteel – but it is very real' (*The Guardian* 14 August 2000). In the academy, scholars can confront that reality by recognizing just how absorbing the conspiracy model that carries this racism is – but also by recognizing that even the most fanciful conspiracy theories are actually based on something comprehensible which must be mapped. In one of the earliest attempts to theorize the role of the press, Theodore Peterson stressed that it is important to remember that any media theory 'is still chiefly a *theory*', but is significant nonetheless as 'some aspects of theory have found their way into practice' (1956: 75). For the Front, its conspiracy theories have found their way into practice when its supporters threaten to kill or violently attack journalists whose writing is hostile to the Front for participating in that conspiracy. Olivier Bertrand of *Libération* received death threats from supporters of the Front while Michel Soudais of *Le Parisien* was attacked and beaten (Hunter, 1998: 69–71). Thus, far from being ineffectual, this conspiracy theory can have serious consequences when one believes in it enough to take action.

When media academics have referred to past scholarship as conspiratorial, with what James Curran calls 'that grand dismissal; that knowing sophistication', it may amount to little more than 'name calling'.[22] However, in a book on the role of media organizations in society, an area that he has identified as under-researched, Curran hinted that much media scholarship, by not considering that role, does smack of conspiracy. He says a common strain in many scholars' work is 'a tacit assumption that control of the media lies outside the media, in forces and agencies external to it' (2000: 10–11). This would suggest that in media scholarship in the UK, conspiratorial readings abound and that sustained research intervention is called for.

Back in France, anti-fascist fringe publications like the monthly *Ras l'front* (Enuf of the Front)[23] have not shied away from making such interventions and explicitly challenge the ideas of the sort found in the Front's *Présent*. In a useful crossover of journalism and scholarship, Nonna Mayer contributed a 20 page analysis of the far Right's performance at the 1999 Euroelections to the July/August edition of *Ras l'front*. Meanwhile, the recovery of France's economy, coming on the heels of France's World Cup and Euro 2000 victories, has not gone unnoticed in the English-language press. That recovery (predictably labelled a Renaissance or Revolution) has made the front page of *Newsweek* (20 March 2000)[24] and *Time* (12 June 2000) magazines and has found its way onto the comment pages of many British newspapers.

The Guardian's Paul Webster has reported on a promising development in French schools that may fill the historical void where French conspiracy theory resides. He writes that France is now confronting its fascist history and 'sixty years after France introduced anti-semitic laws that resulted in the deportation of more than 75,000 Jews, the Holocaust is to become a subject of study in French secondary schools from this autumn ... the latest step in the country's slow recognition of its wartime past' (*The Guardian Weekly* 9–15 March 2000). Both are significant developments and reflect an ability, both in pedagogy and in media research, to respond to Europe's return to the Right.

Notes

1 15% is the figure most often quoted and reflects the Front's performance at the 1995 presidential and 1997 legislative elections. However the Front's potential electorate has been calculated to be even more sizeable. *The Guardian's* Jon Henley reports that the Front National and its off shoots have found themselves 'competing for the votes of the 30% of the French electorate who have, at one time or another, voted for the party' (27 January 1999).

2 From an interview with the author. I am grateful to Mark Hunter for granting me three separate interviews in Paris in August 1998, December 1998 and August 1999.

3 The term (neo)pagan is complex and needs to be qualified. Its elusiveness is reminiscent of the term conspiracy. For the purpose of this chapter, paganism in the Front is characterized, first, by a rejection of Christianity. The pagans see themselves as more in touch with their Greek and

Roman roots. They also hold the belief that the Roman Empire is *actual*. They subscribe to a theory that sees a direct parallel between the state of contemporary France and that of the Roman Empire just prior to its demise. It follows therefore that they should have an affinity for hard core fascist thinkers who have also found inspiration in the Classical period.

4 Australia may become the exception to this. In an appearance on the History Channel's programme Playback, Tony Benn explained that with mass unemployment (citing 15 million in the EU) 'you get Le Pen in France, you get the fascists coming back in Germany, you get Pauline Hanson in Australia. Unemployment creates such despair that it can lead to people moving to the Right' (27 October 1998). However, in developments reminiscent of the Front, Hanson's One Nation party has shown signs of destroying itself from the inside. Christopher Zinn writes that the party is 'riven with highly publicised splits, mass defections to rival parties and damaging court cases' (*The Guardian* 24 January 2000).

5 www.arte-tv.com/thema/19990325/ftext/droite_f.html.
ARTE is a Franco-German channel that shares the terrestrial channel five with La cinquième. The latter broadcasts is the daytime with ARTE taking over in the evening.

6 'Les Coulisses D'une Implosion En Direct', a report by Olivia Buffi. www.lacinquieme.fr/asi/002499/14/2440.cfm.

7 The other is the Union Démocratique Française (UDF). It is seen as more moderate.

8 Michaël Darmon was interviewed by *Envoyé Spécial's* Bernard Benyamin as a postscript to the 1992 episode, re-broadcast on TV5 on 17 December 1998, to offer a context for the split within the Front.

9 *Envoyé Spécial*, no. 282, 20 February 1997. This documentary presented the findings of a six month content analysis project examining the recurring themes in Jean-Marie Le Pen's public statements over a period of 10 years. The principal journalists were Jean-Pierre Metivet and Emmanuel Maquaire. Pierre-André Taguieff, Director of Research at the Centre National pour la Recherche Scientifique (CNRS) contributed to the programme as an academic consultant.

10 An example of this from the world of British politics is that of the United Kingdom Independence Party which 'secured three seats in the European election' and like the Front 'is in danger of splitting amid vicious personality clashes and rows over allegations of infiltration by ring-wing extremists ... the campaign of Rodney Atkinson, a former Tory Party member, has been damaged by the distribution of an open letter by two prominent eurosceptics *accusing* him of being a "conspiracy theorist"' (Pierce, *The Times* 18 March 2000, emphasis added).

11 Ralph Negrine, from an interview with the author 20 January 1999.

12 John Pilger reminds us with a staccato-like insistence that: 'Watergate was a conspiracy. The Iran-Contra scandal was a conspiracy. The 'Gulf of Tonkin Incident' was a conspiracy. The secret bombing of Laos and Cambodia was a conspiracy. The overthrow of Salvador Allende was a conspiracy' (1992: 272).

13 Peter Knight of Manchester University and Alasdair Spark of King Alfred's College. www.wkac.ac.uk/research/ccc.

14 www.front nat.fr

15 Hunter, op cit.

16 John Lichfield of *The Independent* says that until 2000, when a three year official inquiry reported that 'the French state apparatus and leading financial institutions, such as banks, took part enthusiastically in a "persecution [of Jews] whose ultimate goal was extermination"', past French presidents had 'insisted that the wartime Vichy regime was not a legitimate representative of France'. However, in 1995 Jacques Chirac declared 'that the French state had "committed the unpardonable sin" of taking an active part in the Holocaust' (18 April 2000). Patrick Bishop of *The Telegraph* says that, now, 'the Vichy authorities do not hide the past ... The Hotel du Parc where Marshal Pétain had his headquarters ... carries a plaque reminding passers-by of the regime's complicity in deporting Jews to the German death camps' (28 October 1999).

17 This is the precise electoral score, often cited as a rounded 15%, that initially attracted such attention. However, one should note the earlier electoral successes that foreshadowed this result. For Andrew Geddes, the extreme Right's 'breakthrough' came at the 1984 Euroelections

which saw the Front win ten of the 80 seats available in France (2000: 141) while Michalina Vaughan fixes the Front's electoral 'turning point' at 1983 when the centre Right went into coalition with the Front to defeat the Left and win the local election in Dreux (1995: 226–227).

18 www.rpf-ie.org

19 Noam Chomsky, from an interview with the author 23 February 1999.

20 www.mouvement-national.org After some legal wrangling over who owned the rights to the name Front National and its tricolour/flame symbol, Mégret's party underwent several name changes finally settling on Mouvement National Républicain (MNR).

21 This incident has become known as 'le deuxième détail' (the second detail), marking a return to the coded revisionist discourse that Le Pen first used on French TV in 1987.

22 James Curran, from an interview with the author 29 January 1999.

23 www.globenet.org/RLF

24 That spring, *Newsweek's* front page declared 'High Tech and the Pursuit of Wealth are Driving Europe's Leading Economy' (20 March 2000). However in something of a reality check, by the end of summer *The Times'* financial editor Graham Searjeant's headline cautioned 'Eurozone leader France shows signs of slowing' (1 September 2000).

References

Askolovitch, C., (1999), *Voyage au bout de la France: Le Front national tel qu'il est*, Grasset: Paris.

Bishop, P., (1999), 'Vichy in fight to escape shadow of collaboration', *The Telegraph*, 28 October.

Bourdieu, P., (1998), *On Television and Journalism*, Pluto: London. Translated by Priscilla Parkhurst Ferguson.

Copsey, N., (1997), 'A Comparison between the Extreme Right in Contemporary France and Britain', *Contemporary European History*. 6 (1): Cambridge University Press, 101–116.

Chombeau, C., (1999), 'Les émissions politiques contraintes de se fixer des règles d'équilibre'. *le Monde*. 13 May.

Curran, J. (ed.) (2000), *Media Organisations in Society*, London: Arnold.

Downing, J., Mohammadi, A. and Sreberny-Mohammadi, A. (eds) (1995), *Questioning the Media: A Critical Introduction*. 2nd ed., London: Sage.

Eldridge, J. (ed.) (1993), *Getting the Message: News, Truth and Power*, London: Routledge.

Fiske, J., (1990), *Introduction to Communication Studies*. 2nd ed. London: Routledge.

Fleming, I., (1954), *Moonraker*, London: Pan.

Frankel, S., (2000), 'The Great Male Fashion Conspiracy: Nice legs, shame about the frock'. *The Independent*, 29 February.

Fraser, N., (2000), 'In poll after poll, a majority of French voters admitted to holding "racist ideas". The Front National has made hatred legitimate'. *The Guardian*, 26 August.

Freedland, J., (2000), 'Court 73 – where history is on trial'. *The Guardian*, 5 February.

Geddes, A., (2000), *Immigration and European Integration: Towards Fortress Europe?*, Manchester: Manchester University Press.

Glasgow Media Group (1976), *Bad News*, London: Routledge and Kegan Paul.

Glasgow Media Group, Eldridge, J., (ed.) (1995), *Glasgow Media Group Reader volume one: News Content, Language and Visuals*, London: Routledge.

The Guardian, (2000), 'Irving "does not deserve to be called a historian"'. 11 February.

Hartley, J., (1996), *Popular Reality: Journalism, Modernity, Popular Culture*. London: Arnold.

Henley, J., (1999), 'Le Pen to fight party rival's "lunatic" coup'. *The Guardian*, 27 January.

Henley, J., (2000), 'We love you Zizou – but ...' *The Guardian*, 14 August.

Hunter, M., (1998), *Un Américain au Front: Enquête au sein du FN*, Paris: Stock.

Kelner, M., (1999), 'HMV's annual conspiracy to frighten the horses (and Auntie Doris)'. *The Guardian*, 7 December.

Kitzinger, J., (1998), 'Resisting the Message: The Extent and Limit of Media Influence', in Miller, D., Kitzinger, J., Williams, K. and Beharrell, P. (eds), *The Circuit of Mass Communication:*

Media Strategies, Representation and Audience Reception in the AIDS Crisis. London: Sage: 192–212.

Knight, P. and Spark, A., (1998), 'Plots all over the landscape'. *Times Higher Education Supplement*, 25 December.

Knight, P. and Spark, A., (1999), 'Conspiracy Thinking and Conspiracy Studying'. www.wkac.ac.uk/research/ccc/sparkess.htm Site accessed 7 December 1999.

Kuhn, R., (1995), *The Media in France*, London: Routledge.

Lichfield, J., (2000), 'Wartime France stripped Jews of £1bn'. *The Independent*, 18 April.

MacAskill, E., (1999), 'The Livingstone conspiracy: Truth or bluff?' *The Guardian*, 18 November.

Mayer, N., (1996), 'Is France Racist?' *Contemporary European History*. 5 (1): Cambridge University Press: 119–127. Translated by Rosemary Morris.

Mayer, N., (1998), 'The French National Front', in Betz, H-G. and Immerfall, S. (eds), *The New Politics of the Right: Neo Populist Parties and Movements in Established Democracies*. Macmillan: Basingstoke: 11–25.

McCann, P., (2000), 'Judges say Al Fayed Diana claim "absurd"'. *The Times*, 11 February.

McNair, B., (1999), *News and Journalism in the UK: a Textbook*. 3rd edition. London: Routledge.

McQuail, D., (2000), *McQuail's Mass Communication Theory*. 4th ed London: Sage.

Negrine, R., (1994), *Politics and the Mass Media in Britain*. 2nd ed. London: Routledge.

Neil, A., (1996), *Full Disclosure*. London: Macmillan.

Newsweek Magazine. 20 March 2000.

Open University (1996), *Informer, éduquer, divertir*? OU L21012. BBC2 Learning Zone. Broadcast 30 May 2000.

O'Sullivan, T., Hartley, J., Saunders, D., Montgomery, M. and Fiske, J., (1994), *Key Concepts in Communication and Cultural Studies*. 2nd ed., London: Routledge.

Perraud, A., (1998), 'Les forts en anathème'. *Télérama*. No. 2554, 23 December.

Peterson, T., (1956), 'The Social Responsibility Theory of the Press', in Siebert, F., Peterson, T. and Schramm, W., *Four Theories of the Press*, Urbana: University of Illinois Press, 73–103.

Philo, G. (ed.), (1996), *Glasgow Media Group Reader volume two: Industry, Economy, War and Politics*, London: Routledge.

Pierce, A., (2000), 'Anti-EU party heading for split'. *The Times*, 18 March.

Pilger, J., (1992), *Distant Voices*. Vintage: London.

Pognon, O., (2000), 'Les désillusions de l'extrême droite'. *Le Figaro*, 7 February.

Sayle, A., (2000), 'The Great dot.com paper bag conspiracy: the clueless entrepreneurs wasting your money'. *The Independent*, 6 June.

Searjeant, G., (2000), 'Eurozone leader France shows signs of slowing'. *The Times*, 1 September.

Shoemaker, P. and Reese, S. (1996), *Mediating the Message: Theories of Influences on Mass Media Content*. White Plains: Longman.

Sieghart, A.M., (2000), 'Why the French are always up in arms'. *The Times*, 1 September.

Souchard, M., Wahnich, S., Cuminal, I. and Wathier, V., (1997), *Le Pen — les mots: Analyse d'un discours d'extrême droite*. Paris: Le Monde Éditions.

Tévanian, P. and Tissot, S., (1998), *Mots à maux: Dictionnaire de la lepénisations des éspirits*. Paris: Éditions Dagorno.

Time Magazine. 12 June 2000.

Vaughan, M., (1995), 'The Extreme Right in France: "LePénisme" or the Politics of Fear', in Cheles, L., Ferguson, R. and Vaughan, M., *The Far Right in Western and Eastern Europe*, London: Longman: 215–233.

Watson, J. and Hill, A., (1997), *A Dictionary of Communication and Media Studies*. 4th ed. London: Arnold.

Webster, P., (1997), 'National Front will benefit most from debate on European unity'. *The Guardian*, 22 April.

Webster, P., (2000a), 'France at last learns lesson from Holocaust'. *The Guardian Weekly*, 9–15 March.

Webster, P., (2000b), 'Le Pen loses MEP seat'. *The Guardian*, 25 April 2000.

Wieviorka, M., (1993), 'Tendencies to Racism in Europe: Does France Represent a Unique Case, or is it Representative of a Trend?' in Wrench, J. and Solomos, J. (eds), *Racism and Migration in Western Europe*. Berg: Oxford/Providence: 55–65.

Williams, K., (1998), *Get me a Murder a Day! A History of Mass Communication in Britain*, London: Arnold.

Zinn, C., (2000), 'Police seize One Nation party files'. *The Guardian*, 24 January.

The popular culture of conspiracy/ the conspiracy of popular culture

David Bell and Lee-Jane Bennion-Nixon

I want to believe

(Ufology poster in Fox Mulder's office, *The X-Files*)

This chapter centres on the popular TV series (and movie and merchandizing spin-offs), *The X-Files*. In particular, it seeks to interrogate the 'conspiratorial narratives' that *The X-Files* dramatizes in its metatext. To accomplish this, we trace one story arc, or 'cumulative narrative', that crosses the seven seasons of the series broadcast by the end of 2000 in the UK: the story of the abduction of Samantha Mulder, younger sister of *The X-Files*' central character, FBI Special Agent Fox Mulder. This long-running, episodic storyline is especially pivotal to the series, as it is the desire to find 'the truth' of Samantha's abduction that propels Fox Mulder in his single-minded pursuit of answers to the riddles posed by the X-files.

Our reading of the Samantha narrative is set in two contexts. First, as a core motif of *The X-Files*, it is located in the growing 'popular culture of conspiracy' – the production, circulation and consumption of conspiracy theories within the broad realms of popular culture. It is then set in a second context; that of the 'conspiracy of popular culture'. In particular, focus here will be given to the ways in which 'fringe knowledges' such as those about alien abduction (propagated and popularized by *The X-Files*) gain popular currency and mass exposure at the same time that they suffer harsh critical scrutiny from what we might call 'knowledge-keepers'. By looking at critical responses both to 'fringe knowledges' and to their representation and reproduction in *The X-Files*, we want ultimately to think about the forms and functions of 'popular conspiracy culture'.

Trust No One™: Conspiracy in *The X-Files*

The gripping dramatic story is, ultimately, at the heart of conspiracy theory.

(Mark Fenster, *Conspiracy Theories*)

Mark Fenster (1999) argues that all conspiracy theories, whether 'fictional' or 'non-fictional', are organized within a dramatic narrative framework. It is this telling of stories that captures imaginations, piecing together disjointed events to uncover a conspiracy 'theory' that has the potential to produce 'ontological shock' – a radical change in world-view. In this section we will look at *The X-Files* (1993-present), which through seven seasons (160 episodes), plus a feature-length theatrical movie, has featured conspiracy at the core of its on-going narrative. By its very nature a television series needs a dramatic framework, one that works within a restricted timeframe (from 45 to 50 minutes), includes mini-climaxes to carry the viewer through commercial breaks, and highly tantalizing season cliff-hangers to hold audience attention through the summer break. *The X-Files* uses this televisual structure to fuel its continuing fantastical conspiracy metatext:

> There are two main kinds of stories we tell ... the 'stand-alone' episodes; these are the self-contained genre stories; thrillers or science fiction. And then we tell the 'mythology' episodes which deal with Mulder and Scully's pursuit of a conspiracy to hide something from the American public.
> (Chris Carter, Series Creator of *The X-Files*)

Carter calls the conspiracy narrative or metatext of the series the 'mythology'; even though it does not feature in every show, it is this 'mythology' that drives the show's narrative along, and keeps the viewer watchful for signs of its return.

Drawing on Fenster's in-depth analysis of conspiracy theories in American culture, we will use *The X-Files* as a way of mapping a fictional conspiracy narrative. *The X-Files* has proven a popular formula with both American and British audiences, not only featuring on the television and cinema, but also as computer games, books, magazines, trading cards and action figures (see Lavery, Hague and Cartwright, 1996). Looking at *The X-Files* and piecing together one of its key conspiracy storylines, we will see a dense weaving of information, misinformation and disinformation, with an endless deferral of 'the truth' through the escalation of conspiratorial plot twists and *denouements*. *The X-Files* has sustained a long-running and complex conspiracy theory within a conventional format, yet it also twists 'logical' storytelling structures by reworking old narrative threads, going back over previous storylines and making unforeseen connections in the light of new discoveries. It is this narrative structure that interests us here, as the on-going 'conspiracy arc' unfolds unexpectedly through the investigations of the main protagonists, FBI Agents Fox Mulder (David Duchovny) and Dana Scully (Gillian Anderson). Each week Mulder and Scully investigate unexplained criminal cases that the rest of the FBI can neither understand nor solve. These paranormal or mysterious cases, called 'the X-files', are what bring Mulder and Scully into contact with the people and information that feeds their search for 'the truth':

> the motivation in popular conspiracy narratives tends to be a straight forward, unconflicted combination of revenge (often to right a private

wrong), nationalism (restoring public order and a nation's 'honor'), and an abstract desire for 'truth'. (Fenster, 1999: 114)

The X-Files has all three elements Fenster describes; however, the search for 'truth' is the central motivating force for both characters. This is accentuated, almost every week, by the slogan 'The Truth Is Out There' at the end of the opening credits.

A perfect conspiracy?

We had a perfect conspiracy with an alien race – aliens that were coming to reclaim this planet and destroy all human life.

(Cigarette Smoking Man, '*Two Fathers*')

Mulder and Scully have been at the centre of a fantastical conspiracy that threatens the very nature of human existence. As the conspiracy has unravelled over the years, it has been revealed that Earth is being primed for alien colonization. Along with the colonizing alien race has come an alien rebel force that threatens the conspirators and tries to destroy the plans for colonization. (However, it is never really clear who these rebels are, what their motivation is, and if they have plans of their own for the human race.) Although appearing as if Mulder and Scully have been on the periphery of this conspiracy, merely uncovering fragments of information as they investigate the unexplained mysteries of 'the X-files', in actual fact they have been at its heart from the beginning. Scully, assigned to the 'the X-files' to debunk Mulder's work by one of the conspirators (Director Blevin), becomes inexorably linked to the conspiracy when she is abducted and subjected to 'tests'. Following his own lines of inquiry, Mulder uncovers that his father was part of the conspiracy, and ultimately learns that his father is implicated in the abduction of Fox's sister, Samantha.

The two protagonists are portrayed as having different investments in the search for 'the truth' – often picked out as inverting conventional genderings (Wilcox and Williams, 1996). Scully's personal motivation has been one of science and reason: for her, discovering 'the truth' has been about uncovering scientific facts. It has not been a matter of just debunking Mulder's work, but a systematic search for evidence; if that has meant finding facts that substantiate Mulder's argument – as it often has – then this has led Scully to adjust her worldview. As for Mulder, his search for 'the truth' has been more emotional than Scully's, and involves the guilt that he feels over the abduction of his sister. Tortured by the fact he cannot explain her disappearance, Mulder's quest has been to uncover 'the truth' of that night – but what he initially does not know or understand is that his search for Samantha has positioned him in the very centre of the conspiracy.

Samantha! Samantha!! Samantha!!! Mulder's Journey

> I have lived with a fragile faith built on the ether of vague memories from an experience that I could neither prove nor explain. When I was twelve my sister was taken from me, taken by a force that I came to believe was extraterrestrial. This belief sustained me, fuelling a quest for truths that were as elusive as the memory itself.
>
> (Mulder, 'Colony')

Uncovering the facts about the disappearance of his sister has been at the centre of Mulder's motivation and is also an important component of *The X-Files* metatext. Tracking the Samantha storyline as it recurs in the series, we see a pattern of fragmented and contradictory threads. As mentioned previously, Mulder's guilt over losing his sister has caused him great pain; forgoing a high-status career as one of the FBI's top criminal profilers, he is characterized as a loner who has a reputation as an eccentric, and is nicknamed 'Spooky' at work. His obsession with Samantha is simultaneously the driving-force that keeps him searching, and his Achilles Heel, since he will sacrifice almost anything to find 'the truth' about his sister.

The 'classical' conspiracy narrative, according to Fenster (1999: 111), is 'best recognized as putting forth a particular narrative logic that organizes disparate events within a mechanistic, tragic framework'. The Samantha story is typical of the logic that Fenster comments on, and is also a typical narrative arc within *The X-Files*, producing narrative shifts which make new connections and revise previous stories. The arc sometimes offers resolutions, only to unravel them later with the discovery of new evidence, dismissing old conclusions and posing new questions. Nothing is what it seems in light of the conspiracy, and in *The X-Files* there exists only a fragile reality that is constantly shifting. For Mulder, not even the past (his personal history) is sacred; as the conspiracy unfolds fragments of his life, he ends up with a history that proves as elusive as Samantha.

In 'Miracle Man' (1X17) Mulder is plagued by visions of his sister that begin to affect his behaviour and reveal the trauma of her disappearance, opening up the Samantha arc. 'Little Green Men' (2X01) includes a dream sequence that features Mulder's memories of the night Samantha was taken: the Watergate hearing is on television as Mulder and Samantha play – giving a broader conspiratorial landscape for the story (see Graham, 1996). The lights go out and the house begins to shake as blue and red lights pulse through the window from outside. Mulder runs for his father's gun as Samantha calls out for him. Then we see the image that has haunted Mulder ever since: Samantha suspended in thin air, being pulled away into the mysterious light. These fragments of his past reveal the deep motivating force that obsessively pushes Mulder forward, propelling him into the conspiracy.

Samantha next appears in the double episode 'Colony' (2X16) and 'End Game' (2X17), in which an adult Samantha has found her way home. She tells

Mulder the story of her abduction, saying that she was returned three years later with no knowledge of who she was. Raised by the man Mulder and Scully have been investigating, Dr. Dickens (who she describes as 'what you might call alien'), Samantha has come to Mulder for protection against an alien bounty hunter. If Samantha is to be believed, Dr. Dickens is one of a number of alien clones (sent to Earth to live alongside humans) who believe that the stewardship of the planet is being forsaken and that by default they should become its heirs. But their project – mixing alien DNA with human DNA in order to produce a hybrid human/alien race – has not been sanctioned and they are being pursued by the alien bounty hunter. Samantha appeals to Mulder: 'I've got no reason to lie to you. I'm your sister, Fox, you have to trust me' – and he does. Having killed numerous clones who all look like Dr. Dickens, the bounty hunter kidnaps Scully and, in a bungled exchange, both he and Samantha fall into a river. Mulder has regained his sister only to lose her again, but in the following episode it is revealed that 'Samantha' was also a clone and not actually his sister. In a final attempt to gain Mulder's protection, more cloned 'Samanthas' say they know the whereabouts of his real sister. As the bounty hunter systematically kills the clones, the 'Samanthas' vanish, leaving Mulder with nothing but a vague statement from the bounty hunter that Samantha is alive. All Mulder has is the fragmented knowledge of a wider conspiracy that involves a group of humans who are conspiring with the colonizing alien race. The episode concludes with Mulder saying 'I found something I thought I'd lost. Faith to keep looking'. And the quest for 'the truth' continues.

Clones, double agents and 'The Truth'

> I have a feeling we're not being told the entire story here.
> (Mulder, '*F. Emasculata*')

In 'Herrenvolk' (4X10), Samantha appears as an eight-year-old girl. Again she is a clone, part of an agrarian workforce, a drone with no language. Throughout the episode fragmented information is revealed about the mysterious group of men known as 'The Syndicate' (who are conspiring with the alien colonizers, whilst also double-crossing them), and the sinister character known only as the 'Cigarette Smoking Man' (CSM). CSM comes into focus as he continues to be a constant in the conspiracy. When held at gun-point by Mulder in 'Herrenvolk', CSM discloses no more information about the larger conspiracy than to say he knows the whereabouts of Samantha. This makes Mulder draw back, but nothing is revealed that gets him any closer to her or 'the truth'. Here it becomes apparent that Samantha can be used as a weapon against Mulder – a weapon CSM effectively uses to control him again and again.

A CIA agent called Kritschgau reveals in 'Redux' (5X4) and 'Redux II' (5X5) that Mulder has been fed lies and disinformation in order to keep him involved:

> The lies are so deep, the only way to cover them is to create something even more incredible. They invented you. Your regression hypnosis, the story of your sister's abduction, the lies they feed your father. You wanted to believe so badly.
>
> (Kritschgau, *'Redux'*)

Kritschgau suggests that everything Mulder has uncovered is a fabrication, an elaborate ruse to cover up for the US military-industrial complex. Kritschgau's own conspiracy theory is not that aliens are about to colonize but that UFO sightings and stories of alien abductions have been manufactured in order to divert public attention away from a growing weapons war. If Mulder thought he was a player in the game, Kritschgau tells him he is merely a pawn. The conspiracy grows ever bigger and ever darker. Yet as Mulder begins to lose faith in his own convictions, CSM turns up with his sister, telling Mulder that Kritschgau has deceived him with his 'beautiful lies'. According to CSM 'the truth' is that Samantha was returned to Earth, and that he raised her as his own daughter. Face-to-face with evidence – Samantha in the flesh – Mulder is sceptical, but Samantha claims she has had a good life with CSM as her father; however, the meeting gets too intense for Samantha and she runs out. Even though there is a possibility of resolution, the meeting seems like another fruitless encounter; Samantha has appeared only to vanish again, seemingly of her own free will. Although not directly in control of Samantha, CSM lurks in the background, the game playing out according to his rules.

The plot twist is that CSM wants Mulder to work for him, to cross over from his fragmented world to the enlightened world of the conspiracy – and the possibility of a world that includes his sister. Although not convinced by CSM, the vivid connection between these two characters, with Samantha at the centre, is exposed and at the end of 'Redux II' CSM is shot, presumed dead, and left holding a picture of Mulder and Samantha as children. The same photograph finds its way into Mulder's hands and he weeps over the image of his lost childhood. This episode produces another crisis, as Mulder comes face-to-face not only with Samantha but with his own psychological need to find peace. Samantha is the key, he lives to find the pieces of the puzzle that will exonerate him from guilt surrounding her disappearance – that ever-elusive 'truth'.

Fenster (1999) describes the 'classical' conspiracy theory as affirming narrative resolution:

> The resolution returns that which had been either threatened or captured by the conspiracy ... to a relatively secure, stable position free from the centralized power of the conspiracy, and it enables the protagonist to resolve

whatever personal crises established his or her original motivations that led to or were caused by his or her finding the conspiracy. (109)

However, we find little resolution in this arc. Samantha is revealed as bait, used by CSM to try and gain Mulder's allegiance, and although this meeting is an attempt at resolution for Mulder, Samantha remains a fragment of his memory. 'Information has forced on the character a cognitive crisis, and every current and past event becomes subject to reinterpretation' (Fenster, 1999: 112); Mulder's cognitive crisis is Samantha's disappearance; her reappearance always marks a defining moment for him, but it is never sustainable in the trajectory of the conspiracy. Like a ghost from the past, Samantha remains a mystery and this constantly leaves the narrative without conclusion.

Looking for 'Closure'

I just wanted it to be over. (Mulder, '*Closure*')

The narratives around Samantha's disappearance don't seem to enlighten Mulder's path, but instead complicate it. 'The truth' is always in reach but never fully grasped or exposed. Then, in 'Sein Und Zeit' (7X10) and 'Closure' (7X11), all Mulder thinks he knows about his sister unravels before his eyes and the Samantha narrative finally meets some kind of resolution. Through the investigation of a young girl, Amber Lynn LaPierre, who has mysteriously disappeared from her bedroom, Mulder uncovers parallels with earlier cases of suspected child abduction, and he and Scully eventually track down a serial killer who has preyed on children since the 1960s. Unearthing graves and exhuming bodies at the suspect's home, they are surprised to find that Amber Lynn is not among the dead. Mulder also confesses that he is disappointed that they did not uncover the remains of his sister: 'I just wanted it to be over'. Just as Kritschgau called into question Mulder's memories of Samantha's abduction, so now does Scully. Worried about Mulder's mental state, she takes a tape of him undergoing regression hypnosis to an expert within the FBI, who points out that Mulder is feeding his own unconscious desire for his sister to be alive, and tells Scully that Mulder is delusional. The lie has now penetrated Mulder; he is implicated within the conspiracy – the lies no longer lurk in the depths of government, or 'out there', but within him. Mulder's knowledge of Samantha's disappearance disintegrates as he is led by a psychic (Harold Piller) to uncover evidence of another 'truth' within the lie.

In the meantime, Scully uncovers a case file that discloses a high-level investigation into Samantha's disappearance carried out in 1973. CSM signed for its closure. Mulder continues to dig deeper and is led to an Air Force base (by a message from his dead mother, channelled through Piller), where Piller has a vision of children undergoing 'tests' in train cars (the motifs of 'tests' and train cars appear repeatedly in the abduction/conspiracy metatext of *The X-Files*). Although initially sceptical, Mulder finds a handprint in a cement driveway with the name of Samantha written next to it.

Diverting from the conspiracy narrative into spiritual imagery, Piller calls forth the dead, and the ghostly figure of a young boy leads Mulder to find Samantha's diary. Mulder reads that the fourteen-year-old Samantha remembered her brother and family life, but that the 'tests' were stealing her memories, and in the last entry she says she is planning to run away. Searching hospital records, Scully finds evidence of a 'Jane Doe' with signs of paranoia, strange cuts and scars being admitted on the night Samantha ran away. A nurse recalls a smoking man coming to find her – but when the locked door to her room was opened, the nurse said she had disappeared.

Piller's explanation for this disappearance is a spiritual one, rather than anything to do with alien abductions. He explains that Samantha's suffering would have been so great that 'Walk-ins' – 'old souls lurking in starlight who protect other souls from harm that they would have suffered in real life' – came and took her away from this world into the next, saving her from her terrible fate. Mulder follows the ghostly figure of a boy into nearby woods where he discovers the 'ghost' of fourteen-year-old Samantha, who runs into his arms and hugs him. A peaceful Mulder returns to Scully and Piller saying that he is fine, and finally able to say that he is 'free'. A resolution has been reached and closure has been found.

In 'Closure', then, we see a personal revelation for Mulder. There is also affirmation that the main conspirator is CSM, however the conspiracy itself finds no clear resolution and 'the truth' is not illuminated through this narrative:

> Despite its professed intentions of uncovering the plot, the classical conspiracy narrative is inherently ambivalent about uncovering the 'truth' of power and the possibilities of a different future. (Fenster, 1999: 138)

Although the Samantha narrative seems to find resolution, the larger conspiracy of *The X-Files* remains ambivalent, 'the truth' intangible. What seems so ironic about this closure is that the power remains intact, the conspiracy is undeniable and yet Mulder finds himself free. The parting shot of 'Closure' sees Scully framed in the background of Mulder's new-found peace, and in the next conspiracy episode (which marks the last of the seventh season) Mulder is taken away by a mysterious UFO, leaving Scully to uncover 'the truth' of *his* disappearance. Mulder becomes Scully's Samantha and the cycle starts again, the never-ending trajectory of *The X-Files* conspiracy arc continuing, albeit in a new direction.

If we read Samantha as a cipher for 'the truth', then her various appearances – covering different time-frames and at a variety of different ages – raise larger questions about the existence of any tangible 'truth'. Samantha has always eluded Mulder, whether as a clone or as the mysterious figure produced at just the right moment; even in 'Closure' she is a ghostly figure, a faded image that, although comforting, offers nothing more than yet another possible interpretation of her disappearance. Mulder is no nearer to solving the mystery behind her abduction and the larger conspiracy goes on unabated. *The X-Files* seems to confound classical conspiracy structure, ultimately, by endlessly deferring 'the truth'. There is no such thing as unity in *The X-Files* universe, only disparity and confusion as the relentless conspiracy progresses. In this way, then, the Samantha arc, even in its final 'closure', raises yet more questions. We shall return to some of these later in this chapter.

Deceive. Inveigle. Obfuscate: *The X-Files* as conspiracy

All lies lead to the truth

(The X-Files)

Now we have plotted the Samantha arc of *The X-Files*, we want to step back a little, and look at ways the series as a whole has been received and read. Responses to and readings of *The X-Files* have appeared from numerous standpoints, so in this section we want to highlight some of the ways in which the show is understood as indicating something about the age we live in. These readings range from the celebratory to the dismissive, and we want to suggest that they can be read as responses not only to the series itself, but also to the larger 'popular culture of conspiracy' in which we locate *The X-Files*. Let's start with an endorsement for the programme from cyberpunk guru William Gibson, which we can take as representative of one species of *X-Files* reading:

> The show is a chimera. A mutant; a final, brilliantly inbred expression of the Age of Broadcast Television. Like the two-headed dog it is, it manages both to bite the hand that feeds it *and* move phenomenal numbers of units. It is a seamless pop artefact. It is a disturbing and viscerally satisfying expression of where we've come from, where we are today, and all those places where we simultaneously yearn and dread to go. (Gibson, 1998: 9)

Crucial to this kind of reading is the idea that *The X-Files* stands in for, as Lavery, Hague and Cartwright (1996) put it, 'the cultural moment': it is a media product that encapsulates the dreams, hopes, fears and nightmares of our age. Perhaps unsurprisingly, the show is often held up as epitomizing the postmodern, either implicitly or explicitly (Gibson is a good example of the latter). Of course, calling the programme 'postmodern' can itself be a way of celebrating it or of denigrating it – it depends how you feel about postmodernism.

Beyond the description of the show as 'postmodern' (to which we shall return in a while), responses to *The X-Files* often settle on the question of the (cultural) work the series does for its viewers. For celebrants, it offers an all-too-rare moment of intelligent, questioning, unconventional broadcasting:

> I think we live in an age of too much information and easy answers from every kind of expert. Our unsympathetic, materialistic lives have been overly spelled out without the possibility of chance operations or imaginative interventions. Happily, *The X-Files* allows the mass audience, ... habitually held down by numerous institutions like the dreary news reports, to experience the luxury of a questioning imagination. (Lehmann, 1998: 94)

This comment, by the artist Minnette Lehmann, whose work appears in the coffee-table volume *The Art of The X-Files* (1998), is interesting for a number of reasons. Its critique of 'experts' and 'dreary news reports', and its citing of *The X-Files* as the mass audience's moment for questioning are particularly noteworthy in view of the other readings of the show we introduce here.

In a similar vein, the editors of *Deny All Knowledge*, a book of readings of *The X-Files*, write that 'For many viewers, their weekly encounter with the show is an unsettling, sometimes frightening experience that powerfully interrogates a consensus reality that excludes the paranormal' (Lavery, Hague and Cartwright, 1996: 12). Reference to consensus reality – especially as it might be either delivered or complexified by TV – recurs both in Gibson's essay from *The Art of The X-Files*, where it is described as floating, 'like the dollar, the yen, in the irrational moral blindness of market forces' (Gibson, 1998: 10–11) and, in a very different way, in Reeves, Rodgers and Epstein's (1996) essay on cult TV, to which we'd now like to turn our attention.

Reeves, Rodgers and Epstein develop a thesis about the rise of 'cult TV' as a symptom of the transition from Fordism to post-Fordism. This shift, they argue, is indicated by a move from 'lowest-common denominator' network television in the USA (what they name TV I) towards fragmented, niche-marketed programming today (TV II):

> the current prominence of cult TV is ... no harmless freak show in the carnival of American popular culture. Instead, it is a phenomenon that speaks powerfully of a divisive system of taste distinctions that both masks and supports the radical inequalities of the age by dividing the audience into 'insiders' and 'outsiders'. ... In the current prominence of 'cult TV', then, we see evidence of a rewriting of popularity that expresses the deterritorializations and reterritorializations of the decline of television's consensus culture and the weakening of its unifying influences. (Reeves, Rodgers and Epstein, 1996: 24)

In this formulation, TV companies learnt from *Star Trek* the value of a loyal fan-base of 'knowing' viewers, and shifted their production strategies accordingly to tap into 'sophisticated' market-segments with high disposable incomes (in order to milk advertising revenue and licensing agreements for merchandizing). Charting the proliferation of such programming in the US, they single out shows such as *Twin Peaks* and *Beavis and Butthead* as emblematic of this move: these are not 'mass' shows, since they do not mobilize anything like 'consensus culture' (though they may have an impact on the shape consensus culture comes to take). Aligning this slide with the postmodernizing of television, to which they are hostile, Reeves and his colleagues then attempt to salvage *The X-Files* from the postmodern mire:

> *The X-Files* is almost militantly anti-postmodern. Many of the other cult TV shows are contaminated by the tedium of postmodern irony in which cynicism passes for artistry, nihilism is 'cool', sincerity 'sucks', and truth is always already an illusion. ... The assertion that 'The Truth Is Out There' runs counter to postmodernism's doctrine of disbelief. ... Hopefully, the success of *The X-Files* represents yet another rewriting of popularity – only this time, a rewriting whose inclusiveness signals a reinvigoration of consensus culture and a renunciation of the excesses and exclusions of postmodernism. (34–35)

This seems to us a curious reading of the show, given that 'the truth' may be 'out there' but always seems obscured, unreachable, and fakeable. True enough, Mulder and Scully do enact a version of the modern hero quest, exemplified in the figure of the detective (Donald, 1999). But their pursuit of 'the truth' across what Lavery, Hague and Cartwright (1996: 2) call their 'paranormal beat' marks them as different from modernity's detectives, we would argue. Further, the kinds of knowledges and methods that they deploy in order to tail 'the truth' seem to us outside the modern. The shape-shifting Samantha narrative has already suggested that this is no ordinary detective story.

It is precisely that last feature of *The X-Files* that has attracted substantial critical attention from other kinds of 'knowledge-keeper'. In particular, its privileging of 'fringe knowledges' is seen as pedagogically and politically harmful to the viewing public:

> A series called 'The X Files', which pays lip-service to sceptical examination of the paranormal, is skewed heavily towards the reality of alien abductions, strange powers and government complicity in covering up just about everything interesting. Almost never does the paranormal claim turn out to be a hoax or a psychological aberration or a misunderstanding of the natural world. (Sagan, 1997: 351)

For Carl Sagan, then, *The X-Files* is complicit in propagating the irrational in the place of the rational, and for turning people away from 'real' science. As Constance Penley puts it, 'entertainment, for Sagan, is the opposite of enlightenment; popular science and science cannot coexist because popular science ("irrationality") confounds the progress of science ("rationality")'

(Penley, 1997: 5–6). This kind of critique locates the popularity of *The X-Files* in the climate of delegitimation, summed up in one of the show's other famous catch-phrases: *trust no one*. Loss of faith in authority and 'expert knowledge' – governmental or scientific – leaves a space to be filled by alternative explanatory frameworks. The question that might be raised here, is: if we now trust no one, but still need some way to make sense of things, why do we turn to the 'irrational' for answers? This query once attracted the attention of Theodor Adorno, well-known mass-culture-basher, who was troubled by the popularity of astrology in America. We'd like to have a quick look at Adorno's thinking on this matter later, as a way into the question we have posed. First, some remarks to contextualize *The X-Files* in the current 'conspiratorial moment'.

Conspiracy as popular culture

> In the future everyone will be abducted for fifteen minutes.
> (David Robbins, *The Art of The X-Files*)

The X-Files is, of course, only one pop-cultural product currently circulating that has conspiracy at its heart. In this section, we would like to say something about the commodification of conspiracy culture, and also look at the ways in which the growing popularity of so-called 'fringe' beliefs has been critiqued. *The X-Files* is itself heavily implicated in popularizing 'fringe' beliefs, though there were conspiracy culture products in mass circulation long before Mulder and Scully started their mission – many of which have subsequently been folded into *The X-Files* (Graham, 1996). And, of course, outside the 'mainstream' there is a whole conspiracy industry, with countless outlets and products dealing with every conceivable 'fringe' topic (see Fenster, 1999). The possibilities for the production, circulation and consumption of such materials have, in the recent past, been further assisted by cyberspace, itself then implicated in a conspiratorial narrative about the memetic spread of conspiracy culture (Dean, 2000; Thieme, 2000). In the UK, the early success of *The X-Files* helped in the mainstreaming of conspiracy culture, with previously 'fringe' products such as the magazine *Fortean Times* moving out of the shadows of the small press milieu and onto high street newsagents' shelves. For a while, the mass media and popular culture in the UK was swamped by aliens, conspiracies, weird beasts and paranormality. As Peter Knight (1999) notes, of course, a lot of the popular engagement with 'fringe' materials is ironic – epitomized, perhaps, by the SCHWA Corporation's banal, quirky t-shirts and bumper stickers, or by blow-up aliens (see Dean, 1998).

While all this might be read as harmless fad and fun, or – a bit more conspiratorially – as capital's colonization of the counterculture (of which more later), for some critics the rise of conspiracy culture has more sinister overtones. 'Expert' commentaries on the popularization and mainstreaming of

conspiracy culture frequently focus on negative features: conspiracy culture –
like popular culture more broadly – is characterized as at best a distraction, at
worst a wilful misleading (even brainwashing) of the public. Typical of this
mode of critique is Carl Sagan's *The Demon-Haunted World*, cited earlier.
Similar sentiments echo through an earlier work with a different focus:
Theodor Adorno's writing on astrology in 'The Stars Down to Earth'.

Conspiring with Adorno

> People never quite fully believe what they pretend to believe and therefore
> overdo their own beliefs.
>
> (Theodor Adorno, 'The Stars Down to Earth')

'The Stars Down to Earth' offers an analysis of the *Los Angeles Times*
astrology column from the 1950s. Its project, Adorno writes, is the
'investigation of the nature and motivations of some large-scale social
phenomena involving irrational elements in a peculiar way – fused with what
may be dubbed pseudo-rationality' (Adorno, 1994: 34). Given that Adorno is
best known for his work on the culture industry – which we might read itself as
conspiratorial – 'The Stars Down to Earth' traces one way of linking the
'irrational' and popular culture. If we begin by conspiring with Adorno's
reading, we can then maybe move beyond it.

Adorno's study of astrology remains resonant with contemporary culture; in
fact, as Stephen Crook (1994: 1) notes in his introduction to the work's reissue,
the current period, 'in which such irrational phenomena seem to have
proliferated, is also marked by a broader cultural anti-rationalism', witnessed
in New Age cults, religious fundamentalism and deep ecology. 'Adorno's
diagnoses of the authoritarian complicities of astrology and occultism are
directly relevant to these developments' (Crook, 1994: 2) – and we want to see
what light they might shed on conspiracy theory here.

Adorno sees the spread of pseudo-rational thinking – which he more often
refers to as 'semi-erudition' – as a threat to society. He draws parallels between
astrology and popular culture resonant with Carl Sagan's complaints about the
'tabloidization' of science and the rise of 'pseudo-science': 'Much like the
cultural industry, astrology tends to do away with the distinction between fact
and fiction: its content is often overrealistic while suggesting attitudes which
are based on an entirely irrational source' (Adorno, 1994: 50).

Astrology's formula, which Adorno calls 'threat-help' (sounds like trust-risk
to us), has echoes for him in popular culture, too – in soaps and jazz, for
example. And, again echoing his analyses of the culture industries, Adorno sees
astrology as feeding the dependency needs of its consumers:

> What drives people into the arms of the various kinds of 'Prophets of
> Deceit' is not only their sense of dependence and their wish to attribute this

dependence to some 'higher' and ultimately more justifiable sources, but it is also their wish to reinforce their own dependence, not to have to take matters into their own hands. (114)

In the end, for Adorno, astrology is passifying: 'by strengthening the sense of fatality, dependence and obedience, it paralyzes the will to change objective conditions', he writes, adding that 'It can easily be seen how well this suits the over-all purpose of the prevailing ideology of today's cultural industry; to reproduce the *status quo* within the mind of the people' (121).

The receptiveness of people to 'irrational' systems such as astrology is linked, as we have noted, to Adorno's notion of 'semi-erudition'. If, for Fredric Jameson (1995), conspiracy theory is the poor person's cognitive mapping, for Adorno astrology, occultism and other 'fringe' beliefs are 'the metaphysic of dunces' (130): 'Instead of the complicated, strenuous and difficult intellectual processes which might overcome the feeling of drabness by understanding what really makes the world so drab, a desperate short-cut is sought which offers both spurious understanding and flight into a supposedly higher realm' (117). Astrology thus aids the 'semi-erudite', since it offers answers that are 'pseudo-rational' – and that is about the best the semi-erudite can hope for, given Adorno's typologization of that mind-set. Cranking up the conspiratorial narrative which the semi-erudite buys into, Adorno goes on to flesh out this particular world-view, arguing that people's experience of feeling powerless to control their own fates leads them to search for answers in the 'irrational': 'Astrology takes care of this mood by translating it into a pseudo-rational form, thus somehow localizing free-floating anxieties in some definite symbolism'. (Adorno, 1994: 115–116). For Adorno, however, this survival strategy is misguided, and ultimately dangerous, because it is intellectually impoverished.

At one level, there are clear links between Adorno's astrological readings and two works more closely related to conspiracy: Richard Hofstadter's *The Paranoid Style in American Politics* (1965), and Elaine Showalter's *Hystories* (1997). In the latter, 'hysterias' ranging from Gulf War Syndrome to alien abduction are also read as cultural 'symptoms', while *The Paranoid Style* intentionally deploys the term 'paranoid' pejoratively to refer to fringe groups, especially those on the American political right. The diagnoses offered by Hofstadter and Showalter are subject to insightful critique by Peter Knight (1999), who argues that typifying those who believe in conspiracy theories as delusional or paranoid is an inadequate response to the task of thinking conspiracies as 'symbolic and sometimes conscious expressions about society, culture and history' (Knight, 1999: 39). Dismissing conspiracy as a (pre-dominantly psychological) failing – as irrational, sloppy and vulgar, as Hofstadter does – is, for Knight, to miss the social and cultural work that conspiracy theory does. Principally – and here Knight concurs with Adorno – conspiracy culture 'enable[s] a popular engagement ... with notions of global connectedness' (43), even if the connections it makes are unforeseen, unexpected or unorthodox. So, instead of analyses like those discussed so far, which see conspiratorial narratives bolstering feelings of dependency and powerlessness among their consumers, Knight suggests that imagining the world's fate in the grip of conspiring agents at least 'maintain[s] a strategic fiction that contemporary history *is controllable* – albeit by the enemy' (45; our emphasis):

> The proliferation of a popular culture of paranoia needs to be understood not so much as an intellectually impoverished rejection of the complexity of sociological explanation as an attempt to rethink it, to combine a sense of the systematic nature of oppression with a commitment to holding somebody responsible. (Knight, 1999: 45)

Ultimately, Knight calls for a reading of conspiracy that is both symptomatic and sympathetic. Rather than passifying the 'semi-erudite', conspiracy theories can be seen in this way to offer the possibility of agency. Even if readers don't believe in conspiracy theories, instead approaching them ironically, conspiracy culture articulates some kind of critique of the *status quo*, rather than, as Adorno would have it, simply reaffirming it. While Adorno (and, indeed, Hofstadter, Jameson, Showalter *et al.*) recognizes that the 'irrational' helps people order and focus their paranoia ('translating it into a pseudo-rational form, thus somehow localizing free-floating anxieties in some definite symbolism'), this is posited as a distraction from the real conditions of existence (which only science – and social science) can truly reveal. As Adorno writes in 'Theses Against Occultism':

> Superstition is knowledge, because it sees together the ciphers of destruction scattered on the social surface; it is folly because in all its death-wish it still clings to illusions: expecting from the transfigured shape of society misplaced in the skies an answer that only a study of real society can give. (Adorno, 1994: 130)

From the trajectory of our discussion, it should by now be apparent that we think a 'study of real society' must include a study of conspiracy culture, and all its associated 'fringe' beliefs, as a paradoxical but central feature of today's 'social surface'.

Conspiracy as culture

> I'm not entirely certain whether it's better to believe that everything is shaped by discourse, or by the Trilateral Commission.
>
> (Peter Knight, 'A Plague of Paranoia')

Adorno's critique of astrology junkies, then, is heavily underwritten by the stance he takes towards the culture industry as a purveyor of mind-candy. That kind of critique is common among intellectuals writing about conspiracy culture, as we have seen – who too readily consign it to the frivolous realm of popular culture. As Mark Fenster sums up, at the end of *Conspiracy Theories*:

> Although it may be in some way 'resistant' to dominant historical and political epistemologies, 'populist pleasure' becomes a retreat into debilitating fantasies of all-powerful, secret groups and a powerless, virtually hopeless, citizenry unwilling and unable to sense the truth.
>
> (Fenster, 1999: 219)

All-powerful secret groups and a powerless, unseeing citizenry? This sounds a bit like false consciousness, or maybe ideology: 'those who are in ideology believe themselves by definition outside ideology: one of the effects of ideology is the practical *denegation* of the ideological character of ideology by ideology' and so on (Althusser, 1971: 168). You can't tell us that *that* doesn't sound like conspiracy theorizing. As Knight's wry comment suggests, the only difference between the intellectual and the 'semi-erudite' might be in the names we give to the agents of our conspiracies. The kinds of readings produced in the space of the academy about, for example, globalization, or postmodernism, or capitalism, or cultural populism, or multiculturalism, often have more than a trace of the conspiratorial about them. To take one more-or-less random example: Slavoj Žižek's (1997) essay on 'identity politics' as a side-show distracting us from the all-devouring infestations of multinational capitalism doesn't sound to us too dissimilar to the words of Timothy McVeigh or the Unabomber. But one is afforded a certain kind of credibility while the others are dismissed as the rants of maniacs: why is it easier for us to believe in discourse than the Trilateral Commission?

Interestingly, while critical commentaries often side-step the issue of whether or not there is any 'truth' to conspiracy theories, or alien visitations, or whatever, reading them instead symbolically, Erik Davis (1998: 237) suggests that we actually find it *easier* to explain these things away as 'a symptom of some rather tumultuous sociocultural conditions', rather than *believe* them. Similarly, abduction specialist John Mack (1994) argues that the 'ontological shock' experienced by abductees is so extreme, in terms of calling for a realignment of all their beliefs, that it might be 'easier' for them (and the rest of us) to hide behind other, Earthly explanations (though in his view these are primarily the psychological 'explanations' offered by therapists rather than the conspiratorial 'explanations' explored here).

Is that why Mulder's poster says 'I want to believe' rather than just 'I believe'? – because, like the rest of us, Fox Mulder is only ever partially able to escape the rational-sceptical iron cage of modernity. As Davis says, that midway point is where we currently find ourselves,

148

dancing between logic and archaic perception, myth and modernity, reason and its own hallucinatory excess. And it is precisely this tension, and not some abdication of critical intelligence, that now leads so many intelligent and curious minds to conspiracies, alternative histories, paranormal phenomena, and pop science fiction. (Davis, 1998: 235)

In this 'excluded middle', it seems, we can — maybe indeed *should* — believe in discourse *and* the Trilateral Commission, not out of ironic postmodern relativism but out of a commitment to 'challenging what constitutes a reasonable explanation of current events', as Knight (1999: 45) puts it. Davis's formulation certainly sounds to us like a neat definition of the terrain *The X-Files* occupies, traced by the Samantha storyline. If we can begin to rethink conspiracy culture away from paranoia and delusion – if we can begin to use the term non-pejoratively – then we might be able to produce those symptomatic and sympathetic readings Peter Knight calls for. Recognizing *conspiracy theory as social and cultural theory* (and vice versa) seems to us like a good place to start. So, where does that leave us with *The X-Files*?

Coda: watching *The X-Files* with Adorno

Something is behind everything and we wait always, with baited breath, because something is always out there and in the end, the truth is anybody's to invent.

(Collier Schorr, *The Art of The X-Files*)

In the manner of *The X-Files*, then, we would like to end with our own *denouement*; and again like *The X-Files*, this needn't work to resolve all the questions raised in our essay – in fact, it might throw up even more questions, or red herrings, or plot twists, maybe linking in with other aspects of conspiracy culture currently circulating ...

The title of this coda is inspired by two things, apparently a million miles apart, that we want to bring together in our closing moments. The first is an essay by John Hutnyk (1998), who takes Theodor Adorno to 'World Music' festival Womad, in order to think through ideas about resistance, commodification and cultural hybridity with him. The second is one of the works featured in *The Art of The X-Files*, entitled 'Watching X-Files' and made by the artists Komar and Melamid. 'Watching X-Files' is a photographic tableau featuring a badly home-made alien sitting, Coke in one hand and crisps in the other, in front of a big TV in an ordinary-looking living room. It is meant, the artists write, as a commentary on the fact that aliens are currently imagined as of superior intelligence to humans – instead they depict a 'couch alien' doing just what we all do: watching telly. So, in our own small act of textual poaching, we'd like to figure Adorno as our own 'couch alien' – after all, if

Hutnyk can drag him round Womad, surely we can sit with him to watch *The X-Files*.

Komar and Melamid's ironic take on *The X-Files* reminds us of Adorno's emphasis on the dialectic between 'high art' and 'popular culture', which Hutnyk also samples in his attempt to at least partially redeem Adorno's 'maligned' reputation. The problem Hutnyk focuses on, in the context of Womad, is how to think through the value of 'oppositional spaces' carved out *within* commodity culture; bringing Komar and Melamid together with Mulder and Scully (while Adorno nibbles a Twiglet and sips a soda on the sofa) raises, for us, a similar kind of question. Indeed, in terms of some of the ways *The X-Files* is thought about and written about, this question looms large. For William Gibson, as we have already seen, the fact that the show manages (in his eyes) to be both subversive and economically successful is a cause for celebration. To be populist while suggesting alternative worldviews marks *The X-Files*, for Gibson, as one such oppositional space. The fact that it exists within the belly of corporate media culture makes it yet more subversive, since it can grab a more substantial share of the audience than a xeroxed conspiracists' fanzine (of the kind published by the hero of the movie *Conspiracy Theory*).

Hutnyk is more ambivalent on this process in his Adorno-assisted reading of 'World Music', which he reads as inevitably contaminated by contact with multinational capital (he only rates the 'underground' as having political purchase, so presumably he'd prefer xeroxed fanzines to *The X-Files*). This argument seems too limiting – maybe even a bit conspiratorial, as arguments about recuperation and co-option often tend to be. Gibson's line, on the other hand, seems too optimistic, since there are limitations and compromises imposed by working in the belly of the beast.

Reeves and his colleagues, for example, berate cult TV for forcing a 'taste distinction' between those *in-the-know* and those *in-the-dark* – but, to bring Adorno's anti-astrology angle in, the question then becomes one of what it is that those in-the-know know, where they get their knowledge from, and what they then do with it. If what they 'know' is an accumulation of 'fringe knowledges', then for some critics being in-the-know is in fact being more in-the-dark (or, perhaps, 'semi-erudite') than those who are dismissed as being in-the-dark. As with Mulder's quest to find 'the truth' of Samantha's abduction, each fragment of knowledge turns out to be non-knowledge, a dead-end, a wrong-turn. In the end, after longing for (but simultaneously dreading) 'the truth' about Samantha for so long – the same longing that has propelled his search for the other 'truths' contained in the X-files – Mulder says 'I'm free'. But what is he freed from? Free from having to 'want to believe', or from having to 'overdo' his beliefs? Free from having to scrape away the layers of 'lies'? Free to get a life? If this is Mulder's 'closure', then it seems to mark a turning-away from everything that has driven *The X-Files* so far. (Of course, as many X-Philes have no doubt already speculated, offering Mulder 'closure' might be the best way to shake him off the Big Conspiracy he's been chasing –

something which Cigarette Smoking Man has attempted repeatedly through the series, as we've already seen.)

So, while it might seem like an indulgence for us to call up Adorno as a 'couch alien' to watch *The X-Files* with, he has said some provocative and interesting things. His argument against astrology and his figuring of the 'semi-erudite' may have really only given us something to argue with, but he's nevertheless opened up for us a space to consider the intersections of knowledge-forms, commodity-forms and culture-forms that give shape to the contemporary landscape of conspiracy. By exploring how a popular cultural text like *The X-Files* narrativizes conspiracy and 'fringe knowledges' through the contortions of the Samantha arc, we hope to have brought some of these threads together. It might not be closure, but we hope that it adds to the project of rethinking conspiracy theory.

Bibliography

Adorno, T., (1994), *The Stars Down to Earth and Other Essays on the Irrational in Culture*, (edited by Stephen Crook). London: Routledge.

Althusser, L., (1971), *Lenin and Philosophy*. New York: Monthly Review Press.

Crook, S., (1994), 'Introduction: Adorno and Authoritarian Irrationalism', in Adorno, T. (ed.), *The Stars Down to Earth and Other Essays on the Irrational in Culture*, (edited by Stephen Crook). London: Routledge: 1–33.

Davis, E., (1998), *TechGnosis: Myth, Magic and Mysticism in the Age of Information*. London: Serpent's Tail.

Dean, J., (1998), *Aliens in America: Conspiracy Cultures from Outerspace to Cyberspace*. Ithaca: Cornell University Press.

Dean, J., (2000), 'Webs of Conspiracy', in Herman, A. and Swiss, T. (eds), *The World Wide Web and Contemporary Cultural Theory*. London: Routledge: 61–76.

Donald, J., (1999), *Imagining the Modern City*. London: Athlone.

Fenster, M., (1999), *Conspiracy Theories: Secrecy and Power in American Culture*. Minneapolis: University of Minnesota Press.

Gibson, W., (1998), 'The Absolute at Large', in Heiferman, M. and Kismaric, C. (eds), *The Art of The X-Files*. London: Voyager/HarperCollins: 8–11.

Graham, A., (1996), 'Are You Now or Have You Ever Been?' Conspiracy Theory and *The X-Files*', in Lavery, D., Hague, A. and Cartwright, M. (eds), *Deny All Knowledge: Reading The X-Files*. London: Faber and Faber: 52–62.

Hofstadter, R., (1965), *The Paranoid Style in American Politics*. New York: Alfred A. Knopf.

Hutnyk, J., (1998), 'Adorno at Womad: South Asian Crossovers and the Limits of Hybridity-Talk', *Postcolonial Studies*, 1: 401–426.

Jameson, F., (1995), *The Geopolitical Aesthetic: Cinema and Space in the World System*. London: BFI.

Knight, P., (1999), ' "A Plague of Paranoia": Theories of Conspiracy Theory Since the 1960s', in Schultz, N.L. (ed.), *Fear Itself: Enemies Real and Imagined in American Culture*. West Lafayette: Purdue University Press: 23–49.

Lavery, D., Hague, A. and Cartwright, M., (1996), 'Introduction: Generation X – *The X-Files* and the Cultural Moment', in Lavery, D., Hague, A. and Cartwright, M. (eds), *Deny All Knowledge: Reading The X-Files*. London: Faber and Faber: 1–21.

Lehmann, M., (1998), Untitled text to accompany artwork, in Heiferman, M. and Kismaric, C. (eds), *The Art of The X-Files*. London: Voyager/HarperCollins: 94.

Mack, J., (1994), *Abduction: Human Encounters with Aliens*. London: Simon and Schuster.

Penley, C., (1997), *NASA/TREK: Popular Science and Sex in America*. London: Verso.

Reeves, J., Rogers, M. and Epstein, M., (1996), 'Rewriting Popularity: the Cult *Files*', in Lavery, D., Hague, A. and Cartwright, M. (eds), *Deny All Knowledge: Reading The X-Files*. London: Faber and Faber: 22–35.

Sagan, C., (1997), *The Demon-Haunted World: Science as a Candle in the Dark*. London: Headline.

Schorr, C., (1998), Untitled text to accompany artwork, in Heiferman, M. and Kismaric, C. (eds), *The Art of The X-Files*. London: Voyager/HarperCollins: 138.

Showalter, E., (1997), *Hystories: Hysterical Epidemics and Modern Culture*. London: Picador.

Thieme, R., (2000), 'Stalking the UFO Meme', in Bell, D. and Kennedy, B. (eds), *The Cybercultures Reader*. London: Routledge: 230–236.

Wilcox, R. and Williams, J., (1996), ' "What Do You Think?" *The X-Files*, Liminality, and Gender Pleasure', in Lavery, D., Hague, A. and Cartwright, M. (eds), *Deny All Knowledge: Reading The X-Files*. London: Faber and Faber: 99–120.

Žižek, S., (1997), 'Multiculturalism, or, the Cultural Logic of Multinational Capitalism', *New Left Review*, 225: 28–52.

Conspiracy, corporate culture and criticism

Warren Smith

In this chapter I want to engage with the relationship between contemporary corporate culture and recent attempts to criticise its expansionary and increasingly pervasive influence.[1] I use the term corporate culture to suggest the development of global consumerism constructed via international brands and manipulated by transnational corporations whose influence appears to transcend national governance. At the same time, these trends have energized a form of popular critique that attacks both their social and economic consequences. I shall give particular attention to Naomi Klein's (2000) *No Logo*. Called 'the Das Kapital of the growing anti-corporate movement' (Viner, 2000), *No Logo* has, at the time of writing, been given much media attention. Whilst its critique is implicitly informed by critical theory, it shows a preoccupation with how the products of corporate culture both shape and are then shaped by, the forms and methods of critique. However it is uncomfortable with this relationship and consequently searches for a sense of authenticity that, perhaps unlike the critical theorists, it finds difficulty giving voice.

I shall argue that one of the ways in which we can analyse the complicity of this relationship is via the language of conspiracy theorizing. My starting point here is that our engagement with capitalist institutions is, and has always been, a prime site for conspiracy theory. Shadowy cabals like The Illuminati, the Masons, the Bilderbergers, the Insiders, the Trilateralists, the John Birch Society, the Council on Foreign Relations and FEMA have often been proposed as *behind* the workings of capital (see for example Vankin, 1996). Now in the age of globalization, similar arguments are constructed. The production of international trade and investment rights that supersede local interests is, some suggest, being pursued surreptitiously by transnational organizations like the International Monetary Fund, the World Bank and the World Trade Organization that are heavily influenced by powerful corporations. A process is steadily unfolding without scrutiny and where accountability is uncertain. The WTO's multinational agreement on trade, which has been under negotiation for nearly three years, aims to facilitate the unrestricted movement of capital. It will prevent individual countries, regions or towns from imposing specific conditions relating to consumer and environmental protection or employment rights. The WTO, in the words of its director-general, is engaged in a long-term project to 'write the constitution of a single global economy'. Or as one official anonymously told the *Financial Times*, 'This is where governments collude in private against their domestic pressure groups' (De Jonquieres, 1998).

Critics warn of a steady power shift from nation state to multi-national corporations. Within an environment of corporate pacts and secret negotiation between unelected bureaucrats the nature of competition is changing. A new system of regulation serves to minimize competition between companies but maximize it between workers and the wider community. Consumers are unstable elements to be controlled. In a favourite resource of protesters, James Randall, the president of Archer Daniels Midland Corporation was recently secretly taped talking to some of his associates, 'The other corporations are our friends and our customers and our suppliers are our enemies' he admitted (Grossman, 1998).

Yet for this chapter, this is only a stimulus, a provocation. In other words, it notes that globalization is attractive to conspiracy theorists. Certainly, conspiracy theory is active in these areas. However the production of conspiracy *explanations* to explicate or expose is often entertaining, but they are not particularly relevant and should not occupy us for too long. This is for two reasons. Firstly, they do not adequately capture the way we engage with the products of capital. They suggest passivity on *our* part, and omnipotence on *theirs* (whilst assuming of course that there is such a thing as *them* and *us*). This, as I will show, means that we should follow Jameson (1988) and reject this form of conspiracy theory as an *over-determined* compulsion. This is the desire to deal with the complexities of post-industrial society by collecting up its disparate elements in a manageable, if compulsively horrific, package. But by trying to say too much, it ends up saying nothing.

An over-determined approach therefore forgets that the forces of capital are always fragmented. There are many divisions within corporate management. Goals and strategies are never as clearly defined and instigated as over-determined conspiracy theory proposes. Expedience, irrationality and happen-stance are equally powerful explanations. Yet recognizing that management is a fragmented terrain is only part of the story. Another aspect is to point out that market economics requires collusion. This is not the simple pluralist position that some form of mutual dependence leads to (more often than not) a degree of compromise. Instead it recognizes how we work together to maintain certain taken-for-granteds. At a fundamental level the workings of capital require that we must believe that the pieces of paper that we use to signify value are attached to something other than themselves. What gives them value is our acceptance that they have value. Paul Auster (1997) tells of the novelist's H.L. Hume's apparently deranged attempt to initiate an economic revolution by undermining this belief. His strategy was simple. By dividing his substantial inheritance into fifty-dollar bills and then distributing them randomly and liberally he hoped to create a chain reaction of collective doubt about the value of money.

But attempting to dispose of conspiracy theory in this way presumes that the over-determined reading is its only form. Fragmentation and difference applies not only to the objects of conspiracy theory, but also to conspiracy theory itself. A reading of conspiracy theory as over-determined, is itself over-determined. It is often pointed out that the literal meaning of *conspire* is 'to breathe together'. This implies the participation in a social reality. As Paul Auster's story shows, we must work together to maintain the conceit that pieces of paper carry value. But importantly conspiracy theory here does not leave us lost in a social/psychic prison of our own making. For within this mess of oppression and collusion, information and dis-information, there is a belief, a desire, albeit uncertain, of something that stands outside. The classic statement of late 20th/early 21st conspiracy culture is the X-Files '*I Want to Believe*'. In Fox Mulder's heartfelt, but doubting quests, scepticism is combined with the conviction, or at least the hope, that '*The Truth is Out There*'.

Hence the blurb on the back cover of Klein's *No Logo* implores us to 'Forget Generation X and say hello to Generation Why'. It may be uncertain, confused, but it is pursuing *something*. However I will, in my conclusion, present one final twist. Television ratings suggest that we have grown tired of Mulder's never ending search for the truth. In a nice piece of inter-textuality he has been replaced by the completely doubt-less T-1000.[2] I want to tentatively suggest in closing, that some of the prime sites that might, in the recent past, been reasonably associated with a conspiratorial style of thinking are beginning to move in a different direction. Part of this new direction indicates a growing weariness with 'Generation Why's' stumbling for authenticity.

Cycles of conspiracy

A sense of the changing popular forms of conspiracy theory and their relationship to societal trends is provided by Ryan and Kellner (1988). They argue that the cycle of conspiracy motion pictures produced in the 1970s indicated a shift in social and political trajectory from criticism to pessimism as the political radicalism of the 1960s was replaced by a darker, more pessimistic mode. Whilst in the 1960s social attitudes like patriotism, trust and government were attacked from outside by the counterculture, in the 1970s they began to implode via scandals like Watergate. Thus they point out that the 1970s saw a cycle of films in which society is depicted as controlled by corrupt economic and political elites. These include *Klute* (1971), *Executive Action* (1973), *Chinatown* (1974), *The Parallax View* (1974), *All the President's Men* (1976) and *Network* (1976). In *Network* a newscaster, previously a populist critic of society is converted to the ideology of big business, asserting that, 'the world is a business ... one vast and ecumenical holding company, for whom all men will work to serve a common profit, in which all men will hold a share of stock, all necessities provided, all anxieties tranquillized, all boredom amused' (Ryan and Kellner, 1988: 101).

Thereafter, Ryan and Kellner (1988) argue that a more positive sense of the future emerged which manifested itself in the ideological conservativism of the 1980s. But this return of conservatism was borne of something of a paradox.

Although the 1970s saw a liberal-led critique of the institutions of power, the liberal inability to suggest change that was not itself institution-led sowed the seeds of its own downfall. In other words, they had succeeded in undermining confidence in all institutions, including their own. The result was the turn to the market. In other words, the liberal paranoia contributed unintentionally to more insidious developments. This is close to the dangers of conspiracy theory highlighted by Jameson (1984). Jameson warns against a particular fixation with 'immense communication and computer networks' which blind us to the complexity and actual reach of modern day multinational capitalism. The general diagnosis is similar. That a mesmerised, compulsive over-concentration on garish 'horrors' provides a hysterical form of critique that has its own detrimental consequences. In other words, we become distracted. We take our eye off the ball.

It's possible to revisit this cycle. For instance, to argue that the contemporary attempts to apply conspiracy theory to the process of globalization represents a return to the 1970s' paranoid style; an obsession, in other words, with exposing the workings of (corrupt) élites. And whilst I have admitted that this possibility has reenergized conspiracy theory, even that some over-determined conspiracy theories are back in circulation, I don't think that is where conspiracy theory should be, or is, leading us. I have mentioned the role of the *X-Files* in the explosion of conspiracy culture in the late 20th Century and intimated how it plays with the possibility of knowing. Fox Mulder searches for a truth that we, and he, know can never be fully attained. Whilst conspiracy theory in the 1970s tended towards the belief that there are machinations that can be known, more recent contemporary conspiracy theory is preoccupied by the difficulties of knowledge. Like Mulder, our pursuit of truth is grounded, almost thwarted, by the question of whether truth is possible. In this respect, it reflects the uncertainties and complicity of late-capitalist life. Its response therefore is not the over-determined explanations that Jameson rejects. This is nicely expressed by Stewart (1999: 18–19), conspiracy theory, she explains, 'channels the contradictions of a late capitalist world fuelled by difference and uniformity, desire and despair, the bureaucratic self and the romantic action hero ... Conspiracy theory channels both the up side and the down side of things: progress and abjection, enchantment and disenchantment'. Conspiracy theory then becomes about sharing experience in a context of mass information. But it does not as Jameson (1984) seems to suggest seek utility in locating power in labyrinthine networks of information. The problem is that it finds that these orderings are infinite. The result, as Bud Hopkins (1988) admits, is 'I'm so sceptical, that I find it beyond me to deny the possibility of anything'. The question then, is what purchase this form of conspiracy theory has on contemporary corporate culture.

Colonization and consumerism

It is not coincidental that many contemporary conspiracy theories centre on alien activity; of course the foundations of the *X-Files* are built on an abduction narrative. Jodi Dean (1998) has usefully used the alien abduction narrative to reflect upon contemporary society. Metaphors of colonization, she argues, envisage borders to be penetrated and resources to be exploited, but also the possibility of resistance, independence and emancipation. Abduction denies rigid boundaries; things happen behind our backs, things have been done to us that we don't remember and perhaps don't care to remember. These narratives present a preoccupation with truth, but without any promise of resolution. We are left with circling questioning, 'Are UFOs real? Are they responsible for crop circles and cattle mutilations? Does the government know? Is it covering up evidence of crashed saucers? And are aliens really abducting people from their beds and cars, examining, probing, and tracking them through implants? As an ever-proliferating dispersion of statements around the truth of aliens, the UFO discourse lures us into a confrontation with truth. It compulsively repeats questions of truth, whether in its eruptions into currents in mainstream cultures or within the studies, analyses, and testimonials of those working actively to capture and comprehend fugitive alien truth' (Dean, 1988: 14). The difficulty that we find, as Dean finally suggests, is that we cannot fight abduction, merely try to recover our memories. Even then we cannot decide whether we would prefer them to be false or to expose an alien plot (pp. 181).

These are contemporary preoccupations. But I want to begin to develop how they relate to contemporary critical engagements with corporate culture and its products. Earlier I indicated how critical theory has, at least implicitly, influenced these trends.[3] Of course, *colonization* is a central motif here. It represents a concern with authenticity when a sense of authenticity feels threatened. It symbolizes the desire to penetrate the various 'jargons of authenticity' (Adorno, 1964). However I suggest that this confidence, the attempt to get *behind* the 'jargon' of authenticity, is unavailable in a post-colonized world. As conspiracy theory has lost confidence in the capacity to capture some essential truth, so criticism has become more preoccupied with the *possibility* of authenticity rather than the *nature* of authenticity.

Canadian journalist Naomi Klein's (2000) *No Logo* is an important recent document emanating from this environment. *No Logo* describes the creation of what Klein terms 'a third culture'. This is an environment completely colonized by corporate image making, a self-enclosed universe of brand name products, brand name people and brand name media. Here what we once understood as 'culture' becomes suspended in 'arrested development' (Goldman and Papson, 1996). In other words it is increasingly difficult to discern what it would look like without corporate involvement.

Culture is increasingly raided for marketing opportunities. There are a number of advertising agencies – *Sputnik*, *The L. Report* and *Bureau de Style* – that offer reports from the cutting edge of youth culture. Sounding something like stalkers, *Sputnik* founders Janine Lopiano-Misdom and Joanne De Luca outline the importance of tracking key cultural movers, 'how do you know they are the "right" ones – have you been in their closets? Trailed their daily routines? Hung out with them socially? Are they the core consumers? Or the mainstream followers?' At the same time marketing has been absorbed into the attitudes of both the consumers and producers of these cultures. Seabrook (2000) discusses the concept of the 'marketer within'. 'Artists' are so attuned to the marketplace that 'selling out' is no longer meaningful since they produce their art with a marketing angle 'built-in'. Similarly consumers expect the product to be available, packaged and cleverly sold. They notice if tie-ins are absent.

But these skills are often turned back on the instigators. Culture jamming, 'adbusting' and 'subvertising' involves undermining the message of corporate communications through parody and caricature. Yet of course this involves great media knowledge and an undoubted affinity, however ambivalent, for the seductive spectacles of advertising. Culture jammers are able to recognize, interpret and seamlessly twist media messages. This ability produces some tensions. The most famous culture jammers, *Adbusters*, have been criticized for their growing lines of anti-consumer 'products' – not only 'toolboxes' for culture jamming but posters, stickers and T-shirts, some of which somewhat ironically publicized '*Buy Nothing Day*'. The dangers of being compromised by commerciality are strong. Douglas Rushkoff (1994) who in *Media Virus: Hidden Agendas in Popular Culture* was perhaps the first to provide case studies of culture jamming, hacking and media manipulation and also exposed some dubious business links between *Wired* magazine and the *Global Business Network* think tank, was himself soon criticized in the *New York Times* (25/11/96) for accepting large consultancy fees for the secrets of his research. His later *Coercion* (Rushkoff, 1999) reads like a lengthy admission of naivety. His harmless desire to take their money to tell advertisers that the public has become too sophisticated to be taken in by advertiser's messages quickly got translated into courses like 'Giving birth to mutant ideas in a commercial context'. Rushkoff's (1999: 258) original hopes for the Internet as a community-based medium become increasingly threatened by the corporate take-over of bandwidth and their attempts to reconfigure it as 'the next great broadcast technology'.

Likewise since culture jammers show great media awareness, their efforts are increasingly incorporated by marketing campaigns. There are many examples of this. Good examples are the *Nike* campaign which used the slogan 'I am not/A target market/I am an athlete' and *Sprite's* 'Image Is Nothing' campaign which featured a young black man saying that all his life he has been bombarded with media lies telling him that soft drinks will make him a better athlete or more attractive until he realized that 'image is nothing'. Diesel jeans have actually incorporated the political content of adbusting's anti-corporate attacks. One of the most popular methods is to juxtapose conflicting images. Diesel's campaigns consist of a series of ads within ads. In one a glamorous, but extremely thin, blonde is pictured on the side of a bus that is packed with frail workers. The advertisement is selling '*Brand O*' diet with the slogan, 'There's no limit to how thin you can get' (Klein, 2000: 298–99).

Klein's (2000) analysis has different facets. Perhaps its most powerful element is its questioning of the trickle-down assumptions of the so-called Washington consensus. This is the belief that free trade promotes global economic growth that provides poorer countries with infusions of foreign capital and the latest technology. In time, it is argued, greater prosperity will lead to better working conditions and improved human rights. There are some poignant moments when a Mickey Mouse clad Indonesian Nike worker, who had until then had happily bought into the American dream, tries to adjust to the information that the trainers that she produced for $2 a day, sell in the USA for $120 a pair. Klein also argues that the preoccupation with identity politics in the 1980s and 1990s aided the expansion of corporate power and influence. Whilst attention was occupied elsewhere, capitalism became increasingly uncontrolled. Worse still, these identities have been translated into target markets.

It is here that the waters become somewhat muddier. Klein both recognizes the power of the corporate world to absorb and reconfigure cultural identities, even previous points of protest, but retains an optimistic belief that this can be resisted. But there is a more pessimistic reading that is testament to the amorphous evasiveness of capital. This is Adorno's (1973) point that opposition is constantly absorbed, 'It is squirted like grease into the same machinery it once wanted to assail'. As Goldman and Papson (1996) have argued, what is most powerful about the contemporary commodity form is not increasing levels of alienation, but rather, something Marx did not predict. This is how the system of signification that gives the commodity its context for meaning is strengthened by the very knowledge that attempts to create a critical space for opposition. In other words, the contemporary manifestation of the commodity-form has at its roots, critique – a form of knowledge that attempts to resist commodification. Klein seems unlikely to be persuaded to take the corporate shilling to peddle her message (although she has had to fend off criticisms that *No Logo* is published in the UK by Flamingo, part of the Rupert Murdoch owned HarperCollins group). It might be harshly suggested that with a family background securely placed in the North American liberal élite she doesn't have to. But we might consider the probability of a Rushkoff-like, depressed sequel in which she accounts for the dissipation of the protest movements in which she invested much hope and the return to strength of the *Nike* brand. Time will tell. But for now, the most powerful theme emanating from *No Logo* is not the machinations of capital. Nor is it the re-energization of protest. Instead it is the beguiling, but elusive, pursuit of authenticity.

Klein's (2000: xiii–xv) opening to *No Logo* is so problematic in relation to what follows that it has to be deliberate. She tells us that she lives in an old industrial area of garment factories in Toronto. This exists in a state of 'post-industrial limbo' in which the surviving garment producers co-exist with a select group of loft and studio dwellers. These perceptive few know that they are playing their part in a 'piece of urban performance art' but they 'do their best not to draw attention to the fact'. But horrifyingly, this delicate balance was disturbed when City Hall saw fit to commission a series of art installations to celebrate the history of the area. Steel figures of women sewing machinists were sited alongside statues of striking workers carrying placards. But worse, an eleven and half foot high brass thimble was located on the *corner of Klein's block*. The floodgates had opened and subsequently many of the old factory buildings were converted into 'loft-living' complexes with names like '*The Candy Factory*'.

Those readers beginning to become concerned are quickly reassured to read that so far her landlord has refused to 'sell off our building as condominiums with exceptionally high ceilings'. He has a few garment tenants remaining whose businesses are too small to move to Asia and who are holding out against using home workers. The rest of the building is rented out to 'yoga instructors, documentary film producers, graphic designers and writers and artists with live/work spaces'. We are left to assume that the occupants of *The Candy Factory* have rather more mundane jobs and perhaps that this leaves them unequipped to subtly traverse the boundaries of (in)authenticity. In a *Guardian* interview (Viner, 2000) Klein talks about the colonization of space; 'All my parents wanted was the open road and a VW camper ... That was enough escape for them ... (but) now it feels as if there is no open space anywhere' (p. 21). She recalls her frustrated aspirations when she was younger; wanting to be a traveller, the Lonely Planet has done it first. Wanting to produce avant-garde art, she found that it had been made into birthday cards.

Whilst it would be slightly hypocritical to be too sniffy about Klein's dreams of untrammelled virgin pastures, there is something here that suggests the 'most fashionable kid in school'. This involves quickly abandoning anything that has become too popular whether it is a rock band or an avant-garde artist. But of course it is a form of these desires that sustain the whole fashion industry. Is the basic desire leading to uncharted camper van expeditions actually very different to a preoccupation with upgrading your Nike trainers? Well yes, as I have recognized, one is implicated in the exploitation of near-slave labour. This should not be de-emphasized. But there are significant tensions in Klein's accounts of engagement with corporate products. She bemoans the kitsch inauthenticity of certain areas, but recognizes that she performs a more sophisticated version. She regrets the obsession of consumers with brands, but recognizes that they are far from passive recipients of corporate propaganda; for instance, she reports one black 13 year old from the Bronx reacting to the information that his Nike trainers had a 2600% mark-up on production costs with 'Nike, we made you. We can break you'. Indeed as I have acknowledged, the thesis of *No Logo* is that consumers are rejecting or subverting the products and symbols of capitalism. Yet it seems that some can do this better than others. The graphic designers of Klein's condominium clearly are more proficient than the loft-livers of the Candy Store.

Criticism and co-option

This is not meant as a particular criticism of Klein. She has much to say that is worth hearing. It's just that it seems difficult to avoid being finally consumed. We seemed trapped in Jodi Dean's (1998) post-colonized, abduction culture in which any recourse to 'authenticity' seems somehow 'suspicious', somehow 'false'; a conceit, a betrayal, a piece of self-indulgent therapy which serves only to collude with that which it attempts to assail. The dilemma of authenticity is 'that no sooner does something become recognized as a mark of authenticity than it gets appropriated and transformed into a popular sign. As soon as it becomes a hot sign, however, its authenticity is dissipated and lost for those who gave meaning to the sign prior to its mass commodification' (Goldman and Papson, 1996: 143). The current media ubiquity of Klein herself is an obvious case in point.

Klein's optimism is partly invested in new forms of criticism and protest that she suggests, are free from the baggage of existing groups. The recent protests in Seattle, London and Prague lead her to suggest that we are witnessing the birth of a major new movement for social action. These include various forms of direct action targeted at specific products and manufacturers and days of protest like '*Reclaim the Streets*'. It is a characteristic of these protest 'groups' that they lack any clear identity. They have no strong political affiliations and a 'day of action' will consist of a loose coalition of protesters from different backgrounds (from hard-core anarchists to 'concerned citizens') organized, if that is the right word, via the Internet. Klein argues that the looseness of the coalition is precisely its strength. Arguing firstly that the amount of property destruction is overstated by those with a political agenda to protect, she suggests that the disparate backgrounds of the protesters indicates the extent to which their concerns are growing and becoming more widespread. Instead of protest becoming marginalized in 'interest groups' it is moving increasingly into the mainstream.

But for sceptics this is one of the problems. They point out that days of protest lack any clear objective or programme for reform. They criticise the system but do not consider what to put in its place. They therefore usually constitute nothing more than an excuse for vandalism and looting. Around the time of the recent 'riots' in London a number of exposés were published in the national press. One strategy was to reveal the criminal history of protestors. Their 'real' intention is not legitimate protest therefore, but indiscriminate mayhem focused upon property vandalism. Paradoxically some protesters are criticized for being too 'respectable'. In a *Sunday Times* article '*Can't stop mummy, I'm off to join the revolution*', journalist Matt Born (2000) lambasts protestors for the inauthenticity of their 'postmodern political activism'. He contrasts Miles, who is 34, describes himself as 'classic middle class' and rejects 'dot-com' culture, with Jack, 28, 'a dot-com entrepreneur on his first protest'. These are protestors, Born explains, with no purpose other than to protest. On the one hand the protesters are shown to be agitators with hidden agendas, on the other, good time 'Charlies' with no agenda at all.

This, Born argues, is a time when protest appears at least momentarily re-energized, but where the protesters have no coherent identity, no clear sense of what they are protesting against, or, as with our marching dot-com entrepreneur, recognition of their complicity. Marwick (2000) therefore rejects any comparisons with the protests of the 1960s along these lines. Whilst the '60s was a period of coherent cultural revolutions, today's protests, he argues, are 'miscellaneous and contradictory'. What is most depressing is not the sordid reality (if that is the case) of those involved, but that even a cursory glance at history shows that very similar criticisms were applied to the 'coherent cultural revolutions' of the 1960s. Thomas Frank's (1997) account of the '60s counterculture portrays it as a 'stage in the development of the American middle class'. A movement that, far from threatening business, was perceived as an ally in dragging it from the bureaucracy and creative lethargy of the 1950s and 1960s. As Frank's (1997) argues, 'Like the young insurgents, people in more advanced reaches of the American corporate world deplored conformity, distrusted routine, and encouraged resistance to established power. They welcomed the youth-led cultural revolution not because they were secretly planning to subvert it or even because they believed it would allow them to tap a gigantic youth market (although this was, of course, a factor), but because they perceived in it a comrade in their own struggles to revitalize American business and the consumer order generally'.

The counterculture therefore becomes just a 'colourful instalment in the twentieth century drama of consumer subjectivity' (Franks, 1997: 12). Yet Franks is at pains to point out that this is no retrospective judgement. Sounding remarkably like the Sunday Times journalist cited previously, he refers to novelist and adman Earl Shorris writing in 1967, 'Having professed their disdain for middle-class values, the hippies indulge in them without guilt'. Shorris believed that far from revolutionaries, the counterculture betrayed solidly conservative values, 'The preponderance of hippies come from the middle class, because it is there even among adults that the illusion of the hippies' joy, free love, purity and drug excitement is strongest. A man grown weary of singing company songs at I.B.M. picnics, feeling guilty about the profits he has made on defence stocks, who hasn't really loved his wife for 10 years, must admire, envy and wish for a life of love and contemplation, a simple life leading to a beatific peace. He soothes his despair with the possibility that the hippies have found the answers to problems he does not dare to face' (quoted in Franks, 1997: 13).

Writing in the same year, Warren Hinckle argued that hippies were far from alienated. Instead they were 'brand name conscious' and 'frantic consumers'. He wrote, 'In this commercial sense, the hippies have not only accepted assimilation ... they have swallowed it whole. The hippie culture is in many ways a prototype of the most ephemeral aspects of the larger American society; if the people looking in from the suburbs want change, clothes, fun, and some light-headedness from the new gypsies, the hippies are delivering – and some of them are becoming rich hippies because of it'. (quoted in Frank, 1997: 13)

162

Collusions and conclusions

Contemporary accounts of the extension of corporate influence have difficulty because they are accounts of colonization that assume that we remember a time before the occupation. Naomi Klein might well pursue an open space that will 'allow us to rediscover our identities as citizens'. But this is confused even as nostalgia for what Ryan and Kellner (1988: 77) characterise as 'a small-business world of heroic entrepreneurship that existed prior to the rise of corporate capitalism'. Klein, like most of us, has no memory of this. She is, as she readily admits, an 'ex-Mall Rat'. Jodi Dean (1998) might well diagnose Klein's pursuit of that 'open space' as recovered memory syndrome. But if we recognize this, if we realize that the complicit reality of 'breathing together' leaves us uncomfortable, then what do we do? Think more about collusion and co-option? Develop better theories? Assess their prospects? Or can we find more direct methods to manage with our desires and commitments, attachments and detachments?

The editors of the cultural journal *Hermanaut* (2000) have outlined a method. They propose embracing mass culture but with (they think) a sly ironic twist, 'we prefer to concentrate our attention on the independent use of mass culture products, a use which, like the ruses of camouflaged fish and insects, may not "overthrow the system", but which keeps us intact and autonomous within that system, which may be the best for which we can hope ... Going to Disney World to drop acid and goof on Mickey isn't revolutionary; going to Disney World in full knowledge of how ridiculous and evil it all is and still having a great innocent time, in some almost unconscious, even psychotic way, is something else altogether ... Let us revel in Baywatch, Joe Camel, Wired magazine, and even glossy books about the society of spectacle, but let's never succumb to the glamorous allure of these things'.

But what distinguishes their controlled consumption from that of the brutish mass who does succumb to the glamorous allure of 'things'? Why, because it is they who are doing it. As we quickly realize, even 'irony' itself has succumbed to commodification. Metaphorical inverted commas give us the freedom of an 'only joking' get-out. But does this 'knowingness' actually work? There is the danger of a form of irony that becomes almost paralysing in its self-absorption. One response appears to be to give up on this juggling and produce a more wholehearted parodic approach. It is interesting that Ryan and Kellner's (1988: 101) review of conspiracy theory films refers to a short-lived trend between the paranoid style of the 1970s and the ideological conservatism of the 1980s. Here certain films, for instance *Winter Kills* (1979) and *Blow-Out* (1981), began to use the over-familiar conspiracy form to produce 'semi-parodic excesses' devoid of the political critique present in earlier films. Perhaps we are entering a similar phase today. It is entirely consistent then that many protesters signal their disengagement via pranks. Agent Blueberry of the Biotic Baking Brigade throws pies at business tycoons and economists shouting, 'To their lies, we respond with pies'. Even more obviously politically active media social commentators like Michael Moore and Mark Thomas produce their exposés via situationist stunt work.

Consequently, and finally, I want to identify tentatively a developing form of 'antagonistic playfulness' that seems to combine resignation with criticism. Its aim, I feel, is not directed *outwards* towards the standard objects of critique, but *inwards* in order to shake us out of our own indulgences. Chuck Palahniuk's *Fight Club* and particularly David Fincher's film version are exemplars. Here it is interesting that in Fincher's earlier *The Game* (1997) an elaborate conspiracy actually turns out to be what it said it was – a role-playing entertainment purchased as a practical joke by the lead character's brother. It therefore provides a contemporary version of the (apparent) conspiracy film as 'semi-parodic' excess.

Fincher's *Fight Club* (1999) peddles an intoxicating form of designer nihilism that careers wilfully and seductively through a prime selection of contemporary issues: anti-consumerism, emasculation, violence, and generic post-*Generation X* angst. Yet this is not to produce any overarching critique. Instead it strives to force us to confront our hypocrisies and our attempts at managing the tensions of authenticity. By showing the sheer ridiculousness of many of these attempts its message is merely, 'Everyone knows this. Grow up. Deal with it'. As Terence McKenna (1997) implores us, speaking of nothing (and everything) in general, 'They can only work this limited set of tricks upon you three times, four times, six times, before you *get it*. You figure it out, you know? How many art openings, how many Next Great Novels by the geniuses among us, how many filmic triumphs, Nobel Prizes, Booker fiction awards, and on and on and on, can we tolerate in the illusion that we are moving into the truly new and exciting? It works for awhile, is the idea'.

The last words go to *Fight Club's* anti-hero Tyler Durden. He asks,

Tyler: How's that working out for you?
Narrator: What?
Tyler: Being clever
Narrator: Great
Tyler: Keep it up then

Notes

1 Thanks to Debbie Lisle and Valérie Fournier.
2 David Duchovny's reduced filming commitment to the X-Files means that Dana Scully has a new partner played by Robert Patrick. Patrick starred in Terminator II as the implacable T-1000.
3 *No Logo* makes no reference to the Frankfurt School. Of course it is a 'piece of journalism' but it is also self-consciously contemporary. This, I feel, is a strength. It infers its heritage (including 'popular' critics – Packard and Nader also get barely a mention) without being paralysed by it. I've no doubt that Klein is entirely familiar with the pertinent theoretical background. What is the effect of its absence?

References

Adorno, T.W., (1973), *The Jargon of Authenticity*, Northwestern University Press.

Auster, P., (1998), *Hand to Mouth*, London, Faber and Faber.

Born, M., (2000), 'Can't Stop, Mummy, I'm Off to Join the Revolution', *Sunday Times*, 7/5/00.

De Jonquieres, G., (1998), Network Guerillas, *Financial Times*, April 30, p. 12.

Dean, J., (1998), *Aliens in America*, Cornell University Press.

Franks, T., (1997), *The Conquest of Cool*, Chicago, University of Chicago Press. Excerpt available http://www.press.uchicago.edu/Misc/Chicago/259919.html

Freund, C.P., (1997), The Truth Is Out There, *Reason Magazine*, available online at http://www.reasonmag.com/9712/bk.chuck.html.

Goldman, R. and Papson, S., (1996), *Sign Wars: The Cluttered Landscape of Advertising*, New York, Guildford Press.

Grossman, R., (1998), *Challenging Corporate Power*, Interviewed by David Barsamian Provincetown, Massachusetts, August 23, http://www.zmag.org/intgrossman.htm

Hermanaut (2000), Available online at http://www.hermenaut.com/.

Hopkins, B., (1988), *Missing Time*, Mass Market Paperback.

Jameson, F., (1984), Postmodernism, or the Cultural Logic of Late Capitalism, *New Left Review*, no. 146, 53–92.

Jameson, F., (1988), Cognitive Mapping in Marxism and the Interpretation of Culture. In *Marxism and the Interpretation of Culture* (eds), Basingstoke: Macmillan.

Klein, N., (2000), *No Logo*, London: Flamingo.

Marwick, A., (2000), 'The Spirit of 68? Not a Chance', *Sunday Times*, 7/5/00.

McKenna, T., (1997), *Surfing the Fractal Wave at the End of History*, Terence McKenna at The Lighthouse, NYC, April 23. http://www.abrupt.org/LOGOS/tm970423.html

Rushkoff, D., (1994), *Media Virus!: Hidden Agendas in Popular Culture*, NY: Ballantine Books.

Rushkoff, D., (1999), *Coercion*, London: Little, Brown and Company.

Seabrook, J., (2000), *Nobrow: The Culture of Marketing – The Marketing of Culture*, London: Metheun.

Ryan, M. and Kellner, D., (1988), *Camera Politica*, Indiana: Indiana University Press.

Stewart, K., (1999), Conspiracy Theory's Worlds. In Marcus, G.E. (ed.), *Paranoia within Reason*, Chicago: University of Chicago Press.

Vankin, J., (1996), *Conspiracies, Cover-Ups and Crimes*, Georgia: IllumiNet Press.

Viner, K., (2000), *Hand-To-Brand Combat*, The Guardian Weekend Magazine, 23/09/00.

Conspiracy, what conspiracy?: Social science, funding and the politics of accusation

Simon Lilley

Horror is not simply and unambiguously the unbearable Real masked by the fantasy screen ... The Horrible can also function as the screen itself, as the thing whose fascinating effect conceals something 'more horrible than horror itself', the primordial void or antagonism.

    The logic of the horror which functions as a screen masking the void can ... be illustrated by the uncanny power of the motif of a ship drifting along alone, without a captain or any living crew to steer it. This is the ultimate horror: not the proverbial ghost in the machine, but the machine in the ghost: there is *no* plotting agent behind it, the machine just runs by itself, as a blind contingent device. At the social level, this is what the notion of ... conspiracy conceals: the horror of society as a contingent mechanism blindly following its path, caught in the vicious cycle of its antagonisms. (Žižek, 1997, p. 40, original emphasis)

Beginning

Much as I loathe a chapter that begins with a personal odyssey, it is hard for me to get you to see the sense of what follows in the absence of such a trope.[1] Indeed, I am ashamed to say that the chapter as a whole is little more than a series of personal odysseys which only find themselves before your eyes as a consequence of the impulsion to expel the bile that they have produced deep within me. And although I am obviously apologetic for putting you through this, I make no apologies for the productive irony at the core of the chapter's construction. For whilst my aim here is to root out some of the pseudo-antagonisms that I see at work in the nexus of researched, researcher, reviewer and funder, I have only 'decided' to do so to 'cure' myself of the pain that these antagonisms have caused me (see also, Lilley, 1997, 1998a). I have felt myself to be in presence of 'conspiracies' but have, on reflection, realized that I am either complicit in these (or at least their kitschistic reflections (Cooper, 1986; Lilley, 1998a; Linstead, 1996)), or that there is no 'conspiracy' abroad, merely an endless stream of marketed interpretations, relying upon narrativized pseudo-antagonisms that seek to conceal the 'primordial void or [*ur-*]antagonism' which produced them. I have tried to hold the hot potato and I can't – so I am going to try to pass it to you.

Worthy of attention?

You say you want a revolution, well you know, we'd all love to see the plan. You say you want a revolution, well you know, we're all doing what we can.[2]

When I first presented parts of the material that I am playing with here, in an 'ethics stream' of an avowedly 'Critical' conference, what struck me most about the event was the overwhelming and often oppressive sense of *worthiness* that threatened, at every instant, to engulf it. It smacked too much of the union politics of my own student days, during which the self evidently (and I mean *self* evidently) socially concerned would muster quorum, in the Mandela bar, to pass Cnutist motions deploring the latest Governmental, Intergovernmental or Commercial excess. What scares me most about both environments is their potential to degenerate into a form of sincerity that brooks no irony; into an emptily self satisfying (satisficing?) hubris that leaves nothing changed but the 'souls' of participants which are thus ritually cleansed (Burke, 1969). Such a process depends upon a politics of identity which itself seems to derive from a congenitally failing flight from the 'primordial void or [*ur*-]antagonism' that grounds and besets our condition. This flight, at least according to Žižek (1997, p. 10 *et passim*), is operated by that all too human carrier, *narrative*. And whilst in both organizational studies (Czarniawska, 1997; Czarniawska-Joerges, 1995; Czarniawska-Joerges. and Guillet de Monthoux, 1994) and social theory more generally (see, for example, Brown, 1987; the contributions to Brown, 1992), often laudable efforts have recently been made to resurrect the virtue of narration as both a trope and a research technique, for Žižek (1997, p. 10, original emphasis): 'fantasy is the primordial form of *narrative*, which serves to occult some original deadlock'.

> The sociopolitical fantasy *par excellence*, of course, is the myth of 'primordial accumulation': the narrative of the two workers, one lazy and free-spending, the other diligent and enterprising, accumulating and investing, which provides the myth of the 'origins of capitalism', obfuscating the violence of its actual genealogy ... [T]he answer to the question 'Why do we tell stories?' is that *narrative as such emerges* in order to resolve some fundamental antagonism by rearranging its terms into a temporal succession. It is thus the very form of narrative which bears witness to some repressed antagonism. The price one pays for the narrative resolution is the *petitio principii* of the temporal loop – the narrative silently presupposes as already given what it purports to reproduce (the narrative of 'primordial accumulation' effectively explains nothing, since it already

presupposes a worker behaving like a full-blown capitalist) (Žižek, 1997, pp. 10–11, original emphasis).

If we are to draw pseudo-antagonistic lines, and our condition, despite our innumerable flights of narrative fancy, seems to curse us to do so, then I, at least, would like to choose the side of Kierkegaard, whose modest awareness of the 'impoverishment' of the position from which he articulates at least has the virtue of not enlisting the brute power of the 'truth' of his narration to silence his audience. As Said (1997, p. 86, original emphases) renders this position:

fiction alone speaks or is written – for truth has no need of words – *all voices are assumed ones.*

Given such an understanding, for Kierkegaard (1966, p. 270, quoted in Said, 1997, p. 88)

... the outstanding feature of irony ... is the subjective freedom which at every moment has within its power the possibility of a beginning and is not generated from previous conditions. There is something seductive about every beginning because the subject is still free, and this is the satisfaction the ironist longs for. At such moments actuality loses its validity for him; he is free and above it.

And thus perhaps the greatest irony that we witness is in the revolutionary zeal of those who seek to enrol us in their projects with the brute force of the truth of the world, little realizing that it is only when actuality loses (some of) its validity that 'real' opportunities for change begin to open up.

I rather felt it was people who claimed to be the sole possessors of the truth who should be ill at ease for the disruption they caused in others' lives (Barley, 1986, p. 25).

Beginning again

The detour into Žižek's work presented above reveals conspiracy as narrative in the realm of the hyperreal, the Disneyland of stories, that enables preservation of the fantasy that other stories can tell us *something* and not merely 'occult some original deadlock' (1997, p. 10). Now it seems to me, following this vein, that the control of organization is dependent, first and foremost, upon those stories (or conspiracies) of organization whose circulation is organized. The prefixes, brackets and scare marks that both supplement and eviscerate our modernity[3] serve endlessly to remind us that this is so. But 'knowing' that the narratives so produced are 'fantastic' obfuscations does not, in itself, seem enough to ameliorate their power. So one alternative is to use this power to bite the hand that feeds it (see also, Lilley, 1995). To use narrative to display the perversity of its achievements, to antagonise the narrative bases of knowing, to show how it is that 'narrative ... explains nothing' (Žižek, 1997, p. 11).

So, I tell a story. Give you a paratext of organization, of organization that claims to seek the good. It is a story of stories, audiences and reviewers, a story whose conditions I inevitably replay as I tell it to you.

And again

> ... *thrice rejected early in his career, he had reason to believe that something personal and/or political was afoot with the Guggenheim Fellowship committee, and had decided that he'd simply be damned, starve utterly, before he would ever again hire a graduate assistant to fill out the tiresome triplicate Guggenheim Foundation Fellowship application and go through the tiresome contemptible farce of 'objective' consideration ever again* (Wallace, 2000, p. 2)

It is some time ago. I buy a publication whose activities and the surpluses that they generate are intended to improve the lot of the least materially privileged in our society. The publication is *The Big Issue*, the United Kingdom's instantiation of a publishing genre sold in many major cities throughout the world,[4] a magazine which exists to 'help the homeless to help themselves' and is sold by vendors who receive 60% of its cover price. Just inside this cover buyers are informed that ...

> THE BIG ISSUE ... is a business solution to a social problem. It's a private company, limited by guarantee. The Big Issue ... Trust is a registered charity with a business-like approach to ending homelessness.

All this knowledge makes me feel a little bit better about myself as I take my copy home and settle down to read one of its articles. It is a story of organizational conversion. Of *Paperco*,[5] a business that has successfully produced the goods both for its customers and the family who own it. Subtly, before I really notice what is happening, the instrumentalism and performativity (Lyotard, 1984) encouraged by my university employment and its cultural context kick in and I am no longer reading out of 'interest'. I realize that the organization described in the article presents a good opportunity to conduct some 'interesting' research, to attract some funding, to write some words. For the article informs me that an otherwise rather dull family-owned business producing paper-based products is in the throes of transformation. That succession is at hand and liturgies are underway. That the prodigal son has returned and that the future is full of promise. That some amelioration of Capital's cold calculation may be found within frameworks of organization

169

that do not divorce labour from ownership and control of the means of production.

In a page of journalistic text I discover:

1. What the new king looks like.
2. That he has been a revolutionary communist.[6]
3. That he has seen the error of his ways. That his help for the miners has been revealed to himself as hindrance, that dogs bark in China even when you are being told that there are no dogs in China. That Ideology belongs to callow youth.
4. That principles and practices can come together for an adult whose province of influence is small and relatively self contained.
5. That the new king has empowered the workforce, by transferring ownership of the kingdom to his subjects.
6. That inheritance now follows participation rather than descent.
7. That there could be more to know.

Seeking to realize the opportunity that seems to be presenting itself to me, to do some research on an organization that I might be able to admire, I call the company secretary. I flirt, we get on well. I convince her to convince more senior participants to accept my future presence 'so long as you don't need loads of formal information that is going to take us time to drag out and collect'. These preliminaries of knowledge production successfully negotiated, all I need to go further is some time and money.

> Several chapters in this book were written under a pressure of circumstances which afford 'no time' to think ... What was once a necessity to analysis (thought, reflection) is now regarded as a luxury; the means to synthesis (writing as composition) and to communication (publication) have become ends in themselves. (Strathern, 1995, p. 5)

A year later I find some time. I cut out my minimal knowledge of Paperco and paste it onto caricatures of other seemingly worthy organizations I have met and who seem willing to meet me again. I search databases, simulate a grounding in a new field I outline for myself. I promise 'best practice' as I ask governmental mediators at the Economic and Social Research Council (ESRC) for money.[7] They oblige, but their temporary functionaries raise concerns. Concerns which make me laugh – about the location of my intended sites of study, about the lack of clarity over what will be produced.

> *It is unclear what this research will find* (Reviewer's comment sent to me for consideration with the good news that my research will be funded).[8]

Implicitly, they voice concerns about my integrity. I laugh because I know that they are right, implicitly, but also because in the realm of the explicit I know that I will not get called to account, that information assymmetries place all the cards in my hand. Years pass. I visit companies, stay with friends, spend money, write a report, construct and present some papers, get on the radio. I use up two or three of my fifteen minutes.

Zooming in, reeling back

On starting my investigation of Paperco I become disillusioned, just as I became concomitantly disillusioned with charities as I began to understand more about *Heritage*[9] (Lilley, 1998b), a charitable organization who allowed me to crawl about their Head Office as part of the same project. I discover that the family has certainly 'transferred' ownership of Paperco to the work force but has also enobled them with ownership of, and responsibility for, the servicing of millions of pounds worth of long term loan stocks to ensure the family's future financial health in the absence of any need for productive activity on their part.

> The idea was then to find a way of diversifying the family's holding and finding some way of getting liquidity into the family's holding. Which is fine. But the process involved there is for the family to convert their holding into loan stock, which is the process that's been going on, and then the company to purchase that loan stock ... we've made no bones to the employees about the fact that they come third in the list. The first is the family because they've got a commitment, the second is investment in the business particularly to the fixed capital business, ... so they come number three, right, out of three ... (laughs) ... But, given they're getting given it to start with then it's not really unreasonable. (Chairman).

So, on closer inspection we seem to be witnessing business as usual. I begin to feel uneasy, to think that not much control has been passed with the shift in ownership. To feel a little stupid and naïve to have been taken in by an article whose medium and message are now revealed to me as inherently journalistic, in the most pejorative sense. But who do *I* think *I* am and where do *I* think *I* stand to make such accusations? For this is what I told the ESRC in order both to attract the money my chosen research required and to account for its prudent use:

> The research utilised qualitative research methodologies in an exploratory study of practices surrounding *information* in an employee-owned organi-zation ... In the management literature at least, the internal information practices of employee-owned organizations and, indeed, charities, seems to represent something of a lacuna. Given the increasing prominence in, and importance to, the economy of organizations that tend to these forms, a lack of attention to the detail of their organizing practices would seem to indicate

171

an undue focus upon those forms with which we feel we are familiar. The proposed research sought to constitute the beginnings of a rectification of this position.

The research thus sought to contribute to and further develop ... debates around *human communication and the social shaping of technology* by exploring informational practices within a relatively neglected domain.

Such pseudist pyrotechnics which re-present, in italics, my Master's voice, enabled me to present, with almost a straight pen, the following:

Objectives

Through an exploratory study of practices surrounding information in three 'non-conventional' organizations, the research sought:

1. To explore how human communication processes are mediated by information technologies in charities and employee-owned organizations.

2. To examine the particularities of the social shaping of information technologies in such organizations.

3. To contribute to theoretical debates surrounding the social and managerial dimensions of information by examining its use in organizations which are somewhat indirectly embedded in the capitalist economic system.

And indeed I did, or at least I believed that I did.[10] I may not have chosen to use those words if I had been describing my activities in another context, but the time of my entry to the groves of academe means that I am more than inured in the practice of such language games (see also Hill and Turpin, 1995). But is it just words that are at stake here or is something more fundamental at risk in the translation undergone?

The family sold out for less than 'the market' would have paid, although it is not clear that there are that many people clamouring for a previously family-owned paper business. I took my ten grand from the ESRC rather than from any other research funding institutions more tightly tied to business concerns (who again are not obviously scouring the country for research of the sort I conduct), and tried to stay 'critical'. Myself and the family could have taken more. But in selling only part of our virtue, by ignoring (our fantasies concerning) the highest bidders, by distancing ourselves from those more dubious others engaged in the conspiracies we feign to reject, we retain some (albeit grubby) rights to voice. But just as we may ask who owns the company and who controls it (for the two are not necessarily identical as Burnham (1941) informed us many years ago), we may also ask who controls research? The researcher? The researched? Or the funder?

The culture of the marketplace ... crept up on the autonomy of academia ... What was delivered by the end of the 1980s was a culture of production of scientific knowledge that was deeply penetrated by the values of the marketplace towards which the planning process was oriented – both inside and outside the academic world and at the interface between academic and wider domains (Hill and Turpin, 1995, p. 143).

> academics complain ... that the value their research is now being judged by intellectually facile considerations of 'marketability'. (Keat, 1991, p. 216)

(S)he who pays the piper calls the tune?

> Bezos [*Amazon's founder*] makes a show of cherishing the 'Amazon culture' he has created, which is based on the fact that all employees are also owners and therefore have no need of unions. Yet, like many idealists, he assumes that everyone who works for him is *like* him, neglecting the fact that not everyone will see what he sees when he looks to the future of Amazon. This is why idealists often end up behaving like hooligans (Smith, 2001, p. 15, original emphasis).

According to Guest's 'many' (1987, p. 520):

> The unitarist implications of human resource management could only begin to have an appeal following a much more radical shift in ownership and control in industry.

Well, we have here a case of an organization radically shifting its ownership (although the details suck up much of the radicalness). Admittedly we don't have an 'industry' shift. But we should be able to look at how the introduction of shared ownership impinges upon the practices and practicalities of control. We can explore here whether unitarism in one realm – 'ownership', is necessarily reflected in another, that of 'control'. And, surprise, surprise, it isn't. Our logics of separate but parallel spaces of organization suggests that it should be, but it is not. Share councils actively and energetically, through admirably democratic representation and participation, do serve to exert influence upon organizational direction, but in strictly delimited ways, in strictly delimited arenas. Interestingly this seems less the result of cunning tactics on the part of particular managerial bodies (although these are certainly present), more a facet of the nature of a broader 'management' game in which non-managerial employees were certainly complicit. Consider the following account provided by one of the 'share councillors'. Apparently membership of this august body:

> Mainly entails going to the meetings, learning about the business, learning about shares and how we distribute shares. We've tried to make changes and we have actually accomplished that as well ...

As he goes on to note:

> recently we've had a new company strategy so they, they pulled us in before the rest of the company heard about it. Occasionally they say right, we'll tell

you this but you're to keep it under your hat until such and such a date when such and such will be announced. So we're getting more involvement with company things. There are other things. Sometimes they say that it will not be possible to give information. For instance if you were maybe buying another company ... But if they thought that it could be handled by the share council then yes, the information would be passed on ... I think as it goes on and we become more confident then we will be more involved in some decisions but then, we have also been told that it is down to the management to manage them. It's not a share council to stand up and ... rule you there. They have to be allowed to manage ... I think it's because you employ these people on high salaries and if they're not allowed to do their job they could fail I suppose ... and using the skills in the proper area too.

Here then we witness ownership not as being in control but as being kept informed by those who are control, but even then, only so long as market sensitivities allow. Control remains separate from ownership and not only demands higher salaries than those afforded to other 'owners', the very height of these salaries also ensures continued legitimation of this separated locus of 'real' control. This is 'management's' *right to manage* being asserted not in the face of the demands of labour as was its prior mantra, but in that of the owners of the capital assets that are the other object of managerial perogative.

For managers themselves ownership was something of a sideshow, a form of bread and circuses that would only remain acceptable if it could demonstrate its capacity to oil the wheels of managerial control, a control whose disinterested aim was superior performance of the organization as a whole. It was merely another instrumental means to a seemingly self-evident end:

I think you've got to say that the only purpose, in a hard nosed way if you like, of saying why are we doing this, it's not really, it ought not to be purely for the good of mankind, and sheer altruism and making the family feel good, there has to be a belief that it will actually build a stronger company. Therefore I don't think in any way one should get fazed and sort of mesmerised by this company ownership problem. The key feature is, is the company successful? (Chairman)

Increasingly conspiratorial overtones become apparent when we look at the detail:

SL: ... how many share councillors are there?
Share Councillor: There's about twelve in all I think, ... nine, not counting people who are nominated by the management ... They're not voted on.

And as the same councillor went on to note:

There are various topics that we bring up, as I say in the past the share allocation has been mentioned and, a bit of history now, before we did the buy out there was voting shares and non-voting shares, so the share councillor at that time, I think it was all done on salary initially, and the share council at that time said, right, going to have some sort of equal thing so they decided they would make the voting shares which were, like a thirty-seventy split. The voting ones they said right we'll make them all equal so we all got equal shares but that was only thirty percent of the pot, you see ... But you see all the votes were the same. Then when the buy out came along they all had to be the same shares, they all had to be voting shares ... So the company then said that well, keep the split the same, still be thirty-seventy, but, still not too happy about that, still think well, if it's an employee share ownership company then why does everybody not get equal shares? ... But anything that we recommend at share council meetings etc., it has to go in front of the board, the board have to approve it.

So not only was involvement in 'strategy', even strategy concerning ownership as the immediately preceding quote reveals, strictly delimited, wider impacts were, rather unsurprisingly given our enhanced understanding of the context of their expression, also felt to be small, even by those committed to the change. Consider the following exchange with a share councillor:

SL: I mean does it actually affect you in the day-to-day work?
SC: Not really, no.
SL: Do you think it does anybody?
SC: I don't know, I don't know if they have a different attitude or not. You just go out and do your job.
SL: Yes. So in terms of the day-to-day it really makes no difference, it's just at the end of the year and ...
SC: Yes. They say it should, it should make a difference day-to-day, that's, I think that's [*the chief executive's*] thoughts on it
SL: Right. But there's nothing, I mean apart from generally feeling better about the company?
SC: That's true, yes. For me personally I just get on and do my job.

But what are we witnessing here? Has management seduced its new 'owners' to make them accomplices of either an older notion of capital or a newer one of managerialism? Is this a 'bad' company, using the pyrotechnics of employee ownership to ratchet up an ideological screw? Or are the dynamics of control more complicated than simplistic considerations of ownership, seduction and ideology enable us to consider?
This is how I presented 'my' findings for the ESRC's consumption:

The shift in ownership at *Paperco*, and the informational prerogatives seemingly associated with it, was carefully represented and managed in order to ensure that no similarly radical shift in *control* occurred. Rather, the identity of those who control was protected and sustained by a discourse of standardized and professionalized business practice. A discourse in which managers retained special status as a group of employees, a status which combined *their* ownership *and* control as it limited notions of employee shareholding to a status of ownership *without* control (original emphases).

Which seems to capture much of what is going on. But what is not entirely clear here is the identity of the villains in our cautionary tale, for whilst we *can* witness managers manipulating handy discursive resources to maintain their special status, we can also witness similarly conservative discursive manouevres on the part of both the managed and indeed, the 'critical' researcher who would wish to speak in their name. Moves which beg some rather bigger questions. For example, are 'managers' and 'workers' conspiring together to maintain their access to extant discourses of identity that assuage the dread of the 'primordial void or antagonism' with more extensive narrative forms of the beast that enable them to maintain aspects of their identities as collective possessions, as if antagonisms between groups were any less dreadful than than those between those other much loved and hated fictional entities, individuals? Is control of identity through allegiance and membership all that we seek, regardless of the implications of our moves for control of our lives? And perhaps more importantly for the thrust of the argument here, what of my account? Am I only hearing those aspects of the story that allow me to remain comfortably critical, self-deludingly at one with the workers whose activities are almost entirely alien to me, other to those managers who shuffle different sorts of paper about much as I do? Do we merely hear what we want, in order to say, however fantastically given the 'evidence' that confronts us, who we think we are (Lilley, 1997)?

> ... the justification for fieldwork, as for all academic endeavour, lies not in one's contribution to the collectivity but rather in some selfish development. Like monastic life, academic research is really all about the perfection of one's own soul. This may well serve some wider purpose but is not to be judged on those grounds alone. This view will doubtless not sit well either with conservative academics or those who see themselves as a revolutionary force. Both are afflicted by a dreadful piety, a preening self-importance that refuses to believe the world is not hanging on their every word (Barley, 1986, pp. 9–10).

Hyperreal? Hyperbusiness?

When I reported back to the ESRC in order to account for my diligent use of their resources on the project as a whole, I suggested the following (immediately preceded by a simulation of the seemingly mandatory, numerically ordered, vacuum-packed summaries and truisms which I had witnessed in other final reports):

[T]he research suggests that, at least in the limited number of sites studied, that partial amelioration of the structural environment of standard equity capitalism does not provide niches that are protected from business logics and rhetorics, particularly around information collection, deployment and use. Rather the reverse would seem to be closer to the truth. In all three organizations studied under the project, and particularly in the paper manufacturer and the charity Head Office, fears of appearing 'unbusiness-like' in a rhetorical environment in which a private sector model is both implicitly and explicitly raised above all others, resulted in sets of practices being adopted which could perhaps best be described as a form of 'hyperbusiness', which, to me at least, seems a very interesting finding indeed.

Which all seems suitably deft at keeping critical concerns, the continuing importance of 'management' for organizations like the ESRC, and my own concerns for academic rigour in the air. But it is not what I would normally write ... My ownership of the text as signalled by my authorship does not extend to full control. Now, to be sure this has always been the case:

knowledge production itself is already part of a wider system (of progressive application of rational knowledge). Its meanings are negotiated within 'abstract' discourse that individual researchers can enter, but not command. However, with the entry of the commercial marketplace directly into this knowledge system, the symbols that steer knowledge production – 'first discovery prestige', reputational status and attributed authority, and so on – become not 'condensed' into a summary version of wider meanings, but *replaced* by symbols of the commercial market place (Hill and Turpin, 1995, p. 141, original emphasis).

To exemplify this point and to lend weight to the central thrust of my argument here, such deftness was not however what some of the rapporteurs commissioned by the ESRC to review the final report of my research wanted to see. And, as a consequence, the outcome of the research was deemed to be, and graded as, 'problematic'. As my self inflated in the face of such opprobrium, and I faced the prospect of limited future prospects for gaining research funding as a result of this judgement, a new version of a doubtless familiar conspiracy (to some readers at least) began to articulate itself in my mind. A cabal of self-aggrandizing administrators and sympathetic academicians, straddling the divide between government and governed to ensure the future of UK plc. A bolus of functionaries[11] feeling 'briskly in step with the times' (Roszak, 1986) as they manipulate levers of influence which are attached to nothing. A collection of self-satisfied others who know less than me! However, having kicked a few doors and spat out a few expletives, pragmatism began to rein both my anger and my rather dubious imputations back in. It seemed to me important to attempt to restore my reputation and I thus telephoned the evaluation division of the ESRC to inquire about the possibilities of appeal.

Initially, there seemed to be two central thrusts behind the 'problematic' judgement: that I had not done enough to ensure that practitioners had gained benefit from my findings and that I had not addressed the objectives I had set myself.[12] Conversation with the evaluation division lead me to believe that the former was the more substantive point of concern, and given the extensive publicity that my findings had received,[13] I felt on fairly safe ground to launch an appeal. To be fair to both the rapporteurs and the ESRC's publicity machine, the reviewers could not possibly have known about the extent of this success on the making-my-findings-available-to-practitioners dimension, for I have to admit that this happened without too much involvement or planning on my part. The very well-worded ESRC press release concerning my study had clearly hit a nerve with practioners and their mediators – for the publicity I referred to was based solely upon this press release. Rapporteurs could not have known about these outcomes, simply because they were not included in the final report, being the result of the artful condensation of that report by the ESRC's press office. I thus dutifully constructed an appeal which I emailed to the evaluation division.

The response to my appeal generously expressed pleasure at the extent and nature of the dissemination of findings to practitioners, but the undiplomatic tone of my response to the initial grading proved something of a strategic error on my part, given that my appeal had been sent to the most unsympathetic of my original rapporteurs, rather than to an independent reviewer of the process of grading as a whole![14] I had unfortunately said the following in response to concerns about me not meeting my objectives:

Addressing of ... objectives ... relating to the social shaping of information technologies and how these technologies mediate human communication processes, is indeed largely absent if one views 'information technologies' as limited to computers and their connections and thus seeks only to look at human communication processes mediated by such devices. However, in the organizations studied informants made it clear to me that this was not where the action was, that there were few differences in formal IT methods in these organizations from those adopted in more 'conventional' organizational sites. Given that the project was exploratory and ethnographic in nature I did what a good researcher should do, and followed up the concerns and issues which WERE seen to be interesting to practitioners, those concerns that THEY felt revealed where tensions lay with regard to advice as to how information should be organized which originate in more 'standard' private sector organizations. These problems all seemed to turn around the problems associated with incorporating advice derived from private sector, market operation, into activities that could not completely be captured by such imagery.

Unsurprisingly such an insulting tone (see, also, footnote 12) cut little ice. The rapporteur merely reiterated and strengthened their claim that my research was 'problematic'. In response to my playing of the 'exploratory and ethnographic' card, whilst the reviewer could see 'some logic in this', they did not believe:

> ... that the ESRC gives money on the basis (even for ethnographic research) that the researcher will follow up what is interesting or relevant to practitioners at the expense of meeting stated objectives.

The response to my appeal concluded with the following *tour de force*:

> ... in as much as the objectives of the research have not been genuinely addressed, I think it raises rather serious issues related to the use of public money and the point must be very clearly made that *the research grant scheme is not designed to support researchers, however competent, doing what they and practitioners find interesting and important*. It is designed to support research aimed to address particular objectives as set out in proposals. I feel there is no doubt that the overall evaluation grade should be Problematic (emphasis added).

My arrogance about information assymetries was clearly misplaced!

The end is nigh?

> *These systems collect and process. All the secret knowledge of the world ... It means the end of loyalty. The more complex the systems, the less conviction in people. Conviction will be drained out of us. Devices will drain us, make us vague and pliant.* (DeLillo, 1991, p. 77)

> auditing can be regarded as a technology of *mistrust* (Armstrong, 1991) in which independent 'outsiders' must be summoned to restore that trust (Power, 1994a, p. 5,[15] emphasis added)

What are we to make of this story? And why is it included here? Well partly, having nowhere else to go with the ESRC with the spectre of misuse of 'public money' being raised via the insanity of a process that directs appeals to those whose judgement is being called into question by them, it appears here to get it out of my system. But it is also intended to serve a much more important purpose. For it highlights the 'insidiousness' (see, also, Talai, 1996) and endless conspiratorial potential that arises when a politics of accusation organizes relations between researched, researcher, funder and reviewer. This is not a story in which I appear as an innocent. My account of the practices at *Paperco* is just as amenable to indignant description as the rapporteur's account of my practice. Nor would I wish to appear as innocent here, for it seems to me that it is only by engaging in *mea culpas* that we can reasonably hope to rise above the spurious exaggeration of *difference* which sustains the antagonisms upon which critique, in and of the social sciences, depends. In doing so we will seek not just to expose 'the truth' of the dubious practices of others, but also to pause sufficiently in our rush to accusation to remember that we too are often the *same*.

What we are engaged in when we entertain such practices is not a battle for the good or the right – that is merely a side-show, a nice story to tell ourselves as we unleash our venality and bellicosity upon our targets. Rather we are fighting for identity, scapegoating others (Burke, 1969) as they scapegoat us as part of the endless charade of difference and similarity upon which our memberships and identities depend. Good academic/bad manager, unruly academic/ordered administration, whining author/superior reader. The dialectics of identity rely upon the narrativised antagonisms of difference which seek to conceal the 'primordial void or [*ur-*]antagonism' (Žižek, 1997) of the same. I have elsewhere addressed this problem as it relates to the researcher/researched intersection (Lilley, 1997). Here I focus upon the perniciousness of the process as it is played out in the researcher/reviewer/funder nexus, a process that is driven by that form of narrativization that sustains 'the awful idea of accountability' (Hoskin, 1996), in our contemporary cultural *cul de sac*, activity made auditable.

Hill and Turpin (1995, p. 141) highlight the effects of 'the entry of the commercial marketplace directly into [*the*] knowledge system' utilizing an argument which they derive from the work of Habermas (1984, 1987). Given increasing complexity and systematization of a society which seeks to solve its problem of order whilst parading a solution to its problem of scarcity, Habermas contends that a new problem arises, that of interpretation between the newly differentiated systems of the world. As these demands for interpretive action outstrip the capacities of actors:

> 'Steering media' increasingly stepped in to provide relief mechanisms that either *condense* or *replace* the need to interpret and negotiate the meaning of action. Primary amongst these steering media is money, that reduces all knowledge values to bottom line finance, and *administrative power, that indentures knowledge values to the interest of management* (Hill and Turpin, 1995, pp. 140–141, original emphases).

With the emergence of *demands* for 'enterprise culture'[16] around, and thus in, academia, commercial 'steering media' are seen to 'replace rather than condense the traditional values of academic scientific knowledge production' (Hill and Turpin, 1995, p. 144).

The key medium here is not money, although there is undoubtedly a monetary market for research funding and the existence of this market is important contextually. Rather it is administrative power, the medium that supplements money's reach. 'Market values' is a phrase used far too liberally, frequently to curtail discussions of this sort, for even where money 'works' best, in 'market' conditions, we must pay great attention to the specifics of the particular market under question. 'The market' is a fiction, not an (or an increasingly) universal social form, for individual markets represent specific acts of construction.

> ... markets ... do not emerge 'naturally'. Rather, their products and rules of exchange must be socially contracted. This is more than merely 'packaging', for in the act of packaging the product itself is defined. To misappropriate McLuhan, the product is the package (Lightfoot and Lilley, 1999, p. 45)

And the market in academia, such as it is, serves only as a backdrop to the influence of mediating administrative power. This power functions through the influence of a seemingly ever increasing ...

> ... intermediary layer of actors and institutions – like funding agencies and programme bureaus – between research practices on the one hand, and state and societal institutions on the other hand (Rip, 1991, p. 401, quoted in Hill and Turpin, 1995, p. 138)

These intermediaries *produce* administrative power through their demands that the actors who they support render themselves accountable, which in our current 'audit society' (Power, 1994a; see also Power, 1994b), means auditable. Audit supports 'best practice', which, as you will remember, was one of my proposed gifts to the ESRC if they were willing to provide me with the funds to enable my endeavours. But one can go much further here than questioning the virtue of this support, for support seems to seamlessly shift into shaping:

> ... the cultural shift is ... not simply ... increasing pressure to plan and 'relate' the production of scientific knowledge, but ... shaping, and perhaps constraining, the production itself according to managerialist 'best practice' rules (Hill and Turpin, 1995, p. 139)

And 'best practice' in managerialism is increasingly that practice that supports auditability.

> Officially, audit is neutral with regard to ... standards. However, this disguises the fact that it is active in constructing them within a 'politics of best practice' in which the audit functions as much to impose definitions of quality on the local auditee environment as to monitor it. (Power, 1994a, p. 16)

Audit functions, whether on organizations, individuals or other institutions, through the construction of accounts or narratives of self. Hence the claim to neutrality with regard to standards:

> ... it is not ... that individuals are being asked to conspire in their own subordination by accepting the aims of others as their own ... it is their own aims that are externalized and reflected back to them. Each individual (person, institution, enterprise) is being asked to express and make public its own identity ... – to show *it is achieving its own goals* satisfactorily (Strathern, 1996, p. 9)

But only certain sorts of selves with certain sorts of aims will do here. In the audit society, a society in which, through demands for accountability, 'audit tends to become the sole basis for for administrative legitimacy', '"performance" of the auditee is reduced to the possibility of being audited' (Power, 1994a, p. 19). In an inversion of 'the sociopolitical fantasy ... of "primordial accumulation" [which] ... silently presupposes as already given what it purports to reproduce' (Žižek, 1997, p. 10–11), through the construction of auditable selves 'audit creates and sustains the very structures of accountability from which its demand is supposed to flow (Power, 1991)' (Power, 1994a, p. 6).

> ... audit only makes sense within particular *representations* of social arrangements, representations which are reinforced by the imperatives of audit (Power, 1994a, p. 5, original emphasis)

> Auditing 'represents' the auditee and thereby creates the condition of its own functioning. It does not 'passively' observe the auditee but constructs and inscribes it with the material basis upon which audit can operate (Power, 1994a, p. 17).

Audit constructs a simulational world of Baudrillardian proportions, for:

> Auditable systems require subjects to present themselves primarily as auditees ... [N]ot only do audits create and reinforce the conditions of their own functioning, but they seek to do so by creating a new bureaucratic 'surface' or social reality which is highly standardized and which represents the auditee for the purpose of the audit. (Power, 1994a, pp. 19 and 18 respectively)

Audit, literally the hearing of an account, demands a narrativization of self, an observation of self which, in the process of its production, produces an image of self that takes precedence over, and reaches back into, that which it purports merely to represent.

> Audit, as the 'self observation of the economic system' (Luhman, 1989) is a system in its own right. It functions by virtue of an 'auditing logic' which

demands auditable auditees as the condition of possibility of its own functioning. The auditing system of knowledge 'productively misunderstands' (Teubner, 1992) the auditee in order to make it auditable. In turn, auditees are potentially alien disturbances to this system which reacts by rendering them familiar and auditable. But, if auditing is an 'autopoietic' practice in this sense it is itself the disturbing environment for auditees who may adapt their practices in the name of ideals of verifiability, calculability and responsible control (Miller and O'Leary, 1987). (Power, 1994a, p. 21).

(Un)fortunately, however, audit is just like those other forms of narration that we encountered in our introductory comments. Just as narratives outside of the realms of formality that govern auditing provide a congenitally failing basis for identity, so does auditing provide a congenitally failing basis for ensuring the probity of activity that cannot, for reasons of distance, complexity (Flint, 1988) or ideology, be assessed directly:

> ... the production of trust from mistrust via auditing is not automatically effective. Indeed, the production of trust is constantly threatened and is constantly exposed by the continuing visibility of 'healthy' companies which fail, the accumulation of ecological risks, the decline of educational standards, the wastage of public revenues and so on. Ideals of accountability, transparency and control which are undermined must continually reaffirm themselves in a politics of failure which allocates blame and reconstitutes 'failed' practices (Power, 1994a, p. 13)

Rarely does audit express its congenitally failing nature directly, although as Power notes above, it is only through such failure that the goods that audit delivers, and thus its own necessity, can be reaffirmed. And it is rarer still for audit to admit with the transparency it demands of all other aspects of the world that it touches, its interference in the intimacies of the matters it orders through its translation of the activities it purports to merely inspect.

> Audit that so loves transparency conceals one thing: its reduction of external complexity is concealed under the banner of enhancement. It purportedly adds and augments organizations' understanding of themselves. And thus empowerment, the agent's capacity to act and the skills that involves, becomes absorbed into the internal complexifying development of those who want to make sure it it is visible there (Strathern, 1996, p. 13).

But this is precisely what we do witness in that amazingly brazen account of the 'purpose' of the ESRC's research grant scheme articulated in the final lines of the rapporteur's response to my appeal. Mediation by narrative, when coupled with the constructions of accountability that accompany and justify audit's form of the beast, ensures a conspiracy, a plot against the very activity whose probitious execution it promises to deliver.

> *Plots carry their own logic. There is a tendency of plots to move toward death ... [T]he idea of death is woven into the nature of every plot. A narrative plot no less than a conspiracy of armed men. The tighter the plot of a story, the more likely it will come to death. A plot in fiction ... is the way we localize the force of the death outside the book, play it off, contain it.* (DeLillo, 1991, p. 221, emphasis added).

When rapporteurs and assessors are concerned that 'it is unclear what this research will find', we are witnessing the death of interesting research activity. Even activity whose 'relevance' and 'rigor' would seem to meet precisely the demands that auditability seeks to deliver in this realm. For we must never forget that the demands of auditability always come first.

> *... the research grant scheme is not designed to support researchers, however competent, doing what they and practitioners find interesting and important.* It is designed to support research aimed to address particular objectives as set out in proposals.

The plans that constitute proposals are self-evidently plots whose logic must be respected. Audit demands activity that is auditable, activity that brooks no irony or contradiction. And concommitantly demands transformed actors that are capable of delivering it.

> Contradiction is the engine of the intellect. But turn aims into objectives, turn multiple possibilities into plans for action, and contradiction is banished. The institution [or research project or individual researcher] becomes judged by acts that presume unity – by the degree of consensus by which it will actually achieve its aims, and thus by the effectiveness which which it has actually *eliminated* contradictions. The simple model is that 'one' organization [or project] must be defined by one (coherent) mission. In other words the institution [or project] is like a 'self', defined by an identifiable singleness of purpose. Here the loop gets to throttling tautness: the 'self' in the invitation to self-scrutiny turns out to be already a particular kind of self – to be judged by criteria that agree what the self is, that is, the type of agency that propels persons/institutions towards their stated goals. (Strathern, 1997, p. 313, original emphasis).

In such circumstances it is little wonder that 'scrutiny has brought with it an explicit intolerance for open-ended research procedures' (Strathern's (1996, p. 8) account of Talai's (1996) conference presentation) and journals proliferate to house a seemingly endless increase in the number of articles which tell us what we already know.

Audit exacerbates the 'mistrust' its seeks to ameliorate and is forced to return to the 'trust' it supposedly supersedes even to deliver the poor substitute 'goods' that result from its guarantees (Armstrong, 1991). Just as the administration of sound research through assaying the extent of achievement of self-defined objectives exacerbates the need for judgement from which it seeks to shy. Just as narrative's flight from the 'primordial void or [ur-]antagonism' delivers only more antagonism on a grander scale. And life becomes a world of seemingly probitious connections in which:

> *Everyone [is] a spook or dupe or asset, a double, courier, cutout or defector, or was related to one. We [are] all linked in a vast and rhythmic coincidence, a daisy chain of rumor, suspicion and secret wish.* (DeLillo, 1991, p. 57).

Conspiracy revisited: learning from *Libra*?

> *The intoxications of power began to break apart under waves of discomfort ... His orders were being carried out even before they were given, even before he thought of them, and they always went much beyond what he would have dared have them do* (García Márquez, 1978, p. 140)

> Self-referential systems are inherently restless and disposed to reproduce (Nowotny, 1990)

Audit is an inherently self-referential system to be sure, but it is also a system with a history and antecedents, many of which are themselves only now falling under the sway of their well travelled progeny (Strathern, 1997; Hoskin, 1996). Immediate antecedents to the 'audit explosion' (Power, 1994b) are certainly to be seen in the realm of financial accounting and its seemingly natural link to accountability, but as Hoskin reminds us, the latter is the product less of finance, more of its antecedents in the *mélange* constituted by those formalized written examinations that could turn words into numbers and numbers into grades.

> *A word is a magic wish. A word from anyone. With a word they could begin to grid the world, make an instant surface that people can see and touch together* (DeLillo, 1991, p. 414).

Such moves enable the conflation of 'is' and 'ought' that Hoskin sees as characteristic of accountability, the ingratiation of 'enhancement' (Strathern, 1996) and 'improvement' (Strathern, 1997) into the fabric of administration and the activities it oversees. And it is this progressive impulse that remains rudely alive in the managerialism from which auditing derives its current impulsion. The busy-ness of business, the seeming *sine qua non* of the 'professionalism' required of all activities in our current accountability regime of endless improvement, means that all activities that must be rendered auditable (and that is pretty much *all* activities) and all of the entities that seek to perform them, must be rendered in a business-like and organized way.

> audit ... makes sense of an institution *as* an organization, and requires that it 'perform' *being* an organization, focusing on those parts that indicate performance ... auditing practices are a literal embodiment of ideals of organization ... Audit wants to see organization at 'work'... Hence audit elicits a self-description of the organization in terms of constant activation, as though every component of the organization were in a state perpetual self-awareness and animation. And in a constant state of explicitness (Strathern, 1996, pp. 12–13, original emphases).

In the absence of any other legitimized narratives that count, we must all account for ourselves, and do so only in ways that simulate the hyperrealities of hyperbusiness:

> The hyperactivity of an audit produces a description of the world as hyperactive (Strathern, 1997, p. 319)

Such accounts of the world are just what my informants produced as I conducted my ESRC funded research. For many of these informants they were deeply problematic, but for all of them there was no alternative available that could do the same work. Presenting this as a finding to an organization whose demands for auditabilty had already resulted in the embodiment of such imagery, exhibits something of the nature of the action of a 'strange attractor'. The mimetic pre-figuring of my results was always going to render them at best, old news, and at worst, sacrilegious, given that they had arisen through profance means. But this is not a problem of the ESRC alone, it is an inevitability of our mediated connections and distributed and ephemeral control in a world of narration and judgement. In such conditions, conspiracy will always be present, even when we are not. But what it will look like will depend upon where, and how, we stand to observe it.

> *If we are on the outside, we assume a conspiracy is the perfect working of a scheme. Silent nameless men with unadorned hearts. A conspiracy is everything that ordinary life is not. It's the inside game, cold, sure, undistracted, forever closed off to us. We are the flawed ones, the innocents, trying to make some rough sense of the daily jostle. Conspirators have a logic and a daring beyond our reach. All conspiracies are the same taut story of men who find coherence in some criminal act.*
> *But maybe not ... .* (DeLillo, 1991, p. 441).

> *There is enough mystery in the facts as we know them, enough of conspiracy, coincidence, loose ends, dead ends, multiple interpretations. There is no*

need ... to invent the grand and masterful scheme, the plot that reaches flawlessly in a dozen directions (DeLillo, 1991, p. 58)

Notes

1 This research was made possible by a grant from the ESRC, Award Reference Number R000221859. An earlier version of this paper was presented at the 1st International Critical Management Studies Conference, Manchester, July, 1999, and I am grateful for the helpful comments I received from other participants at this event. It has also benefitted from some invaluable input both from the editors of this volume and my colleague, Gavin Jack. Inadequacies that remain are all my own work.

2 Entirely italicized quotes in this chapter are taken from novels or, in this case song lyrics (*Revolution*, written by John Lennon and Paul McCartney of *The Beatles*). As the text surrounding these quotes should make abundantly clear, I believe such a distinction to be entirely arbitrary but follow it to demonstrate a measure of respect for standard academic convention.

3 ('post' –?

4 *The Big Issue* is a member of the International Network of Street Papers. Further details of INSP, and indeed of *The Big Issue*'s equivalents in other cities and countries can be found at http://www.bigissue.com/international/Default.htm

5 As usual, *Paperco* is a thoroughly unimaginative pseudonym.

6 The Left feature heavily in accounts from this organization's participants. For example, I have been informed on numerous occasions, by staff at all levels, that the organization's head office is situated in the last constituency in Britain to return a communist member of parliament.

7 Further details on the activities and remit of the ESRC *should* be available from its website, http://www.esrc.ac.uk/. However, rather delightfully for the purposes of this chapter, numerous attempts at the time of writing to connect to this site in order to quote the precise *raison d'être* claimed by the ESRC, all resulted in a message informing me that I have selected a 'BAD GATEWAY'.

8 'I assumed ... that what was necessary was to show a grant-giving body why proposed work was interesting/new/important. Nothing could be further from the truth. When an inexperienced ethnographer pushes this aspect of his (sic.) research, a grant-giving committee begins, perhaps on the basis of sound experience, to wonder how the research is standard/normal/a continuation of previous work. By stressing the vast theoretical implications of my little bit of research for the continued existence of anthropology, I was putting myself in the position of a man extolling the quality of roast beef to a party of vegetarians' (Barley, 1986, p. 14).

9 Another pseudonym.

10 But confronted by the practices of my involvement I am forced to pause, feel obliged to join in the minutes silence that reflexivity demands (Steve Brown, personal communication, but see also Stenner and Brown, 1997). Not for too long mind. Just enough to take not only the moral high ground but also the back door exit from these heights to offer up a paper and the opportunities it provides nonetheless (see also, Lilley, 1997; 1998a).

11 It is important to note here that I am also one of these functionaries and was so during the events described here. Wearing my application assessor's hat I am more than capable of producing similarly irritating texts to vex potential fundees, although I may choose different grounds on which to base my accusations.

12 A third issue related to the 'obviousness' of what I had discovered – it was already clear, at least to reviewer A, that there were 'markets' at work in the voluntary sector, the only difference with the more conventional business world being that these markets were multiple. Responding to this concern in the following acerbic tone clearly did little to facilitate my intent of changing the grading provided on the final report: 'The managers I spoke to were clearly less able than

reviewer A to adopt an Archimedean position from which they could be certain that there was indeed a "tripartite" market environment for voluntary organizations. They struggled a great deal with such an understanding. Some newer members of the organizations shared reviewer A's views, some wholeheartedly, some with reservations. But even those who thoroughly agreed with such a characterization of their activities were at pains to point out the endless problematics they faced when adapting advice designed for one "market" to uses in others in which very different goods are exchanged. In essence then, neither my informants nor myself share the arrogance of reviewer A in assuming that they know what is there before they have looked at the detail of a situation. If the confounding of my initial assumptions had been as simply achieved as reviewer A believes, I would of course happily accept this criticism, but it seems to me that the assuredness of this reviewer's tone belies the fact that the detail of my accounts of these sites is unamenable to characterization in the mode s/he prefers. The priority of their market view simply precludes them from seeing what the informants have said'.

13 At least four write ups in practitioner magazines of which I am aware, along with two radio appearances – there's nothing like blowing one's own trumpet!

14 To be clear here, this is the *only* aspect of my experience with the ESRC which I highlight in order to make a point that derives its legitimation through invocation of 'bad' (not 'best'?) practice. My aim in writing this paper is NOT to suggest that the ESRC is some sort of monstrous beast that inevitably and deliberately produces unworthy research, far from it. Rather, as I hope I make clear in my concluding remarks, I am seeking to suggest that when narrativization spreads accountability through *any* network of activity, that a form of conspiracism arises between otherwise unconnected and entirely probitius individuals, to the positive detriment of whatever activity that network is intended to accomplish. In short, that narrativized mediation of activity, enabling accountability and its concommitant, audit (Strathern, 1997; Hoskin, 1996), is inevitably conspiratorial.

15 Page references to Power (1994a) refer to a mimeographed version of the article distributed at a presentation to the Department of Accounting and Business Method, Edinburgh University.

16 The italicization of 'demands' here is intended to indicate a level of agnosticism with regard to the extent to which individuals are actually 'constituted' by a supposedly hegemonic cultural context such as 'enterprise' (see, for example, Fournier and Grey, 1999; Armstrong, forthcoming; and indeed, Kelemen, 2000 who takes up this point with regard to TQM regimes), or at the very least, the difficulties involved in establishing evidence for such a claim (Armstrong, forthcoming).

References

Armstrong, P., (1991), 'Contradiction and Social Dynamics in the Capitalist Agency Relationship', *Accounting, Organizations and Society*, 15 (1): 1–25.

Armstrong, P., (forthcoming), 'Styles of Illusion', *Sociological Review*.

Barley, N., (1986), *The Innocent Anthropologist: Notes from a Mudhut*, London: Penguin.

Burke, K., (1969), *A Grammar of Motives*, Berkeley: University of California Press.

Brown, R.H., (1987), *Society as Text: Essays on rhetoric, reason and reality*, London: University of Chicago Press.

Brown, R.H., (ed.) (1992), *Writing the Social Text: Poetics and Politics in Social Science Discourse*, New York: Aldine de Gruyter.

Burnham, J., (1941), *The Managerial Revolution: What is happening in the world*, New York: John Day.

Cooper, R., (1986), 'Notes on Organizational Kitsch', Working Paper, University of Lancaster.

Czarniawska B., (1997), 'A Four Times Told Tale: Combining Narrative and Scientific Knowledge in Organization Studies', *Organization*, 4 (1): 7–30.

Czarniawska-Joerges, B., (1995), 'Narration or Science? Collapsing the Division in Organization Studies', *Organization*, 4 (1): 11–33.

Czarniawska-Joerges, B. and Guillet de Monthoux P., (eds) (1994), *Good Novels, Better Management. Reading Organizational Realities in Fiction*, Chur (Switzerland): Harwood Academic Press.

DeLillo, D., (1991), *Libra*, London: Penguin.

Flint, D., (1988), *Philosophy and Principles of Auditing*, London: Macmillan Education.

Fournier, V. and Grey, C., (1999), 'Too much, too little and too often: a critique of Du Gay's analysis of enterprise', *Organization*, 6 (1): 107–128.

García Márquez, G., (1978), *One Hundred Years of Solitude*, London: Pan.

Guest, D.E., (1987), 'Human Resource Management and Industrial Relations', *Journal of Management Studies*, 24 (5): 503–521.

Habermas, J., (1984), *The Theory of Communicative Action, Vol. 1: Reason and the Rationalisation of Society*, trans. T. McCarthy, Boston: Beacon Press.

Habermas, J., (1987), *The Theory of Communicative Action, Vol. 2: Lifeworld and System: A Critique of Functionalist Reason*, trans. T. McCarthy, Boston: Beacon Press.

Hill, S. and Turpin, T., (1995), 'Cultures in collision: the emergence of a new localism in academic research', in Strathern, M. (ed.), *Shifting Contexts: Transformations in Anthropological Knowledge*, London: Routledge.

Hoskin, K., (1996), 'The "awful idea of accountability": inscribing people into the measurement of objects', in Munro, R. and Mouritsen, J. (eds), *Accountability: Power, Ethos and the Technologies of Managing*, London: International Thomson Business Press.

Keat, R., (1991), 'Consumer sovereignty and the integrity of practices', in Keat, R. and Abercrombie, N. (eds), *Enterprise Culture*, London: Routledge.

Kelemen, M., (2000), 'Too Much or Too Little Ambiguity: The Language of Total Quality Management', *Journal of Management Studies*, 37 (4): 483–498.

Kierkegaard, S., (1966), *The Concept of Irony: With Constant Reference to Socrates*, trans. Lee M. Capel, London: William Collins.

Lightfoot, G. and Lilley, S., (1999), 'Fixing Futures?', *Emergence*, 1 (3): 37–50.

Lilley, S., (1995), 'Disintegrating Chronology', *Studies in Cultures, Organizations and Societies*, 2 (1): 1–33.

Lilley, S., (1997), 'Stuck in the middle with you?', *British Journal of Management*, 8 (1): 51–60.

Lilley, S., (1998a), 'Wisdom and Understanding? Would you Like Fries with That?: A View from Behind the Counter', in Jary, D. and Parker, M. (eds), *The Dilemmas of Mass Higher Education: Issues for a post-Dearing HE System*, Stoke-on-Trent: Staffordshire University Press.

Lilley, S., (1998b), 'Mass Needs Existential Philanthropy: The Counterfactual Construction of Care', Centre for Social Theory and Technology Conference on the *Consumption of Mass*, Prince Rupert Hotel, Shrewsbury.

Linstead, S., (1996), 'Administrative Science as Kitsch', paper presented at the *Translations* Conference, Malahide, Co. Dublin.

Luhman, N., (1989), *Ecological Communication*, trans. J. Bednarz, Cambridge: Polity Press.

Lyotard, J.-F., (1984), *The Postmodern Condition: A Report on Knowledge*, trans. G. Bennington and B. Massumi, Manchester: Manchester University Press.

Miller, P. and O'Leary, T., (1987), 'Accounting and the Construction of the Governable Person', *Accounting, Organizations and Society*, 12 (3): 235–266.

Nowotny, H., (1990), 'Actor-networks versus science as a self-organizing system: a comparative view of two constructivist approaches', in Krohn, W. *et al.* (eds), *Selforganization: Portrait of a scientific revolution*, Dordecht, Netherlands: Kluwer Academic Publishers.

Power, M., (1991), 'Auditing and Environmental Expertise: Between Protest and Professionalisation', *Accounting, Auditing and Accountability*, 4 (3): 30–42.

Power, M., (1994a), 'The Audit Society', in Hopwood, A. and Miller, P. (eds), *Accounting as Social and Institutional Practice*, Cambridge: Cambridge University Press.

Power, M., (1994b), *The Audit Explosion*, London: Demos.

Rip, A., (1991), 'The R&D system in transition: an exercise in foresight', in Cozzens, S.E., Healey, P., Rip, A. and Ziman, J. (eds), *The Research System in Transition – to What?*, Dordecht, Netherlands: Kluwer Academic Publishers.

Roszak, T., (1986), *The Cult of Information*, Homewood, IL: Dow Jones-Irwin.

Said, E., (1997), *Beginnings: Intention and Method*, London: Granta.

Smith. A., (2001), 'Brought to book', *The Observer Magazine*, 11th February, 8–15.

Stenner, P. and Brown, S., (1997), 'Psychology as history and philosophy: implications for research', *The Psychologist*, 11 (4): 172–175.

Strathern, M., (1995), Foreword to Strathern, M. (ed.), *Shifting Contexts: Transformations in Anthropological Knowledge*, London: Routledge.

Strathern, M., (1996), 'A Case of Self-Organisation', paper presented to the workshop on *Complexity and the Social Sciences*, Centre for Social Theory and Technology, Keele University.

Strathern, M., (1997), 'Improving ratings': audit in the British University system', *European Review*, 5 (3): 305–321.

Talai, (1996), 'The insidiousness of bureaucratic banalities: some implications for anthropological fieldwork', paper presented at the *IV EASA Conference*, Barcelona.

Teubner, G., (1992), 'The Two Faces of Janus: Rethinking Legal Pluralism', *Cardozo Law Review*, 13 (5), 1443–1462.

Wallace, D.F., (2000), *Brief Interviews with Hideous Men*, London, Abacus.

Žižek, S., (1997), *The Plague of Fantasies*, London: Verso

Human science as conspiracy theory

Martin Parker

Our newspaper is delivered by a middle-aged Iranian driving a Nissan Sentra. Something about the car makes me uneasy – the car waiting with its headlights on, at dawn, as the man places the newspaper on the front steps. I tell myself I have reached an age, the age of unreliable menace. The world is full of abandoned meanings. In the commonplace I find unexpected themes and intensities. (DeLillo, 1986: 184)

My mission, should you choose to accept it ...

I believe that I have uncovered a conspiracy – a coincidence that is too perfect to be an accident – and I have a great deal of circumstantial evidence that supports my claim. In this chapter I will document a series of systematic connections between conspiracy theories and elements of the human sciences.[1] Putting it simply, my argument will be that contemporary theories of conspiracy share a narrative structure with much of human science generally. On investigation, it is clear that both are attempts to provide explanatory myths for mass societies in that they claim to uncover (supposedly) 'hidden' plots or machineries which have caused a particular state of affairs or event to take place.

There are conspiracies everywhere nowadays. UFOlogy, crime fiction, the assassinations of Princess Diana, Martin Luther King, Marilyn Monroe; the figure on the grassy knoll; cash for questions; photographs of fairies; the search for the holy grail; the fiction of Pynchon, Eco and De Lillo; the *Men in Black*, *Dark Skies*, *X Files* and *Roswell High*; the TWA 800 crash; the New World Order, GATT, WTO; the 'Heavens Gate' suicides; Waco; the Turin shroud; alien abductions; computer viruses; the beast of Bodmin; the Majestic 12; freemasons; the Templars; the Trilateral Commission; international terrorism; the face on Mars; crop circles; black helicopters; Loch Ness; Watergate, Irangate, Whitewater, Monicagate; the Roswell incident; *The Matrix*; Area 51; gulf war syndrome; Lockerbie; the Nazca plain markings; the CIA, AIDS, crack cocaine and the ghetto; Mad Cow disease; Elvis is alive and well and living in ... (Don't you KNOW about all these? Why not?[2])

W.H. Auden's second world war poem, *The Age of Anxiety*, is set in a time 'when everybody is reduced to the status of shady character or a displaced person, when even the most prudent become worshippers of chance' in response 'to the universal disorder of the world outside' (1948: 7) That was then, this is now. But, as this book evidences, in the last half century North Atlantic culture has not moved beyond this kind of diagnosis. Auden's 'age of anxiety' is now DeLillo's 'age of unreliable menace'. The role of the seemingly ubiquitous conspiracy '*theorist*' is to connect things which were previously unconnected – to posit causes, motives, plans and plots. Importantly, the grammar of these theories is not insane speculation – or a romantic poetic wildness – but a form of detective work which uses the tools of the hypothetico-deductive method. Photographs, documents, eye witness accounts and so on are used to demonstrate that a particular explanation successfully draws together a series of events and causes. The popularity of these accounts is huge, and the heat generated by arguments about particular conspiracies is often quite intense. Yet at the same time conspiracy theories are often treated with derision by commentators who claim to be more rational and scientific. Indeed, claiming to believe in a particular conspiracy in the wrong company can produce some alarming effects. So, how can we explain this culture of conspiracy, this age of anxiety?

But why should I want to answer that kind of question? Why should I want to explain the big conspiracy that holds together all these little conspiracies? So perhaps one way to avoid the question might be to celebrate conspiracy, rather than condemning it or explaining it (away). After all, it seems rather unreflexive to point at other people's paranoia, at 'them', as if this exempted myself from the diagnosis. Physician, heal thyself. Instead, perhaps what is is required is that one becomes paranoid oneself. So, in this chapter I will argue that much of sociology, psychology, economics, geography and so on shares the same project and narrative structure. For example, the holy trinity of Marx, Durkheim and Weber – and the many others who preceded and followed them – all claimed access to some level of explanation which was somehow beyond the apprehension of ordinary persons. By invoking causes such as capitalism, evolution, convergence, patriarchy, human nature, imperialism, functional prerequisites, mythological structures, *homo economicus*, complexity and so on, all these theorists of the human have claimed to be able to explain what was not previously understood. These are explanations that somehow reached beyond the skin of everyday life to expose the machinery at work 'behind people's backs'. 'Theory' then, as a seeing from a distance, as a way of seeing what those who are too closely implicated cannot themselves see.

So I have three aims in this document. Firstly, to ironize certain forms of theory by comparing them to a form of popular cultural explanation which is widely dismissed. Secondly, to think about the atmosphere of an age of anxiety. It seems to me that the desire to find explanations, to theorize events, the 'will to connect' is centrally implicated in a culture that must explain everything. And so, my third aim will be to gesture vaguely towards (and suggest the limitations of) a form of thinking which might be predicated on no longer searching for *an* explanation, but instead attempts to disseminate as many wild explanations as possible. Both the celebration of many conspiracies, and the doubting of all of them, would seem to follow from such a position.

Revealing the logic of conspiracy

How might we think conspiracy? And is conspiracy in some way different from the unfolding of a plot, or a plan? The latter two terms were originally, and are still also, ways of describing a piece of land, a flat surface, plateau, plate or plane. The slippage of meaning towards something more nefarious seems to occur when some kind of representation intervenes, a ground plan, scheme or design (of a building for example). Any representation suggests a particular way of seeing the ground, one that accounts for it (and its past and future) in a different way. Representation is architectural, in that sense of constructing a perspective from which to look towards the earth (Kallinikos, 1995). Correspondingly, if you can not see the plan then the plot will not be clear. A comprehension of the past and the construction of the future will be beyond your understanding. Importantly then, in order to see the plan, you must be elevated, lifted, from the terrain. Standing on the earth will not do for a plan – the earth must be represented from above, from somewhere else.

There is something quite curious going on here. It seems that elevation from the 'here and now' allows for time to be thought. Once time can be thought, then so can lineages of explanation which separate 'events' and 'causes', 'precedents' and 'ante-cedents'. Plots, plans and conspiracies share this grammar of a series of 'events', and some 'causes' to tie them together, but they also share the sense of an elevated place for the observer. This seems to be a rather paradoxically useful logic, so let me use it on this other word – 'event'. For something to take on the status of event, it must be in some way 'unexplained'. To explain is to provide causes, to account for the antecedents or intentions of the event, and being unexplained suggests that all causes posited so far have not yet stuck to the event in a convincing way. Oddly, the recognition of an event as an 'effect' might 'cause' causes to become an issue – might think them into being. So, recognizing the 'unexplained' requires that we understand that certain causes did not cause, rather that they were contingent to the event, or epiphemonema of the event. Once again, elevation is crucial in order to see the way that explanation works. You cannot see how the billiard balls are clicking against each other, falling into pockets and bouncing off cushions, if your line of perspective is on the green felt. You will not be able to see the event.

So here is the point. A conspiracy theory creates and ties together a series of events in relations of cause and effect. Conspiracy is predicated on uncovering a specific form of order and structure. Once we inhabit the elevated universe of conspiracy there can be no unexplained residues, everything has a cause, everything has meaning and nothing can be left out. As one of Umberto Eco's characters puts it, 'every earthly object (...) must be read as the hieroglyph of something else' (1990: 576). Everything must mean something, nothing can mean nothing. Like a detective looking for evidence – a stray hair, a missing minute, a footprint – everything is a clue. Once Sherlock Holmes has us trapped within the web of causes there can be no uncaused event.

But conspiracy theory in our age does not merely echo the detective novel, partly because it embraces far more than it used to. The detective novel takes a delimited set of characters, puts them on a train and then something happens. A murder usually of course, and the question that follows is a simple 'whodunnit'? Once we have discovered 'whodidit', the puzzle is solved and the case closed. Contemporary conspiracies are harder to solve, because they are not simple puzzles which can be answered with an accusation of 'Miss Scarlet, in the library with a knife'. Instead they are ramified, interconnected nets of events and causes with a wide variety of possible solutions and agencies. To add to the complexity, there are counter-agents who may be consistently laying false trails and putting out dis-information in order to confuse our attempts at explanation. The single 'twist in the tail/tale' that comes at the *denouément* of the detective novel becomes amplified into a more pervasive and endless trope in the conspiracy. We can never be sure that our theory is accurate, or whether this is just what 'they' want us to believe. Where the conspiracy ends is unclear.

So, plots, schemes and conspiracies imply some kind of agency which is preventing us from discovering the truth, from connecting events and causes in a correct manner. Now, this sounds rather like the old problem of being tricked by the devil. Consider Descartes version of it for example.

> I shall suppose, therefore, that there is not a true God, who is the sovereign source of truth, but some evil demon, no less cunning and deceiving than powerful, who has used all his artifice to deceive me. (...) That is why I shall take great care not to accept into my belief anything false, and shall so well prepare my mind against all the tricks of this great deceiver that, however powerful and cunning he may be, he will never be able to impose on me. (Descartes, 1968: 100)

Yet the point of conspiracy thinking is that we can never be sure that our minds are well prepared, that the clues are not merely tricks. In other words, though we might have a faith in reason – for why else would we theorize – it cannot be an unconditional one for the truth statements that make up our logical syllogisms might always be false. Descartes felt he could reason his way out of this problem, but in doing so invokes an even bigger cause – God. But if God is dead, then all we have left is the evil demon.

Another way of putting this is to say that conspiracy theories are never falsifiable, but they are never verifiable either. Indeed it seems that the elevated position they require, the perspective that is their condition of possibility, does not guarantee any firm contact with the ground at all. They are entirely self-confirming belief systems. Now these kind of beliefs have been described in other contexts too, and a rather well known one is Evans-Pritchard's account of witchcraft beliefs amongst the Azande of the Sudan (1937, see also Skinner, this volume). The question here is again one of event and cause. Why has my crop failed? Why did my uncle fall ill? Why did the grain store fall on my child? One kind of answer to the latter might be – 'because termites had weakened its supports'. But why did the termites weaken the grain store? Because that is what termites do. The manifest inadequacy of this final answer for a grieving parent suggests that these are simply not the causes needed. In order to discern these, *benge*, the poison oracle must be consulted. And, if the procedure is applied correctly, then a witch will be discovered and a suitable accusation and form of reparation will follow. Since witchcraft can be an unconscious practice, the *benge* accusation is deemed to be sufficient proof of the practice. According to Evans-Pritchard, 'smelling out' a witch is a matter of public credibility, and if the answer was deemed wrong (due to its lack of public credibility) there was a fault in the procedure, in the fowl, the poison or whatever. The logic of witchcraft causes and effects is unharmed.

So this is a self supporting, reversible argument. How do you know there are conspiracies? Because they don't want me to know about them, which proves that conspiracies exist. Let me take an example. In a recent book on UFOs the author is pointing to the long pedigree of similar stories in human history. After citing Vedic literature, tales of Greek Gods, stories of magical flight and extraordinary powers he says:

> Skeptics would say that this only indicates that UFO lore is itself a kind of folklore. Others would argue the opposite – that such widespread themes demonstrate that folklore and myth are based on actual events – in these cases, on actual UFO experiences. (Brookesmith, 1997: 12)

It seems that, whatever the evidence, the explanations can be connected. Once the 'event' needs a 'cause', or a witch, one can usually be found. It is the very asking of questions of 'events' that makes some attribution of cause necessary.

Conspiracy and science

So far this might easily be taken to imply that conspiracy thinking is somehow deficient, that it is irrational, a perverse manifestation of Lévy-Bruhl's 'primitive mentality' in the late twentieth century. Diagnoses like this are certainly common – Carl Sagan's *The Demon Haunted World* (1996) for example. Once we rid the world of demons and hauntings, of astrology and fortuna then we will be able to produce a clearer, more transparent, society. Mysticism is an obstacle to modernization and must be swept away by science. But this kind of response doesn't really attend to the texts of conspiracy very closely, because it seems to me that such texts are often very decidedly rationalist in their ramified logics. In that sense we might suggest a double move in the literature on the unexplained and conspiracy – it both suggests that modern science and authority doesn't explain everything *and* that new science will.

It seems to me that conspiracy thinking is not mysticism, is not easily characterized as Sagan's rural nostalgic primitivism alive and well in the late modern city. (Though this also exists.) Indeed, publications like *Fortean Times* and *UFO Magazine* are decidedly rationalist – with extreme criticism for the hoaxers and much play given to the academic/scientific qualifications held by authors. Issues of trust and credibility are obviously central here, with the internet (almost the spiritual home of conspiracy theory) being treated with considerable scepticism, and even hostility, for the bad name it gives to respectable investigators. My point here is not simply that conspiracy theories 'ape' science in a child-like way, but that they model themselves on it. Take *UFO: The Complete Sightings Catalogue* again for example.

> I have avoided single-witness cases, as they are less reliable than those involving two or more observers. (Brookesmith, 1997: 8)

The book is full of such cautionary statements, together with citation of authorities and attempts to limit wild speculation by others. His arguments do not celebrate poetic invention or imagination, but attempt to deal with 'the facts'. Towards the end of his book, Brookesmith presents eight causal hypotheses to explain UFO sightings, and outlines the evidence for and against each one: 'Extra-Terrestrial Hypothesis', 'Alien Cohabitants', 'Atmospheric Animals', 'The Federal Hypothesis', 'The Earthlights Hypothesis', 'From Other Dimensions', 'Hallucinations', 'Psychic Intrusions' and 'Psychic Hardware' (Brookesmith, 1997: 166–169). Each of these hypotheses is, in principle, testable – even if there might be severe difficulties in actually operationalizing such a test. And this, of course, is a particular problem if there are agencies who do not wish for these matters to be uncovered – whether they be 'evil demons' or the military-industrial complex.

Organization and conspiracy

Conspiracy comes from the latin root *conspirare* – literally to breath together, to co-ordinate, to organize. My thesaurus makes these links with 'planning' laterally without recourse to any archaeological etymology.

> **623. Plan – N.** *Plan*, scheme, design; planning, contrivance; organisation. systematization, rationalization, centralization.

In that sense organization is conspiracy, and (as several chapters in this book exemplify) big organizations form a major element of conspiracy thinking. What Brookesmith calls the 'Federal Hypothesis' is a component in many of his other hypotheses too – that sinister corporations, the military-industrial complex, secret agencies and so on are working in various ways to ensure that we do not discover the truth. The emblematic status of the *X-Files*, the insistence that the 'truth is out there', seems to embody this sense that modern conspiracy has translated Descartes 'evil demon' into a demonology of the Machiavellian organization. I and others have written about this with reference to contemporary science fiction and culture in other places so I don't propose to dwell on its textual ramifications in this chapter (Parker, 1998, 2000; Parker and Cooper, 1998; Smith *et al.*, 2001). Here, I want to treat it as a fact.

This is because there are cameras watching. There is a security camera watching my building now. If I slide back from the computer I can see a pylon on a grassy bank. It is elevated above the terrain. On top of it is a white camera, with two infra-red lamps. It turns to watch buildings, car parks, my office. Someone, somewhere, is controlling it, but I don't know who they are, or where on the Keele campus they are located. This is a fact.

They are always watching you. The government, big brother whatever you want to call it. (Paraweb, 1998)

Mine is an 'organizational society', one in which citizens are being continually counted, monitored, examined and surveyed. This is not a Kafkaesque nightmare, but a description of what is actually happening. Last night I had a phone call from an employee of 'Kwik-Fit' to ask me whether I was happy with the service I received last week, and whether I would be interested in hearing about other services they could offer me. She was obviously reading a script. Why did she phone? Why is that car waiting outside with its engine on? As Baudrillard suggests, 'the Stealth Agency' – 'invisible, anonymous and clandestine' is a terribly pervasive trope of the times.

This could equally well be called:
ANATHEMATIC ILLIMITED
TRANSFATAL EXPRESS
VIRAL INCORPORATED
INTERNATIONAL EPIDEMICS. (1994: 14)

Our lives are organized for us between Keele University and Kwik-Fit. Just as one audits my research output, so does the other audit my spending patterns. So surely it would be foolish to imagine that there are not other institutions which are attempting to monitor and manipulate in clandestine ways? Recent work by a variety of anti-corporate writers gives ample evidence for such a claim, for the insinuations of stealth marketing or the corporate takeover of state institutions (Klein, 2000; Monbiot, 2000; Smith, this volume).[3] And of course they don't want me to know about this. After all, if I knew what they were doing to me and for me my responses might be less predictable or, as Noam Chomsky would have it, they would be revealed as greedy utilitarian capitalists set on market domination. As the main character (played by Mel Gibson) in the 1997 film 'Conspiracy Theory' puts it:

> A good conspiracy is an unprovable one. If you can prove it they must have screwed up somewhere along the line.

I don't feel betrayed by this. Its just a fact of life.

The 'masses' and conspiracy

It is hardly surprising then that a pervasive psychologization of this mood of conspiracy can be found in the diagnosis of paranoia. The megalomaniac assumption that the world rotates around yourself, that there are cameras watching, that what you do *matters* in some way to somebody. But the root of the word – *para* – suggests that one is beside one's mind, not fully inhabiting one's head. In other words, the diagnosis pathologizes the condition, positions it as something abnormal rather than as a fact of life. It seems to me that this is rather a common diagnosis of a particular kind of modern sickness, one that can be found in Marx as 'alienation' and Durkheim as 'anomie'. Importantly, what all these terms do is to conjecture a split self as problematic, as an unity which has been severed by the conditions of modern life. And this putative split produces perspectives which are not accurate responses or understandings of what is 'really' going on.

Elaine Showalter's book *Hystories* (1997) follows this line in suggesting that the 'plague of paranoias' which US culture suffers from effectively displaces responsibility for social problems. There is a sense here that something is being mis-recognized, or that we are being distracted. In looking to the skies we misplace our attention when, for Showalter, we should be concentrating on the salient material features of late capitalism. In other words, the real cause of conspiracy events are insecure labour markets, global capitalism, the collapse of the local and so on. Frederic Jameson (1988) has quite a similar line. For him the trope of conspiracy is a 'poor person's cognitive mapping' of the postmodern age. It is a hopeless attempt to map the ramified logic of late capital, to think the impossible totality of the world system. 'They', the masses, seem to need the comforting simplicity which is invoked here, one that implies a childlike faith in simple explanation. But of course Showalter and Jameson are not childlike because they 'know' where the real explanation lies. Their elevation allows for a better perspective on such matters, they understand that the simple conspiracy theory is actually a much more complex one. So finding causes for conspiracy can often seem like a infinite regress. You displace one form of explanation by another, larger, explanation. The role that 'global capitalism' plays in Showalter and Jameson's accounts is a common one, simply because Marxism in general has functioned as a pervasive conspiracy theory for most of this century. And this works in both ways – it is again a reversible argument – since Marxism can be a theory of conspiracy (for Marxists), or a conspiracy itself (for anti-Marxists). Or even (for Featherstone, this volume) the pervasive need for a 'master of puppets' in the application of conspiracism to forms of Marxism disguises the fact that our deepest senses of identity are now structured by individualizing forms of thought and hence 'secretly related to the paranoic system of delusions' which plagues non-dialectical thinking (Adorno, 1995: 296).

But there is another, now more fashionable, form of conspiracy explanation too – the invoking of some version of the 'postmodern'. In an essay which eschews the poverty of cognitive mapping type of explanation, Alasdair Spark suggests that the popularity of conspiracy thinking is related to:

a postmodern collapse of distinctions between the literal and the metaphorical, the factual and the fictional, the paranoid and the persecuted, the plausible and the incredible. (Spark, 2001: 4)

Now, instead of economics, we have a kind of culturalist determinism here, one that suggests that the flattening of the hierarchies at the heart of postmodern culture is providing fertile ground for forms of thought which are predicated on mixing different genres. Thus the 'believe it or not', 'mysteries of the unexplained' genre dissolves into the social reporting and political concern genre. Spark's colleague in this 'conspiracy culture' research – Peter Knight – suggests that:

A postmodern form of paranoid skepticism has become routine in a world in which the conspiratorial netherworld has become hypervisible, its secrets just one more commodity. (...) This reconfigured form of popular paranoia is in effect one of the defining characteristics of what has come to be known as postmodern culture. (2000: 75)

In other words, people believe in conspiracies because they no longer have much else to believe in. The old stabilities of state, community, expert and authority have been washed away by the inexorable tides of postmodern scepticism. Once again, it seems that there are issues of trust and credibility being raised here, and the 'certainties' of conspiracy explanation provide some kind of life raft to hang onto whilst the grand liner of Western modernism sinks without trace.

Now whilst I am not attempting to ironize any of these contributions – well, not much anyway – it seems that Showalter, Jameson, Spark and Knights are all essentially engaged in the same logic. In order to stand above conspiracy theory, in order to see the real plot, they invoke another level of explanation. In this way Karl Popper argued, for example, that conspiracy thinking is caused by abandoning God but not fully embracing science (1969). Whatever the form of the argument, these writers are positioning their explanations, their surveillance cameras, above the 'mass' who believe. They would disavow such an explanation of course, invoking perhaps a certain kind of reflexive playfulness on the part of conspiracists, but they would say that wouldn't they? Spark and Knight (both in this volume) are populists, but still academics attempting to account for matters that everyday people do not fully understand. This allows them to suggest alternative explanations for the problematic event, but of course the 'event' this time is not the assassination of JFK, but the proliferation of theories about the assassination of JFK. So, in other words, they end up invoking a larger conspiracy – a diagnosis that the patient is paranoid; is falsely consciousness; is playfully reflexive; or is even suffering from a nasty collapse of faith in metanarratives. Conspiracy is explained (away), and the treatment is truth.

Human science and politics

But, as should be fairly clear by this point, I am not at all convinced about the distinction between 'conspiracy theories' and 'theories about conspiracy'. They seem to me to be both based on a very similar logic of elevation and plotting. Indeed, they even share a logic of improvement, a narrative of intellectual progress through the uncovering of better descriptions or explanations. Hence, just like human science, theorizing about conspiracy can easily be justified as a task intended to preserve liberalism and democracy.

> Believing in conspiracies doesn't make a person anti-government. In fact, it may be just the opposite. Seeking out the corruption, if it exists, helps in the quest for a better society. (Paraweb, 1998)

And, reversing this logic once again, so can investigative journalists bemoan the state obsession with secrecy that itself produces websites like Paraweb.

> A child in the dark will imagine things – creepy, scary things. So it is with a nation kept in the dark. The obsession with secrecy has bred a population vulnerable to conspiracy theories and sinister imaginings. (...) If the country wants to get a grip on its secrets, it must first check its compulsion to lock up everything. (Gup, 2000: 14)

So whether from conspiracy junkies, or liberal journalists who want freedom of information, the quest to discover the truth, against all odds, is a very familiar trope in the texts of conspiracy. A standard film plot, for example, involves the 'fugitive' attempting to find out who framed them, who they can really trust, who is one of 'them'. The resolution is (almost always) a victory for truth, justice (and the American way). Even if the resolution is not achieved, as in the *X Files*, (see Bell and Bennion-Nixon, this volume) the journey continues. It seems as if discovering that the conspiracy is more labyrinthine than we imagined merely encourages us to explore further, to keep asking more questions.

So the search for explanations can be posited as a heroic one. The more 'we' know, the less 'they' can control us. This is the 'quest' for knowledge, the question that begins a journey with trials and tribulations, but one that takes us to a better place. Erich von Daniken puts it nicely in the opening to his *Chariots of the Gods?* – a book which posits that the earth has already been visited by aliens.

It took courage to write this book, and it will take courage to read it. (...) scholars will call it nonsense and put it on the index of those books which are better left unmentioned. Laymen will withdraw into the snail-shell of their familiar world ... (1971: 11)

If you have the courage, and who is going to admit that they do not, then you might attempt to look beyond the boundaries of your certainties. But we don't need to invoke extra-terrestrials in order to be engaged in a heroic un-masking. Lee Richards, writing in the home produced Stoke-on-Trent UFO magazine *Beyond Blue Book* (1998) suggests that the Roswell incident was faked by the US government. This was in order to convince other governments – primarily the USSR – that the USA had alien technology, and hence gain a strategic advantage in any potential hostilities. My point here is that this is a perfectly credible explanation, one which relies on many features of the world which most of us assume and that does not invoke any agency or mechanism which we do not have knowledge of. We know that states often behave in Machiavellian ways; that various state agencies (CIA, MI6, Mossad) use propaganda; and that the cold war was a time of remarkable tension between the USA and the Soviet bloc. These are all matters of historical record, of common knowledge. Why then should we not believe this particular account of attempts at ideologically driven control through fear and suspicion? As Ronson (2001) documents, in his *exposé* of the Bilderberg Group, there is nothing particularly surprising about the idea of wealthy industrialists and politicians meeting in secret to discuss matters of common concern. Indeed, it would be rather surprising if they did not attempt to use their power in concert to achieve outcomes that they collectively believed to be desirable.

It seems here that the logic of conspiracy creates some strange bedfellows. This is not to say that the causes, events or teleologies are all the same, rather that the attempt to uncover the truth, to find the hidden mechanisms, is one that can be found on both the right and the left. Indeed, perhaps as Quinn argues (this volume), some form of conspiracy thinking is a condition of politics itself. Both Noam Chomsky and the US militias are suspicious of the military-industrial complex and the emerging new world order (see Spark, and James, both this volume). What is common here is not only the diagnosis of modernity gone off the tracks, but also the faith in a form of explanation which is capable of pulling apart the fabric of what appears to be real in order to uncover the pattern behind the order of things. This is to show that *tout est lié*, that everything is in someway connected to everything else. What appears in the everyday, that which is commonplace, then takes on a sinister sheen. The everyday assumptions held by everyday people about what causes what are ironized. When what we see, think and do is treated as an epiphenomena, the question of what counts as 'real' phenomena becomes urgent, indeed becomes a political necessity. And so a multiplicity of substrates, of grounds, are proposed as being more foundational.

And so, our economic decisions are not 'ours' but caused by the hidden hand of markets. The market imperatives of globalizing capitalism are resulting in convergence on a form of democratic liberalism. The movements of populations, weather and water droplets can be mathematized as a science of complexity. The law of the tendency of the rate of profit to fall is causing greater and greater fluctuations in the world system which will eventually result in its downfall. Pathological personality development follows from unhealthy Id, Ego and Superego alignments. Anomic suicide is most common in Protestant countries because of a decline in the density of community. Our personalities, mating rituals bodies, hair colour are caused by evolutionary biology, or even the human genome. The dialectic of enlightenment turns all our dreams of emancipation into hollow consumerist fakes. Employees are naturally self interested and best motivated by financial incentives. History is a cyclical process. Capitalism occurred in Western Europe because of an elective affinity with non-conformist religions. All our institutions and interactions are being MacDonaldized. Our senses of subjectivity in late modern societies are effects of a narcissistic society of surveillance. Cities and their peripheries are taking new forms according to the availability of transportation mechanisms. For psychological reasons people tend to buy brightly coloured packages. And so on ...

Not only are many of these postulated substrates tangential to one another, or even contradictory, they are also vying with each other for the prize of which is 'deepest', the most 'penetrating', or perhaps (given the metaphor I have been employing) the most 'elevated'. At this point you might think I am simply stretching things too far. Suggesting that economics, geography, sociology and so on are forms of conspiratorial thinking is lumping together a collection of very diverse forms of thought as if they were connected in some way. So, in response, let me push the argument even further. Does a 'hermeneutic of suspicion' (a scepticism that exceeds all reason) escape the net of conspiracy? If we accept the premise that the world is not as it seems, that there is (or could be) something else going on, then any attempt to re-describe that world is in constant danger of representing itself as another place away from the world. In that sense, so much of what is casually labelled as 'the postmodern' (though often that which is careless with its reading of certain philosophy) tends to read 'suspicion' as a sophisticated form of 'ideology critique'. Thus does an anti-foundational strategy easily slide into becoming a foundational position with a heroic agent resisting the linguistic traps of modernity.

The truth trap opens wide. The question mark always seems to lead me there. So how can I summarize the moves that always seem to end up at its jaws? First, conspiracy thinking always insists that there must be an answer to the question. Whatever answer is discovered, there are always more questions to be asked, even questions about the 'truth' of the answer. Denying you are a witch makes you a witch. Insisting that your decision to buy a pot noodle was an unconstrained act of creativity, and yours alone, does not prevent the logic of economics from relating the purchase decision to class, gender, lifestyle choice and so on. In that sense it doesn't matter what the question was because the response is always a variant on (as I said of Spark and Knight earlier) 'well they would say that wouldn't they?', and then an endless stream of further questions. Second, what would the human sciences be if they were *not* a quest for the elevated position? What would be the point of all that thinking, talking and writing? It seems that a condition of possibility for allowing question mark thought into the canon of human sciences, indeed, for allowing it to constitute that canon, is that it should be engaged in a battle of the substrates. The search for the structures, systems, mechanisms, causes, teleologies that describe what is 'hidden' from everyday view is constitutive of our understanding of what can be included as sensible, as comprehensible, as legitimate within enquiry itself.

So what are we left with to answer the question I began with? How can we explain the culture of conspiracy, the age of anxiety? Only by deploying more forms of conspiracy thinking. Either there are more conspiracies now (for whatever reason), or there are now conditions which encourage such beliefs (but they are false beliefs). Alasdair Spark wishes us to embrace a new term for thinking about conspiracy in the latter way – 'dietrologia' – which literally translates as 'behindology' (Spark, 2001; Knight, 2000: 230).[4] Whilst I am sure he has more modest aims, for me this could be the science that embraces all the others, a generalized project of looking behind things, of assuming there is a behind to things. Dietrologic has no faith in surfaces, and always assumes that the interesting things are happening behind the skin of the world. But as a self avowed hermeneutician of suspicion,[5] I am no longer certain that this is a project I have much faith in, so (how) can I escape this dietrologic? Can I stop myself from looking behind things?

Revelation

I have come to believe that the world is an enigma, a harmless enigma that is made terrible by our own mad attempt to interpret it as though it had an underlying truth (Eco, 1990: 95)

So here is the twist in the tale, the end of the book. That this entire argument is no more than another version of conspiracy logic. The conspiracy of conspiracies, and I am the one who has put the clues together. My etymology of plot and plan, my nefarious description of the human sciences, my appropriation of a few selected texts (including those carefully selected in this book) as 'clues'. My 'unexplained' is the growing number of conspiracy theories, and the co-incidental rise of the human sciences. And because the two seem to grow together, and seem to be related in their logics and ambitions, I claim to have found the plan. Indeed, Simon Lilley's entanglement with the Economic and Social Research Council (this volume) demonstrates my point perfectly. The structures of accountability in the very bodies that fund research in the human sciences produce the logic of explanation they claim to uncover. But, once again, is there no escape from this dietrologic, no place to stand beyond being enrolled in the schemes of the world as I have described it? One character in Auden's *Age of Anxiety* is described as finding:

... his path is blocked
By Others from Elsewhere, alien bodies
Whose figures fasten on his free thoughts,
Ciphers and symbols secret to his flesh,
Uniquely near, needing his torments (1948: 37–38)

How can I conclude by suggesting that the path of enquiry is always blocked by the question mark, when it really leads nowhere? That, as Hamlet despairingly suggests, all this sound and fury ends up 'signifying nothing'? How would you feel, as a reader who has got this far, perhaps all this way through this book, if I leave you with just another question mark?

In the novel *The Name of the Rose*, after William of Baskerville has followed all the clues to the mystery he finally discovers, almost by accident, that the murders were committed by a diverse group of individuals for quite distinct reasons. He had been:

... pursuing the plan of a perverse and rational mind, and there was no plan ... when I should have known well that there is no order in the universe. (Eco, 1983: 492)

According to this reading, perhaps it is the very quest for a semblance of order that makes the world seem terrible. The insistence on looking for the pilot, Žižek's 'captain or any living crew', and finding there is no-one there is exactly what leads us to see 'the horror of society as a contingent mechanism blindly following its path' (in Lilley, this volume). Perhaps to avoid confronting this horror, we ask questions. But asking 'what are the functions of witchcraft?', or 'who shot JFK?', or 'what explains conspiracy?', simply shuts the trap by seducing us into the mysteries of the behind. It assumes there is an order to the messy shape of the earth, and that things can be become clear when we can properly see the plan. This is what Hetherington has called 'the will to connect', the desire to make a line of sight which attaches diverse objects in patterned ways (1997). So do the stars become constellations, and the 'event' only becomes 'unexplained' precisely because we are looking for explanations for events. All this relies on the same (dietro)logic.

But, again as this volume testifies, perhaps *the* plot and *the* plan are only plateaux, and there are thousands of those. Thousands of places to see from, and a multiplicity of different plots and plans to be uncovered and buried. So, perhaps a more deliberate and ironic strategy would be preferable to this endless search for the big conspiracy. This is exactly what Baudrillard's 'Stealth Agency' is actually intended to achieve. In a deliciously paradoxical turn, the agency's mission is 'to lift the veil on the fact of events not taking place', of 'the storm of events of no importance'. The 'radical desimulation' propogated by this organization is intended to counter the idea of a 'sequencing of things as though they had a meaning' (1994: 14–15). Such a fictional agency might use any means at its disposal, perhaps Alfred Jarry's 'pataphysics' (*Evergreen Review* 1960), Lyotard's 'paralogic' (1984) or Burrell's 'humuments' – hidden messages in the text (1997), to counter the dis-information being put forward by the proponents of conspiracy, whether they masquerade as human scientists or UFOlogists. In an attempt to make the fantastic even realer than the real, secret societies (Jarry's 'College of Pataphysicians'; Bataille's 'College of Sociology' and 'Acéphale' (Richardson, 1994); or Baudrillard's 'Stealth Agency') might manufacture a parody of explanations, a parody of scientific reason. As with much of the internet, the inauthenticity of such thinking is beyond doubt, but the point is that a blizzard of inauthenticity should cast a shadow on the authenticity of Reason. To be clear, this would be no attempt to discover what lies on the far side of conspiracy, but a form of the hermeneutic of suspicion that seeks to de-legitimize Reason itself. And that would include all reasonable attempts to ask questions of Reason in the name of something that lies beyond. If we must have faith, then let it be a faith in fakes.

The point here is not that we can do without conspiracy thinking of some kind, of a search for explanations, but that ironic hyper-conspiracism might make this logic more transparent to us. In using the word 'transparency' here, I am echoing Vattimo's characterization of modernity's urge to transparency. Vattimo suggests that communication in general (and the media in particular) is predicated on the idea of 'the ideal of emancipation modelled on lucid self-consciousness, on the perfect knowledge of one who knows how things stand' (1992: 7). The search for clarity – in democracy, ethics, economics, thought – is the search for transparency. Yet, for Vattimo, the media now actually generate such a plurality of truths that they are now eroding this axiomatic principle through their polymorphous practice. So instead, we might become dimly aware of 'an ideal of emancipation based on oscillation, plurality and, ultimately, on the erosion of the very 'principle of reality'. We might not accept Vattimo's version of cause and effect, or indeed his suggestion that this is a 'new' possibility (and Auden's poem would suggest that it is not). However, the metaphor is one I would to conclude with. It suggests that the 'will to connect' cannot be switched off, but it can be multiplied. Through its multiplication, and consequent generation of partial connections and open secrets[6] more questions can be asked. So find the hidden message, and then work out who or what put it there, and then do it again, in another context, or in reverse. This is the restlessness of genuine thought. The attempt to connect everything, however improbable, and hence make the very act of connection into a practice that exposes the true relationality of knowledge. Here then is what this chapter is intended to achieve, and now you know why I wrote it, and who put me up to it.

Is this true? Why did I say it? What does it mean? (DeLillo, 1986: 26)

Notes

1 Earlier versions of this chapter were presented at the 'The consumption of mass' conference in 1998, and at a seminar at Glasgow Caledonian University in 1999. Thanks to the participants in those events, and Bob Cooper, Valerie Fournier, Bob Grafton-Small and Brenda Parker for their comments and help. Thanks also to Ben Courtney for his work on the cover.
2 See Knight (2000: 25) for a longer list.
3 For more stories 'they' don't want 'us' to know, see www.projectcensored.org.
4 The term is borrowed from Don DeLillo's novel *Underworld*.
5 In this context anyway. I usually lack this suspicion in most of my everyday activities.
6 On the impossibility of not having secrets, see Sedgwick (1994).

References

Adorno, T., (1995), 'Cultural Criticism and Society', in Tallack, D. (ed.), *Critical Theory: A Reader*. Hemel Hempstead: Harvester Wheatsheaf, 287–297.
Auden, W.H., (1948), *The Age of Anxiety*, London: Faber and Faber.
Baudrillard, J., (1994), *The Illusion of the End*, Oxford: Polity.
Brookesmith, P., (1997), *UFO: The Complete Sightings Catalogue*, Leicester: Blitz Editions.
Burrell, G., (1997), *Pandemonium: Towards a Retro-Organisation Theory*, London: Sage.
DeLillo, D., (1986), *White Noise*, London: Picador.
Descartes, R., (1968), 'First Meditation', in *Discourse on Method and the Meditations*, Harmonds-worth: Penguin.
Eco, U., (1983), *The Name of the Rose*, London: Secker and Warburg.
Eco, U., (1990), *Foucault's Pendulum*, London: Picador.
Evans Pritchard, E., (1937), *Witchcraft, Oracles and Magic among the Azande*. Oxford: Oxford University Press.
Evergreen Review (1960), 'What is Pataphysics?', 4/3.
Gup, T., (2000), 'When Everything is Secret, Nothing is Safe'. *Newsweek*, Oct 30th: 14.
Hetherington, K., (1997), 'Museum Topology and the Will to Connect', *Journal of Material Culture*, 2/2: 199–218.
Jameson, F., (1988), 'Cognitive Mapping', in Nelson, C. and Grossberg, L. (eds), *Marxism and the Interpretation of Culture*, Urbana: University of Illinois Press, 347–360.
Kallinikos, J., (1995), 'The Archi-tecture of the Invisible: Technology is Representation', *Organisation* 2/1: 117–140.
Klein, N., (2000), *No Logo: Taking Aim at the Brand Bullies*, London: Flamingo.
Knight, P., (2000), *Conspiracy Culture*, London: Routledge.
Lyotard, J-F (1984), *The Postmodern Condition: A Report on Knowledge*, Manchester: Manchester University Press.
Monbiot, G., (2000), *Captive State: The Corporate Takeover of Britain*, London: Macmillan.

Paraweb (1998), 'Conspiracy'. Internet document accessed 30/10/98 at http://theparaweb.com/Conspiracy/body_conspiracy.html

Parker, M., (1998), 'Judgement Day: Cyborganisation, Humanism and Postmodern Ethics', *Organisation*, 5/4: 503–518.

Parker, M., (2000), 'Manufacturing Bodies: Flesh, Organisation, Cyborgs', in Hassard, J., Holliday, R. and Willmott, H. (eds), *Organising the Body*, London: Sage.

Parker, M. and Cooper, R., (1998), 'Cyborganisation: Cinema as Nervous System', in Hassard, J. and Holliday, R. (eds), *Organisation – Representation: Work and Organisation in Popular Culture*, London: Sage: 201–228.

Popper, K., (1969), *Conjectures and Refutations*, London: Routledge.

Richards, L., (1998), 'Roswell Theories', in *Beyond Blue Book*, Stoke-on-Trent: Potteries Organisation for Paranormal Investigation.

Richardson, M., (1994), *Georges Bataille*, London: Routledge.

Ronson, J., (2001), 'Who Pulls the Strings?', *Guardian Weekend*, March 10th, 10–20.

Sagan, C., (1996), *The Demon Haunted World*, London: Headline.

Sedgwick, E., (1994), *The Epistemology of the Closet*, London: Penguin.

Showalter, E., (1997), *Hystories: Hysterical Epidemics and Modern Culture*: London: Picador.

Spark, A., (2001), 'Conspiracy Thinking and Conspiracy Studying'. Internet document accessed 15/03/01 at http://www.wkac.ac.uk/research/ccc/index2.htm.

Smith, W., Higgins, M., Parker, M. and Lightfoot, G., (eds) (2001), *Science Fiction and Organisation*, London: Routledge.

Vattimo, G., (1992), *The Transparent Society*, Oxford: Polity.

Von Daniken, E., (1971), *Chariots of the Gods? Unsolved Mysteries of the Past*, London: Corgi Books.

Contributors

David Bell is Reader in Cultural Studies at Staffordshire University. His publications as author or editor include *Mapping Desire* (Routledge, 1995), *Consuming Geographies* (Routledge, 1997), *The Cybercultures Reader* (Routledge, 2000), *City Visions* (Prentice Hall, 2000) and *The Sexual Citizen* (Polity, 2000). His current work includes an introduction to cybercultures, and a number of essays on rural cultures. Email: d.bell@staffs.ac.uk

Lee-Jane Bennion-Nixon is currently completing a PhD in Film and Cultural Studies at Staffordshire University. Her research uses visual ethnography to explore women's relationships to contemporary representations of femininity in mainstream film. She is also a practising film-maker, and co-runs the company Altiplano Productions. Email: ljbn@mac.com

Mark Featherstone teaches Sociology at Keele University. He is due to publish his doctoral thesis, *Knowledge and the Production of Non-Knowledge*, with Hampton Press later this year. Apart from his PhD study, he has also written various papers on the logic of conspiratorial thinking and social theory. This work includes articles published in the journals *Ctheory* and *Anthropoetics*.

Nigel James is currently in his final year as a part-time PhD student. His research involves a statistical analysis of Patriot websites, emphasizing those belonging to real-world organizations such as militias, plus an online questionnaire targeted at Patriot webmasters and online activists. His purpose is to explore the underlying meanings of contemporary American nationalism, from the perspective of cultural identity theories, and to examine the role of the internet from a New Social Movement perspective. 'Nigel James' is an academic pseudonym.

Peter Knight is Lecturer in American Studies at the University of Manchester. He is the author of *Conspiracy Culture* (Routledge, 2000), and the General Editor of the forthcoming *Encyclopedia of American Conspiracy Theories* (ABC-Clio).

Simon Lilley is Senior Lecturer in Management Information and Organization, Director of MBA Programmes and an active member of the Centre for Social Theory and Technology at Keele. Simon has taught previously at the Universities of Edinburgh, Glasgow and Lancaster and at the Manchester School of Management, UMIST. Research interests turn around the relationships between (human) agency, technology and performance, particularly the ways in which such relationships can be understood through post-structural approaches to organization. These concerns are reflected in a continuing focus upon the use of information technologies in organizations and he is currently pursuing these themes through investigation of the regulation and conduct of financial and commodity derivatives trading.

Jane Parish is Lecturer in the School of Social Relations, Keele University. She has carried out fieldwork in West Africa, looking at the relationship between witchcraft and misfortune among shrine priests and their clients in a large town in Ghana. Her particular interests are in conspiracy discourses, witchcraft and morality.

Martin Parker is Reader in Social and Organization Theory in the Department of Management and Centre for Social Theory and Technology at the University of Keele. His background is variously in philosophy, anthropology, cultural studies and sociology. He has published widely on ethics, organization theory, postmodernism, higher education, and the sociology of culture. His recent books are the monograph *Organizational Culture and Identity* (Sage, 2000) as well as some edited or co-edited collections – *The New Higher Education* (Staffordshire University Press, 1998), *Ethics and Organization* (Sage, 1998) and *Organization and Science Fiction* (Routledge, 2001).

Adrian Quinn is a print journalist by training and an alumnus of Cardiff University's Centre for Journalism Studies in Wales. He has worked and studied overseas, in Canada and France, and currently lectures in the School of Politics and Communication Studies at the University of Liverpool. He has previously taught journalism at the University of Teesside in north east England and at Liverpool John Moores University. Adrian's contribution to this volume comes from an ongoing research doctorate examining French news media and carried out in collaboration with Glasgow Media Group.

Jonathan Skinner is a social anthropologist lecturing in the Division of Sociology at the University of Abertay Dundee. His interests are in narrative and biography, performance, postmodernism and ethnographic representation. Previous publications have brought these interests into subject areas such as health, risk, and calypso and Carnival representations of Montserrat, a British Dependent Territory in the Eastern Caribbean. He is grateful to those at the University of Abertay Dundee and The Sociological Review Editorial Board at Keele University for his 1998/9 Fellowship which gave him the space and the environment in which to relate his material to this new subject area.

Warren Smith is a lecturer in Organization Studies at the Management Centre, University of Leicester. For all his protestations he would prefer to read a good, old-fashioned, over-determined conspiracy theory any day. However he is increasingly less preoccupied with questions of authenticity.

Alasdair Spark is head of American Studies at King Alfred's College, Winchester, UK. His interests are focused particularly on contemporary

American culture, and he has published articles on subjects relating to the Vietnam War, science fiction, and conspiracy theories. The latter is his particular interest at present and his previous work has focused on the 'black helicopter' and UFO conspiracy theories. He runs a webpage on conspiracy at www.conspiracy-culture.com, but finds that teaching, learning and bureaucracy conspire to keep him from maintaining it properly.

Index

215